COMPUTER-MEDIATED COMMUNICATION

COMPUTER-MEDIATED COMMUNICATION

ARUN BHATIA

AKANSHA PUBLISHING HOUSE
NEW DELHI-110059 (INDIA)

AKANSHA PUBLISHING HOUSE
R 37-B, Vani Vihar, Uttam Nagar
New Delhi-110059
Email: ektabooks@yahoo.com

Showroom
4649/21B, Ansari Road
Darya Ganj
New Delhi - 110 002
Ph.: 23269193 / 9811582579

Computer-mediated Communication

First Edition 2005
ISBN 81-8370-024-1

PRINTED IN INDIA

Published by M.P. Misra for Akansha Publishing House, New Delhi and *Printed at* : Mehra Offset Press, New Delhi.

Contents

Preface

Computer-Mediated Communication (CMC) is any form of communication between two or more individual people who interact and/or influence each other via separate computers through the internet or a network connection. CMC mostly occurs through e-mail, video, audio or text conferencing, bulletin boards, list-servers, instant messaging, and multi-player video games. Switching communication to a more computer mediated form has an effect on many different factors: impression formation, deception and lying behaviour, group dynamics, disinhibition, and especially relationship formation.

CMC is examined using three main aspects of any form of communication, that are altered by the medium used; these aspects are synchronicity, persistence, and anonymity. Each of the aspects vary widely for different forms of communication. Instant messaging is highly synchronous, while not persistent. Message boards are low in sychronicity, but high in persistence. Anonymity depends more on the context and particular program/web page being used. It is important to remember the psychological and social implications of these factors, instead of just focusing on the technical limitations.

The present volume provides a comprehensive analysis of CMC, geared at professionals and students in the field of communication. It will assist the readers to become aware of the opportunities and challenges of CMC.

Editor

1

Introduction to Computer-Mediated Communication

Humans communicate in order to share knowledge and experiences. Common forms of human communication include sign language, speaking, writing, gestures, and broadcasting. Communication can be interactive, transactive, intentional, or unintentional; it can also be verbal or nonverbal. In addition, communication can be intrapersonal or interpersonal. There are a number of theories of communication that attempt to explain human communication.

Communication Technology

In telecommunications, the first transatlantic two-way radio broadcast occurred on July 25th 1920. As the technology evolved, communication protocol also had to evolve; for example, Thomas Edison had to discover that hello was the least ambiguous greeting by voice over a distance; previous greetings such as hail tended to be lost or garbled in the transmission. As regards human communication these diverse fields can be divided into those which cultivate a thoughtful exchange between a small number of people (debate, talk radio, e-mail, personal letters) on the one hand; and those which disseminate broadly a simple message (Public relations, television, cinema).

Our indebtedness to the Romans in the field of communication does not end with the Latin root "communicare". They devised what might be described as the first real mail or postal system in order to centralize control of the empire from Rome. This allowed Rome to gather knowledge about events in its many widespread provinces. As the Romans well knew, communication is as much about taking in towards the centre as it is about putting out towards the extremes.

In virtual management an important issue is computer-mediated communication. The view people take toward communication is changing, as new technologies change the way they communicate and organize. In fact, it is the changing technology of communication that tends to make the most frequent and widespread changes in a society - take for example the rise of web cam chat and other network-based visual communications between distant parties. The latest trend in communication, decentralized personal networking, is termed smartmobbing.

Anxiety associated with communication is known as communication apprehension. Such anxiety tends to be influenced by one's self-concept. Besides apprehension, communication can be impaired via bypassing, indiscrimination, and polarization. Failing to share a common language is also an important barrier in many parts of the world.

Nature of Computer-Mediated Communication (CMC)

Computer-Mediated Communication (CMC) is any form of communication between two or more individual people who interact and/or influence each other via separate computers through the Internet or a network connection. CMC does not include the methods by which two computers communicate, but rather how people communicate using computers. The way humans communicate in professional, social, and educational settings is different, depending upon not only the environment but also the method of communication in which the communication occurs, which in this case, is through the use of computers. CMC mostly occurs through e-mail, video, audio or text conferencing, bulletin boards, list-servers, instant messaging, and multi-player video games. More recently, weblogs and wikis have come to provide interesting alternatives.

Switching communication to a more computer mediated form has an effect on many different factors: impression formation, deception and lying behavior, group dynamics, disinhibition, and especially relationship formation. CMC is examined and compared to other communication media through three common aspects of any forms of communication: synchronicity, recordability, and anonymity. Each of these aspects vary widely for different forms of communication. For example, instant messaging is highly synchronous, but rarely persistent since one loses all the content when one closes the dialog box unless one has a message log set up or has manually copy-pasted the conversation. E-mail and message boards are similar; both are low in synchronicity since response time varies, but high in persistence since messages sent and received are saved. Anonymity and in part privacy and security, depends more on the context and particular program/web page being used. It is important to remember the psychological and social implications of these factors, instead of just focusing on the technical limitations.

In a study conducted by Dr. Jeffrey T. Hancock, director of the Computer-Mediated Communication Research Laboratory at Cornell University, deception in commonly used communication mediums, the telephone, email, and instant messaging, was examined to determine how communications technology affects lying behavior relative to Face-to-Face (FtF) interactions.

The three design aspects studied were "synchronicity" (the degree to which messages are exchanged instantaneously and in real-time) of the interaction, the "recordability" (the degree to which the interaction is automatically documented) of the medium, and whether or not the speaker and listener are "distributed" (they do not share the same physical space). What was found in the study was that synchronous media increase opportunities for deception.

In a FtF, instant messaging, or telephone conversations, people lie more often because most lies are unplanned. In a less synchronous medium, such as email, the opportunity for spontaneous lying is much less, thus lies occur less often in email. Another finding of the study was that users will be hesitant to lie in a medium which can be recorded and reviewed. Instant messages can be logged by services such as DeadAIM and [[AIM+]], third-party add-ons to the instant messaging program AOL Instant Messenger, emails are saved by both sender and receiver.

Users are more likely to lie when using FtF or telephone interactions which are typically not recorded in order to avoid being caught. Lastly, participants restrain from lying if the media is not distributed because being copresent limits deception concerning issues contradicted by the physical setting. The example from Dr. Hancock's report is "I'm working on a case report" when in fact the speaker is surfing news on the web. The more synchronous and distributed, but less recordable, a medium is, the more frequently lying should occur. Of the four mediums studied, lying occurred most frequently on the telephone, followed by FtF and instant messaging, and least frequently in e-mails.

Modes of CMC

Computer-mediated communication refers to human communication via computer. The emphasis is on interaction between humans using computers to connect with one another. The computers may be central repositories for human messages, or they may comprise a network of links and nodes facilitating the transfer of human messages. Various modes and media can be combined to facilitate the communication process.

Presently, most applications and much of the research into CMC is focussed on text-based communication. With the increasing sophistication of computer and communications technology, however, additional modes and media are being utilized. Ultimately, in support of human communication via computer, "the human intellect and sensorium are entitled to the fullest array of media we can muster". Further, computer technologies that support human intellectual activity as well as mediate communications should be given appropriate attention in the realm of CMC as their power and usefulness increases.

There are numerous incarnations of text-based CMC. Foremost among the asynchronous types is computer conferencing (CC). CC usually refers to those systems that reside on large central computers to which numerous users can connect directly via inhouse terminals or indirectly via home computers, modems, and telephone lines. Messages are composed and saved to files that are designed to permit multi-user access.

As such, groups of people can establish "conferences", or "special interest group" (SIG) areas to which they send the messages they wish to share with others. In this manner, the "conference" resembles an ongoing discussion or meeting that does not require the physical presence of the participants in one place. Nor does it require that contributions to the discussion be synchronized with the attendance of other members of the group. All members can link into the conference discussion when they log in, at their own convenience.

Electronic mail (EMAIL) is another form of text-based CMC that has seen tremendous growth in business organizations. With EMAIL, there is no group-accessible central repository of messages. Rather, messages are sent to individual addesses just as conventional mail is sent to individual addresses. Of course, bulk mailings by individuals or by automated message handling software are becoming as common as their counterparts in the conventional mail systems. One variation on this theme, which is popular in higher education networks, is the LISTSERVER. Listservers function primarily to receive messages from individuals and then to distribute them according to mailing lists. Members of these mailing lists, then, constitute a group of communicants who can carry on asynchronous discussions much the same way as users of computer conferencing systems do.

Electronic bulletin board systems (EBBSs, or BBSs) are an emergent form of CMC activity. The original concept was that of the conventional community bulletin board as an area where public messages could be posted and read. In the early 1980s, BBSs were primarily established by computer user groups for the purposes of online distribution of software and related information. The messaging feature became increasingly popular as members found that the posting of bulletins soon resulted in interactive discussions.

That is, bulletin messages could either be initial postings, or response postings. The group discussion potential of BBSs led to a broadening interest in the medium. With the advent of post-hobbyist home computers and the availability of inexpensive communications software, BBSs by and for the general public emerged. Many of these new BBSs were no longer oriented to computer enthusiasts. Instead, they came to be used as local fora for educational activities, special interest groups, writer collectives, and academic discussions.

One popular feature of BBSs and of the larger commercial conferencing systems is the "CHAT" mode of interaction. This feature is conceptually based on another more conventional public communication system: Citizen's Band Radio. On a small BBS, users have the option of requesting a real-time, text-based chat with the SysOp. On larger systems, numerous simultaneous users can interact in real time and all participants can observe the contributions of the others as they occur. Just as the radio waves provide for multiple simultaneous users, the CHAT mode of large conferencing systems allows for similar interaction in text.

CHAT mode is an example of synchronous text-based CMC. Most computers used for communications have at least a rudimentary form of this feature installed. The various incarnations of synchronous CMC differ primarily in the way the exchange is presented on the screen, and in the number of simultaneous users who can participate in any one group activity. The exchange can be character by character, line by line, or in multiple-line blocks. In character by character mode, the recipients see each character as it is typed by the sender. In line by line mode, the message is not sent until the sender presses the key (or), and in the multi-line blocks mode, several lines are composed before the message is sent. In all cases, however, the transaction occurs immediately and is not held in a mail system or conferencing space for future retrieval. This is not to say that transcripts of the interaction cannot be collected (logged) for future review of the discussion; it is just that the exchange is intended to be in real time.

The user interface for synchronous text-based interaction often involves some partitioning of the terminal screen into window areas. A common design for two simultaneous users involves splitting the screen horizontally. If the top half is used for receiving messages, the bottom half may be used for composing and sending messages. Systems with more advanced GUI (graphical user interface) features can allow for multiple windows of variable size and location to appear on the screen with any or all of them being used to receive or send messages. The CSILE Phone utility developed for the synchronous dyads in the present study used one window for both receiving and sending messages character by character. Other window space was reserved for future uses such as review of previous transcripts or access to information files.

Asynchronous CMC

In The Third Wave, Alvin Toffler documented many of the current trends in society and projected future scenarios. His discussion of "flextime" included the following:

> Indeed it is the computer which has made flextime possible ..., but it also alters our communications patterns in time, permitting us to access data and exchange it both 'synchronously' (ie: simultaneously) and 'asynchronously'.
>
> What that means is illustrated by the growing number of computer users who are today engaged in 'computer conferencing'. This permits a group to communicate with one another through terminals in their homes or offices. Some 660 scientists, futurists, planners, and educators today in several countries conduct lengthy discussions of energy, economics, decentralization, or space satellites with one another through what is known as the Electronic Information Exchange System [EIES]. Teleprinters and video screens in their homes and offices provide a choice of either instant or delayed communication. Many time zones apart, each user can choose to send or retrieve data whenever it is most convenient. A person can work at 3:00 A.M. if he or she feels like it. Alternatively, several can go on line at the same time if they so choose.

EIES was designed by Murray Turoff and had its test period in 1977-1978. Turoff also designed and implemented the very first computer conferencing system in 1971. It served as an automated Delphi conference for the Office of Emergency Preparedness in the Executive Office of the President of the USA. Starr Roxanne Hiltz, a sociologist, began reporting on the effects and impacts of computer conferencing in 1975. Together they wrote the now classic The Network Nation which remains important because of the breadth of analysis and insight it delivers. Hiltz and Turoff defined, clarified, or predicted many of the issues and problem areas in CMC that remain as the focus of questions and investigation more than ten years later.

The wave of the future in human communication, however, is more than Toffler's characterization of "flextime" as a simple matter of convenience. In fact, asynchronous CMC (computer conferencing) was propelled to the leading edge of a new communications revolution primarily because of the way it alters human communication patterns.

As early as 1975, with relatively unsophisticated conferencing software (FORUM), Jacques Vallee, Robert Johansen, and Kathleen Spangler of The Institute of the Future were able to report on computer conferencing as an altered state of communication with significant social implications. Their report presented many of the same factors and impacts that continue to be discussed in the more recent CC literature. Three main themes or issues predominate: alterations in time and place, text-based interaction, and socioemotional content.

Turoff is particularly concerned with the use of computer conferencing for group support. He contends that the asynchronous mode of interaction is most important. This is not necessarily because of time and place convenience, but because "the potential for real improvement in the group process lies in the fact that individuals can deal with that part of the problem they can contribute to at a given time, regardless of where other individuals are in the process". The result, he claims, "is to free the individual to deal with the problem in ways consistent with his or her cognitive style".

It appears then, that Turoff is discussing a particular type of problem or decision task, or perhaps a certain phase in the problem-solving or decision making process. This phase would be one that involved exploration of possibilities and ideas for general consideration. It would have to be a phase where the consensus of the group would not yet be necessary, since once consensus is needed it becomes more important for individuals to synchronize their contributions with those of other individuals in group activities. Turoff suggests the software should be designed to synchronize the asynchronous interaction of the group.

With regard to text-based interaction, Rapaport states that it "addresses a potentially wider set of domains than any other teleconferencing or office automation system. Its purpose is the association of ideas and experience of people, communicated in written words". Feenberg, in his paper "The Written World" adds, "A group which exists through an exchange of texts has the peculiar ability to recall and inspect its entire past". In these two statements we have the makings of a natural hypertext: the association and recall of ideas in text. With the aid of computer based utilities to facilitate the linking and association of ideas, we can presumably make a quantum leap beyond any bandwidth constraints on text-based communication. Besides, whereas a picture is said to be worth a thousand words, one might also proclaim that certain combinations of words can elicit a wealth of images, sounds, feelings, and other sensations.

Provenzo refers to the proliferation of electronic text and information networking opportunities as the "electronic scriptorium" and he predicts that:

> As we go beyond the Gutenberg Galaxy and enter a post-typographic culture, we will see the traditional methods

> and results of scholarship redefined. Through the establishment of information networks and knowledge pathways made possible by the microcomputer and telematic systems, we will have the potential to extend and refine intellectual discourse in a manner that has never been possible before.

Considering CMC in the context of the evolution of media, Levinson describes the development of communications technologies in three historical stages. First, there is the stage of natural communication that takes place within the confines of biological boundaries. The next stage involves the development of technologies which help transcend the physical limitations of human biology. Writing is a technology of this second stage. It evolved in order to facilitate communication across greater distance and through time.

According to Levinson, however, new communication technologies in the second stage often result in the sacrifice of certain features and qualities of communications in our natural environment of the first stage. The written word, and ultimately the advent of the printing press, resulted in the loss of interactivity in our communications. In the third stage, technologies evolve in a manner that recaptures features of natural human function; a process that Levinson refers to as "anthropotropic". Therefore, computer conferencing is proclaimed as "the first progress in the evolution of media since the mass application of the printing press in fifteenth-century Western Europe" because it recaptures the lost interactivity in text.

Without encompassing the full range of human sensory and expressive capabilities, text-based interaction is often thought to be an impersonal medium devoid of social context cues and nonverbal communication. Experience and research, however, are demonstrating that socioemotional content can be communicated in text. Steinfield states that: "Evidence continues to mount showing that CMC will be used for emotional interaction. People seem to work around the nonverbal cue limitations and actively provide their own text-based translations of nonverbal cues".

In terms of cognitive effects, very few studies address the issue directly. Most report on social relations, interaction and outcomes of problem-solving tasks. Kerr and Hiltz, however, surveyed the most prominent CMC projects of that time by soliciting opinions and observations from key representatives of the various groups and organizations utilizing this technology. In line with much of the research preceding their study, and much that would come after, a fairly standard set of factors and effects were analysed. These included system software design factors, and factors affecting user acceptance of new systems.

Kerr and Hiltz also gathered information about the cognitive impacts of CMC on individuals and groups. They reviewed the existing literature, and used reports from evaluators to confirm or disconfirm their expectations . They found that, "the more socially significant cognitive impacts, such as those including conceptual skills and learning [were confirmed], whereas those which may be more trivial, such as spelling and typing skills, and those which are clearly negative in impact, such as information overload [were not confirmed in the literature and reports]".

Synchronous CMC

Most computer supported communication systems have some capability for synchronous text exchange. Strom notes, interestingly enough, that the PARTY-LINE system developed by Murray Turoff was the first to implement a synchronous exchange facility. Rapaport confirms this and goes on to state: "Initially, synchronous support was expected to provide the system's primary value. Dr. Turoff quickly discovered, however, that most of the real work was done asynchronously". Hiltz and Turoff also state: "Of all the communication forms and conditions permitted by computerized conferencing, the synchronous discussion seems to cause the most difficulty and feelings of confusion" . The evidence provided by Hiltz and Turoff is rather slim. They relate the experiences of people in one real-time "party" where insufficient computer core memory allocation resulted in line by line messages taking up to 30 seconds to transmit. There was no structuring of the communication protocols. In fact, there was overt refusal by Roxanne Hiltz, who initiated the "party", to take a leadership or moderating role.

Dobos and Grieve studied the decisional productivity of synchronous online conferencing by comparing the ratio of decisional output messages to messages representing social presence, task related input, and group procedural input. Their results suggest that the use of turn-taking protocols and the use of rotating moderators (with each participant "handing-off" to the next when their contribution was finished) increases decisional productivity. Further investigation demonstrated increased participant satisfaction when turn-taking protocols where implemented in online synchronous groups.

Kiesler and co-workers at Carnegie-Mellon University investigated the social psychological aspects of computer-mediated communication. Their 1984 paper was published in American Psychologist, became very popular, and is often cited. It was also selected for inclusion in an important collection of papers on computer-supported cooperative work four years after its original publication. In fact, it is a very well presented report of research that carefully delineates the factors and effects studied.

The problem with this account, however, is that they failed to clarify one very important point. Whereas they used the terminology of computer-mediated communication, they did not emphasize the fact that most of their data was drawn from synchronous text-based interaction, not asynchronous computer conferencing. Further, although they did present a portion of their work comparing users of the synchronous mode with users of electronic mail, they continued to confuse the issue by referring to their synchronous mode as "computer conferencing."

The effect of this combination of a popular scholarly report and the confusion in terminology relevant to the field, is that some of its main findings have been misapplied to the more widely implemented and researched asynchronous mode of computer conferencing. Most significantly, the issue of uninhibited verbal behavior, reflected in the fiery term "flaming", came to be associated with CMC in general.

The truth of the matter is that the data presented in Kiesler et al. show higher levels of uninhibited verbal behavior in synchronous CMC, but the levels for EMAIL (an asynchronous mode) are more comparable to the lower levels found in face-to-face interaction.

An important new perspective is offered by Ferrara et al. who refer to synchronous CMC as interactive written discourse (IWD) and suggest that it represents an emergent linguistic register. The concept of "register" deals with language variations in the context of language use, as opposed to "dialect" which refers to language variations according to user. Ferrara et al. studied synchronous text-based CMC in the form of message exchanges between a travel planning agent and 23 computer professionals (or their spouses) who were making travel arrangements. Their findings support three claims about IWD:

> ... first, that it is a naturally occurring register, perhaps a reduced register; second, that it is a hybrid language variety, displaying characteristics of both oral and written language; and third, that norms of its use are in the process of becoming conventionalized.

"Reduced register" refers to registers that frequently omit components of the language such as copulas, articles, and pronouns. Note-taking is a reduced register that is generated under real time conditions with pressure on the writer to save time and minimize effort. Ferarra et al. point out that IWD is a register comparable to Note-taking in the type of register reduction it exhibits; except for one crucial difference. IWD is interactive and there is need for somewhat improved clarity in the communications because the audience is other than the self.

Computer-Supported Cooperative Work (CSCW)

Most human work involves both individual effort and group participation. The "personal" computer and common applications software such as database managers, wordprocessors, and spreadsheets have provided significant support to people working independently in various organizations. These people, however, must step out of their computer support environment whenever group activities such as meetings are scheduled. In response to this problem, and in conjunction with developments in media and communications technologies, a new area of research and practice has evolved. "Over the last half-dozen years, Computer-Supported Cooperative Work has emerged as an identifiable research field focussed on the role of the computer in group work".

CSCW has drawn together research interests from a variety of fields in order to investigate groups of humans using groups of computers in their work. Sociology, anthropology, and organizational behaviour offer methods and knowledge about the study of humans in groups. Computer science offers methods and knowledge concerning computer-human interaction (CHI), interface design, and communications networking. Together, the integration of these perspectives have resulted in the development of applications that provide research information about group work in shared multimedia spaces. The general direction presently suggests the use of advanced multimedia technology to facilitate group interaction concerning the shared objects of work.

The strength and importance of this trend is revealed in the fact that the latest operating system and user interface for the Macintosh computer incorporates shared document and workspace capabilities as a standard feature of its networking environment. Tocco Gives an example of the use of System 7 features for group work. With the combined effort of several people on a shared document, he states that the document seems to come alive as it evolves with the completion of each participant's contribution.

It appears that the time for individual, "personal computing" software applications is fading away (at least in organizational settings). Document sharing and computer-mediated discussions in support of group work are on the rise. The term "groupware" is being applied to various commercial applications packages that integrate facilities for document sharing and messaging with the more common text-processing, database, and spreadsheet functions. Greif declares,

> All software will be groupware. But CSCW as a research field will still be addressing the larger questions of how to design and refine good groupware - software that will allow people to work together with the best help they can get from the computer.

A related development in the field of management science is the work involving group decision support systems (GDSSs). This represents a variation on the CSCW theme. After the groupware model, GDSSs attempt to integrate group sharing and communication structures with management software. In particular, GDSSs are best understood as the groupware version of more conventional decision support systems (DSSs). DSSs use operational data from an organization to provide simulations and models to help inform management decisions.

Baecker provides a taxonomy of CSCW technology that classifies applications according to synchronicity on one dimension and geographical dispersion of the group on the other dimension. He classifies computer conferencing in the asynchronous, multiple-site cell; electronic meeting and decision rooms in the synchronous, single-site cell; and media spaces, telepresence, and synchronous groupware in the synchronous, multiple-site cell. It is interesting that the cell for asynchronous, single-site applications is left blank, because it is certainly possible to have a messaging system or a group note-making system located at one site but used intermittently by the members of the group as an alternate mode of communication for certain tasks.

Computer conferencing, for example, is often used at university sites as a supplement to face-to-face discussions held in the classroom. Similarly, online courses that utilize CC have participants working from the same site as well as distributed locations. In another example, CSILE establishes a variation of asynchronous, single-site group interaction as the students of one classroom can enter notes, as well as review and comment on the notes of others in their class.

The concept of a single-site asynchronous utility may represent an area of knowledge and interest dissonance between proponents of CSCW and proponents of CC. In fact, the blank cell in Baecker's taxonomy may indicate a lack of appreciation for the asynchronous text-based interaction promoted by Turoff and others. Turoff on the other hand, is quick to downplay the importance of GDSS and CSCW by suggesting that computer conferencing already offers GDSS via a flexible, tailorable system and that CSCW, being mostly synchronous in nature, cannot match the group support power of asynchronous CC. It should be clarified as well, that Turoff has good grounds for his view that work in CC has already addressed a lot of the issues now arising in the GDSS and CSCW work.

Infrastructural Issues

A fully networked society, with capacities for one-to-one, one-to-many, and many-to-many communications, provides a fertile incubator for the development of next-generation information services and for the development of next-generation information workers. Many facets of the infrastructure are already in place, however, the parts remain scattered across networks, operating systems, and computing platforms.

Computer communications can be used to simultaneously join multiple users across hundreds of networks. Recent advances in networking technologies enable diverse computer, information, and telecommunication systems to co-exist and integrate on the networks. While there has been a dramatic increase in the use of wide-area networking technologies, these systems have yet to achieve a full integration into organizations and society.

If fully implemented, network applications might dramatically impact intra- and inter- organizational communications to improve company operating procedures, create strategic advantages, or forge new business alliances. Internet resources have recently come within reach of most organizations and computer users. Recent advances in the technologies of regional, long distance, and value-added telecommunications carriers have similarly created new opportunities to enhance communications. Organizations and individuals may connect to the infrastructure through public, private, or value-added network providers.

Business, industry, government, and education can all claim adoption of sophisticated information technologies able to adequately serve internal operations. Effective organizational communications increasingly involves the integration of resources distributed across organizations, and networks, with the objective that users be able to share all information within a total information environment. External communications for trade, research, and intellectual pursuits are becoming increasingly important. However, effective applications of wide-area, inter-organizational communications are still relatively rare.

Electronic Environments

The goal of telecommunication planners is to create a global digital highway, open to all telecommunications users, with universal access into totally open networks. Users will be able to economically access voice, data and images, in any combination, anywhere, and at any time. Such capabilities exist today.

However, effective use of the resources has too often become dependent on information policies and the culture of the organization. Adoption has entailed a rather difficult process of unscrambling old procedures and attitudes, moving to new ways of performing intellectual tasks and of thinking about communications, and then installing the new processes into the daily agenda of individuals and groups.

While 83% of U.S. Government workers would prefer to work via computer at home or at a near-home remote office, only 14% have the opportunity. Organizations have yet to decide whether office technology has produced measurable increases in productivity, or even whether traditional productivity measures adequately assess quality and quantity of work. Strategists implementing information projects must consider not only systems development needs, and the required skills of employees, but also the degree to which information services are supported by the organization.

Traditionally, implementation problems have been caused by differing interface standards and modes of human-computer discourse. Fortunately, graphical user-interfaces have somewhat alleviated these concerns by standardizing screen displays across multiple platforms, networks, and operating systems. In addition, new network applications allow intelligence to be programmed into the user-interfaces to enable systems to maintain and apply information about the user to further ease communications.

Online Communities

Online communities that will be instrumental in the realization of an advanced learning society. Within these communities, users will access remote computer systems and resources which are fluid, evolving, and continuously expanding. The resources may be used to improve communications, stay abreast of current developments, maintain contact with business partners or external specialists, and to establish future business opportunities.

Difficulties arise because inter-organizational communications services are often not immediately recognized as critical for business functions. Future 'opportunities' are sometimes difficult to justify, thereby hindering wide-spread adoption. Thus, while technology may progress rapidly, the human processes to successfully implement and employ that technology may not.

Implementation problems are compounded because of the somewhat unusual nature of 'networking.' Namely, with network technologies, information flows throughout organizations, and among different organizations, freely and without regard to corporate interests. Some argues that the ultimate impact of the new technologies is to give end-users greater power to shape their computing systems and to manage their information needs. This is very different from traditional 'top-down' communication patterns and can cause concern for top management. Yet, it is this empowerment of the end-user, and their interaction with fluid and dynamic resources, that will drive future organizational innovation.

As users acclimate to network-based communications and information access, they also become increasingly aware of data organization and retrieval issues, and are thereby introduced to current practices in database design, development, and maintenance. Thus, computer-mediated communications may evolve the culture of the organization as the workforce becomes more adept at capitalizing on institutional information investments to increase economic productivity.

Human-Network Issues

The primary modes of computer-mediated communication have been classified as either immediate (teleconferencing), delayed (correspondence), or simulated (computer-tutorial). In addition, new 'groupware' applications are a natural outgrowth of computer communications and enable multiple users to simultaneously interact on the same computer project at the same time.

Groupware applications can improve inter-organizational communications, be used for in-service training, and can improve overall productivity. Employees will need training in the use of the networks. Fortunately, online systems are increasingly adept at supporting in-service training and education. National mailing list services can support network training and alleviate a need for internal funding.

Online information may also be customized to satisfy the needs of participants. And, throughout the development, implementation, and training process, there is little need for administrative costs as users at desktop workstations manage their personal communications, resource sharing, and business transactions.

Network communications are pervasive, reaching into the daily activities of users wherever they work, live, or attend class. Users may access the network at a variety of times, from a variety of places, and participate for a variety of reasons. As this convenience is realized, electronic technologies will increasingly influence program-planning and development strategies as representatives of the target population become more deeply involved in information development and presentation.

In addition, computer communications are dynamic, enabling current knowledge to be integrated into organizational communications. As employees share new knowledge and information, they garner new perspectives and thereby drive innovation. Throughout this process, the medium can itself be used to coordinate the creative contributions of the individuals.

Infrastructure Development

The Internet is excellent for wide-area data transfer and automated online services, but poor for real-time multimedia communications. Private common-carrier networks provide viable multimedia solutions, but offer little, if any, public information. Value-added networks offer some solutions for both Internet and multimedia communications, and some provide online resources. An effective infrastructure may require a mix of networking technologies and services.

In areas of the country with an abundance of high technology companies, such as California's Silicon Valley, many employees have Internet access at the desktop. However, they are not active users. The University of San Francisco, College of Professional Studies, is actively involved in educational programs for mid-career information systems professionals in Silicon Valley. The following network overviews have proven helpful when discussing the roles of infrastructure service providers.

Networking has become a national priority. Compatibility and interoperability standards are established under the Government Open Systems Interconnection Profile. The National High Performance Computing Technology Act will evolve the Internet into the National Research and Education Network (NREN). NREN will extend network technology into homes and organizations, establish comprehensive online information services, and create opportunities for partnerships among government, education, and business. Organizations may connect to the National Science Foundation backbone through one of the regional public networks. Participation often depends on the needs of the organizations, the aggressiveness of the local sales force, and company motivations.

The Silicon Valley area has several public and private Internet providers, and many of the high technology companies themselves make networking products. The BARRNet regional Internet network, in addition to connecting the universities, has active participation by over 70 prominent Silicon Valley high technology companies. However, while Internet communications with employees within these companies is possible, and even somewhat common in certain situations, the Internet is not being used to its fullest potential. Individually, interest among employees is very high, especially once they have seen some of the capabilities of the network.

Internet information services are a valuable resource and solve many of the training and acclimation problems inherent in learning the Internet. Fortunately, such training is available, free-of-charge, through mailing list services, and as self-contained instructional modules for downloading from public domain facilities. Useful training media, such as BBN's 'Internet Tour,' and Merit's

'Navigating the Internet,' have proven quite popular with information systems professionals. Downloading these resources from anonymous ftp sites, using a graphical retrieval and translation utility is also a useful experience.

'Telnet' exercises in which users login to remote computer systems and evaluate national and international library, public information, and government computing resources serve to teach students about network database structures. The Hytelnet library navigation program is a useful telnet demonstration utility. Subscriptions to mailing list services, such as NETTRAIN, Interpersonal Computing and Technology (IPCT), and Comserve, can help organizational innovators learn more about the Internet.

For more advanced users, demonstrations of the new network access, retrieval, and processing utilities impress even the most seasoned information systems professional. A Wide-Area Information Server (WAIS) search can illustrate the power of wide-area network database systems by retrieving information from distributed databases using a natural language query. Internet 'Gopher' software can be used to demonstrate a technique to search and display files structures from remote sites. A 'World-Wide Web' hypertext search can aid research in network-based, human-machine interaction.

In the private sector, new telecommunications switching technologies are melding previously incompatible systems and connecting diverse networks and computing platforms. This is timely since multimedia communications are spurring a demand for faster, more efficient, and more compatible networking. A trend is clearly underway as modem users require more capacity and evolve into online X.25 packet networks. X.25 users are demanding multimedia and evolving into higher capacity services such as Frame Relay, Switched Multimegabit Data Service, and Asynchronous Transfer Mode (ATM).

Multimedia communications are increasingly driven by desktop conference systems able to integrate voice, image, and video into computer-mediated messages. Such multimedia communications can be built into the physical apparatus and wiring in systems such as the Integrated Services Digital Network (ISDN). Or, they can be software-based and achieve multimedia interactivity through desktop systems developed by Northern Telecom, AT&T, IBM, and professional multimedia publishers. Multimedia has become a major force advancing the technology of organizational communications. Another interesting opportunity results from the systems upgrades of the regional and long distance carriers to digital switching and SS7. These technologies enable users to program network functions on both a regional and national level. And, as the networks become increasingly 'intelligent,' programmable network applications will enable users to define personalized, intuitive, multimedia services customized to individual needs.

Value-Added Solutions

Organizations may also connect to the Internet through several value-added network providers. Some of these services actually improve on some of the basic Internet communication capabilities. In conventional Internet switching, the TCP/IP data grams are encapsulated in X.25 or frame relay networks. The value-added providers switch TCP/IP in native format, using routers as switches, thereby eliminating switching delays. These providers include Advanced Networks and Services, UUnet, Performance Systems International, CERFnet, and Sprint. A liberalization and commercialization of the Internet, and public demand, have expanded opportunities for Internet access for individual users. Anyone with a computer and modem can now access full Internet services. Following is a list of the basic Internet functions provided by private online services and available for individual use:

Service	Cost	Mail	Telnet	FTP	Netnews
AOL	$8	yes	no	no	yes
CompuServe	$8	yes	no	no	yes
Infoserv	$14	yes	no	yes	yes
MCI	$5	yes	no	no	no
Netcom	$18	yes	yes	yes	yes
Prodigy	$15	yes	no	no	no
Well	$15	yes	yes	yes	yes
Delphi	$13	yes	yes	yes	no

All of the services offer mail boxes and Internet mail. Most are accessible through a local telephone call. In addition to the listed monthly subscription, hourly charges can vary depending on the service. Telnet and ftp are sometimes a minor additional charge. Of course, with the basic mail service, users can access the Internet listservs to find network training media. Usenet Netnews is also available through many of the suppliers. Most of these services provide bulletin boards and online databases so a subscription includes access to those services. Internet operations are a new but rapidly growing part of their services, and many of their databases contain Internet information.

The evolution to network-based information delivery seems a certainty. The success of the systems and programs will be dependent on the degree to which the processes are integrated into the information infrastructure of the organization and into the daily agenda of participants.

Wide-area network services may involve a mix of networking technologies and services. Too often, the academic community downplays the potential of private networks, and industry underestimates the potential of the Internet. Presently, organizations have needs for simultaneous information, conferencing, and multimedia communications which can only be satisfied through hybrid public-private wide-area network solutions.

Computer conferences, online databases, and bulletin board services afford users the opportunity to complete network training at their own pace and personal convenience. The media may be online text, or independent multimedia or hypermedia instructional modules. Group software, with members operating locally or at a distance, is an exciting area for exploitation and a natural outgrowth of online conference systems. Some of the more interesting aspects of the new network technologies derive from their potential to enable users to shape their personal information environments.

Future research may help to determine the proper mix of the various network and communication technologies, the impact of network-based communications on traditional information structures, and design processes for the distribution of information to various home, work, and social environments.

Use of CMC in Education

Throughout the history of human communication, advances in technology have powered paradigmatic shifts in education. Technology changes both what we can do and what we decide is best to do; big shifts in culture cannot occur until the tools are available. The printing press is an example. Before its invention there were people who could read and write; yet not much reading and writing took place because, for one thing, books were costly and scarce. The press enabled widespread literacy, with books accessible and more affordable for all. The spread of literacy in turn changed both the educational system and the class structure, with consequences that still shape our attitudes today. When people began to accumulate knowledge through the technology of writing and reading, they found a way to preserve it through succeeding generations without relying on memory — greatly changing the way education was conducted.

The impact of the printing press on students of the time has been analyzed and reanalyzed. No longer did students have to write or remember everything the teacher delivered; students could use books. But they did not completely give up the oral/aural connection; witness the popularity of lecture classes even now. As new technology enables shifts at the level of delivery, old technologies are augmented, not totally replaced. Even though many of us have computers at our disposal, we still use books, speech, and pen or pencil writing in education.

The general availability of electricity has fostered an almost universal use of such inventions as radio, television, and, increasingly, computers. For decades, educational technologists have likened the impact of television and other electronic ways of presenting information to the impact of the printing press on learning. Although to date television has not had nearly the impact on school learning that books have had, we have yet to determine whether its impact on education as a whole will be as great and long lasting. Schooling is only a part of education.

Much of education takes place outside of schooling, both as planned activities and unplanned learning. We may not understand the instructional goals of the Music Television (MTV) channel broadcasts, and those goals may differ from those of educators, but that does not mean MTV viewers do not learn anything. Ultimately we must consider what kind of world we as educators want to build. If we envision the merger of computers and telecommunications as a new tool for teaching and learning, now is the time to clearly articulate and promulgate our goals in order to shape future uses of instructional technology.

For communications to take place, at a bare minimum, there must be a sender, a receiver, and a message. If this message is intended as instruction, then besides student, teacher, and content, we must also consider the environment in which this educational communication occurs — an environment that benefits the educational system in some ways and constrains it in others. Part of this learning environment can include various technologies and media. If "the medium is the message," that is, if technology changes what we can do and how we think about it, then the various media enabled by instructional technology also change both what we can do in education and how we conceive of it.

For many years, educators have been exploring ways to combine theories of differing learning styles and student-constructed knowledge with the theory of practice-centered learning. Instead of being passive recipients of knowledge, we now consider students capable of constructing their own knowledge with guidance from the teacher. We can offer part of this tutorial guidance by setting up an environment that will provide students with the resources necessary for independent exploration. In using emerging computer-based technology as a resource, students are encouraged to explore their own interests and to become active educational workers, with opportunities to solve some authentic problems.

As an agent for socialization and collaboration, the networked computer has an even greater potential in education than does the stand-alone, knowledge- server type of computer. The active environment of social learning provided by a computer with access to local, national, and international networks increases interaction and communication among students, their teachers, peers, parents, and other members of the world community. Although there are some differences between distance education and classroom education, the significant issues concerning the use of computer networking and other emerging technologies to promote learning in both are similar.

Distance Education

In addition to being entertained, viewers seem to learn from the Music Television (MTV) channel's eclectic mix of music videos, news, instruction, and information on the world of popular music and performers. Broadcast at a distance, MTV's educational content appears largely unplanned in the sense that educators are not directly involved. However, the distance education now originating from universities and colleges attempts to plan educational content and activities for students removed in place and time from their instructors.

Historically, we have not done a very good job of implementing the concept of learner-centered education in distance education. As Thornburg points out, it is difficult, at best, to instill a mindset of lifelong learning in others if we do not understand it and demonstrate it ourselves. One of the reasons that we have failed in this area has been that the tools were not available to do much besides deliver education (as opposed to enable learning) at a distance. Now, computers and telecommunications have opened the way to formats other than pen- and-paper correspondence courses and allow for a more interactive, integrated learning environment.

The type of change enabled by computer-mediated communication (CMC) does not just involve adding new technology to old ways of organizing teaching and learning . Although the perennial problem is still one of instructional content and design, we must not pave over old cow paths.

Another notion current in educational circles is that we need to develop motivated, skillful, lifelong learners. As knowledge in many fields increases exponentially, we cannot hope to fill up students as if they were passive, empty vessels. During formal schooling, aspiring professionals can only begin to take in the amount of information that they will need during their career life times. The knowledge base of certain fields may have appeared static for decades, but we can no longer accept that view. Therefore, we must teach students to become lifelong learners by helping them locate the resources to continue learning.

Distance educators are now beginning to focus on a related set of notions: (a) there are different learning styles, (b) students create their own meaning when learning new things, and (c) what makes a difference in content retention and transfer is not so much what is done by teachers, but what students as learners can be encouraged to do themselves.

Much has been written about the importance of accommodating the learning styles of different kinds of students. Suffice it to say here that too often students have little choice in what to learn, how to learn it, or when to learn it. The body of literature on constructivism which has emerged over the past few decades has also contributed to our understanding of learning styles. When content is meaningless to the students' world view, when they are taught as if they were passive recipients of knowledge, or when they have little engagement in the instructional tasks, students have no incentive to construct their own knowledge and little motivation to retain information or transfer its use to novel situations.

The notion of practice-centered learning (PCL) is also important to distance learning. As we learn more about how learning occurs, it becomes increasingly clear that the educational process takes place in a complex internal and external environment. One of the teacher's roles is to become the creator of an effective external learning environment that stimulates the environment within. How do teachers and developers of instruction create environments that are conducive to and enhance student learning?

The technology that can help provide these new environments for education is emerging. This technology allows us to utilize such methods as cooperative learning, to recognize such concepts as interdisciplinary needs in education, and to provide an environment in which collaborative efforts are rewarded. These methods foster a view of knowledge in which expertise is distributed and created among the different participants. Now there is no shortage of technology, only a shortage of the educational vision necessary to use the technology to create new educational environments.

Use of Computers and Telecommunications in Classrooms

What we have been discussing is a reengineering of education, not only in the sense of rethinking the organization of site-based schools, but also in the sense of finding ways to unite computers and telecommunications and bring down the schoolhouse walls; to deliver instructional content when and where it is needed-whether in the home, the workplace, or the school.

Computer-mediated communication (CMC) promotes a type of interaction that is often lacking in the traditional teacher- based classroom. It allows learners the freedom to explore alternative pathways-to find and develop their own style of learning. What if content could be delivered in the form of graphics, text, and/or full-motion video, whenever and wherever in the world it is requested? How do we, as teachers and educators, responsibly participate in and make use of the inevitable technological changes at hand?

Computers are not a threat to the teacher (although the role of the teacher must change when using them), but computers may threaten the chalkboard. Computer technologies allow professionals to share with students tools that we use daily. Further, as educators, we can provide guidance to help students develop meaningful ways to construct their own knowledge, much as we ourselves do.

Technology enables us to implement these new visions in distance learning. Berge (in press) points out that:

"[T]echnology makes it possible that these investigations are not limited to students from one classroom, school, grade, or country necessarily-nor to exclude experts in the field of inquiry from the collaboration. Effective learning hinges on active engagement by the student and the construction of knowledge on their own leads to understanding (Sheingold, 1991). This learning is not a solitary process. Rather, it occurs in a larger world of people and technology."

CMC and networking in general can promote long-distance collaboration among students and content specialists in many different areas. The integrated use of technology offers many educational opportunities and possibilities when driven by sound visions of learning. The students' ability to create knowledge can be enhanced when their instructors use varied instructional delivery formats to provide a richer environment than is used in most distance education practiced today.

However, as Sheingold points out, these ambitious new goals for student learning, along with radical changes in the students' roles those goals bring about, must be met with radical, ambitious changes in the educational process. Indeed, information technology offers options for reorganizing and refining distance education. But our new visions of distance learning must drive our decisions about our use of technology, not vice versa.

Although major cultural shifts do not occur without the tools that make them possible, once those tools are at hand, the shifts are inevitable. Emerging technologies, such as interactive television and the "superhighway" for information exchange, may look different depending on who builds them (e.g., telephone companies, cable television companies, federal governments), but we may be assured that they will be built by someone. How we as educators will participate in this enterprise is a issue that deserves our closest attention. More than merely a shift within education, our participation in this movement will bring about major shifts in society and culture. As the number of students outside the ages of 18 to 25 increases, and the number of persons requiring off-campus classes rises, the very existence and future of a university or college may hinge on serving this newly defined and diverse population. In this book, we hope to show how CMC can help serve that population.

In combination with other media, computers can utilize an instructional design that teaches to the multiple intelligences that Gardner speaks of in Frames of Mind (linguistic, logico-mathematical, intrapersonal, spatial, musical, bodily kinesthetic, and interpersonal). The idea behind this instructional design is to use as many methods and formats for instruction (e.g., small group discussion, graphics, lecture, hands-on labs, writing/reflection, sound, CMC, and conferencing) as possible, provided that instructional goals and design dictate their use.

Use of CMC in Workplace

The compter technology reinforces existing hierarchies within organizations, or at least does nothing to break them down. For librarians, especially those in the corporate environment, the question of whether technology may or may not democratize the workplace has much relevance for two reasons: As implementers of information technology, we may consider ourselves as corporate and social do-gooders helping to break down status and power-related barriers by providing access to information to anyone in the company. As employees, and thus users of new technology, we may believe that our voices have a further reach and that our input is taken more seriously.

Collectively known as computer-mediated communication (CMC), it includes e-mail, teleconferencing, electronic bulletin boards, Internet/Intranet access, Internet relay chats, and group decision support systems (GDSS).

Lee Sproull and Sara Kiesler are among the most vocal proponents of the thesis that CMC has democratized the workplace. In their book, Connections: New Ways of Working in the Networked Organization, they argue that computer-mediated communication reduces information gaps by providing a tool for peripheral employees (employees that are removed from the core management structure) to be connected to all people within the organization. They examine passive and active connections in the CMC environment. Passive connections is where employees choose to be an observer only of messages being posted to distribution lists or e-mail. Active connections is where employees partake in the electronic interchange and discussions posted on listservs or e-mail.

The benefit of computer-mediated communication, suggest Sproull and Kiesler, is that it gives a "voice to the voiceless," and, therefore, increases "emotional and informational connections" among employees by creating more active participation in exchanging messages and establishing collaborations in electronic discussion groups. Giving people a "voice," the authors suggest, is part of our democratic culture. Information in organizations now flows more freely in the CMC environment and employees are more willing to participate beyond their stated duties.

Libby Bishop and David Levine, in their article "Computer-mediated Communication as Employee Voice: A Case Study", also examine the "employee voice through computer-mediated communication," supporting some of the findings of Sproull and Kiesler. They conclude that CMC creates easier access to people and information and provides a new vehicle for employees to address concerns to management in the hopes of resolving problems or effecting change. They examine the effects of CMC at a high-tech firm that was an early user and advocate of computer-mediated communication.

After collecting data and conducting interviews over a two-year period, their findings suggested that technology had eroded the hierarchical structure of management and gave employees more of a voice in the decision-making process of the organization. But has the impact of computer-mediated communication really democratized the workplace? Has it weakened or softened the hierarchical structure of organizations? Are librarians now free to interact and exchange information at all levels within or beyond the organization? And do librarians have a more "active voice" in the virtual environment in being part of the decision making process that they did not have in the past? Some researchers contend that CMC does not lead to a democratized workplace.

Susan Herring, in her study, "Gender Participation in Computer-Mediated Linguistic Discourse", was one of the first to challenge the position that modern information technology opens the communication path to a more egalitarian communication structure. Focusing on gender participation in the CMC environment, she observed two electronic discussion lists at an academic institution. She examined two issues for her study: 1) to see if the communication process was democratic in the electronic environment, and 2) to determine if computer-mediated communication increased gender equality.

Herring focused primarily on the degree to which males and females participated on these discussion lists. Her findings revealed that there was a difference between the female to male participation ratio. Male participation showed minimal interest in female postings, which resulted in a decline of female participation. Female postings to the discussion lists tended to be brief or ignored if certain subjects were not of interest or topics discussed did not encourage female participation. Herring concluded that "...although the medium theoretically allows for everyone with access to a network to take part and to express their concerns and desires equally, a very large community of potential participants is effectively prevented by censorship, both overt and covert." In this particular academic environment, computer-mediated communication was found to be male dominated, power-based and hierarchical.

Like Herring, Giuseppe Mantovani is critical of the egalitarian democratic effect of CMC. Focusing on a corporate, rather than an academic environment, he explores the conditions under which CMC may or may not promote democratic patterns. He challenges the arguments made by Sproull and Kiesler in his article, "Is computer-mediated communication intrinsically apt to enhance democracy in organizations?".

Much of how CMC is used depends on the culture of the organization, rather than just the technology itself. He suggests CMC is effective in overcoming physical barriers (geographic location), but not social barriers (structure of the organization). Social inequalities that exist in organizations are not solved by integrating technology. Computer-mediated communication, Mantovani believes, is determined by an organization's history and the rules that are implemented by management. Taking this into consideration, he says, CMC "does not generally foster democracy in organizations."

A more recent study by Frank Symons examines how traditional hierarchical structures are now reproduced electronically. In his article, "Virtual department, power, and location in different organizational settings", he says that technology gives management even more power than they had before by tracking production and efficiency with greater accuracy, less margin of error, and increased monitoring of employees' activities at work.

Hierarchy in the electronic realm depends on the degree to which organizational members have access to the Internet or company Intranet, electronic files or databases. To test the relationship between hierarchy, power, and location, Symons conducted a 10-year study that examined virtual departments in various organizational settings of firms with 3,000 to 5,000 full-time employees. Out of this research emerged three to seven different hierarchical categories, which were characterized by the complexity of the information that was accessible or shared among different departments. The question he raised was whether traditional hierarchies are really being eradicated by virtual departments, or are they merely being changed under the guise of technology.

Symons concludes that hierarchical models still exist in many organizations and are now just electronically reinforced. He notes that organizations practicing different management styles, such as centralized vs. decentralized, still show evidence of hierarchical structures because management holds the power in how the technology will be used, despite geographic location.

William Wresch, like Symons, supports the notion that management has power over technology. In his book, Disconnected Have and Have Nots in the Information Age, he discusses how information technology in many organizations has become the old "panoptican - an optical instrument that allowed an observer in the middle of a prison to see into all the cells yet remain unseen."

In the context of organizations today, this is how upper management controls the use and implementation of information technology - by the type of network administration software to be used, which is dependent on the server and connection an organization has, and who will administer and run these systems. Because of this control, Wresch states there is no "semblance of privacy" for employees anymore. Managers can physically be located anywhere and still have the ability to monitor and track organizational activities. He describes this control over technology as being very powerful for management since they now have tools to put employees under blind surveillance. The issue of power, technology and rights to privacy in the workplace is hotly debated today.

Studies supporting the democratizing impact of CMC are flawed. From the very outset, they fail to consider how the power structure in organizations controls how CMC is implemented and to what extent it is used or what restrictions are placed on it. There is an assumption that all information flows from top-down or vice versa, and that all employees are on the same level playing field as management in the virtual world.

Although technology provides us with a new method to transmit messages as senders and receivers, it does not ensure that these messages are heard or even considered. The reality is that technology, for the most part, has not changed behavior. In most companies, traditional power structures are still in place; messages can be ignored; and electronic activity is monitored.

Issues that confront librarians in an environment that is not democratized through CMC could include: e-mails ignored by upper management, monitoring Internet sites visited and e-mails sent, limiting access to information for certain employees, and information that should be posted in a visible location is buried under layers of directories and files that makes it difficult to find. Who has not personally experienced or heard from colleagues about suggestions repeatedly e-mailed to superiors that are ignored? Who has not encountered management's disapproval in one of its various forms from mild resistance to clear prohibition in response to an attempt to make company information accessible to all employees? And who has not heard about frightening reports of management monitoring Internet sites visited and e-mail traffic?

Technology itself does not shape the culture of an organization, as Mantovani states, although it is certain to have an impact on day-to-day transactions. There is no doubt that technology has changed how business processes and decisions are acted upon in organizations. However, the organizational culture is embedded by the vision of its leaders, and therefore, technology is adapted to "fit" into the culture—not the other way around. Computer-mediated communication has given employees a virtual illusion that there are fewer boundaries and less control placed upon them.

Computer-mediated communication is said to "enhance" and "empower" employees, but they cannot see how management exercises its power by controlling, maintaining and directing the use of technology. Under what conditions, then, can computer-mediated communication be a means in democratizing the workplace? Librarians need to be active participants in attempting to change the way in which existing power structures use technology.

Much of how we leverage knowledge and disseminate information will depend on the culture in which we work. Our desire to help in breaking down barriers is only successful if it is supported by the organization that employs us. In a setting where the power structure controls much of how the technology will be used and our input in the decision making process is not considered, our jobs as librarians is more difficult in trying to serve and meet the needs of our clients and, unfortunately, there are no quick fix answers.

What can librarians do in their organizations to realize some of the potential of computer-mediated communication for democratization within a more traditional hierarchical structure? The answer again depends on the organizational culture. One way to create more of a "voice" in a controlled and closed-communication setting is to establish a group or coalition of clients that support and value the services we provide for them. As a collective group, we have better leverage and can form a more powerful informal network that may have a greater impact in getting management to listen to our concerns. Another consideration in realizing the potential of CMC for a democratized workplace is that it will take time. More face-to-face communication is necessary in proving our value and stating our concerns or goals to management. Also, providing information to management illustrating, for example, the difference between abusing the Internet and using the Internet for information seeking purposes and better decision making may eventually open the door to more equal access to information for everyone in the organization.

2

Use of Information and Communication Technologies

Information and communication technology (ICT) is the technology required for information processing. In particular the use of electronic computers and computer software to convert, store, protect, process, transmit, and retrieve information from anywhere, anytime. In the 1980s, the expectation that innovations in telecommunications and computer technologies would improve industrial performance and increase economic productivity in the industrialized nations became firmly established among the leader of the developing countries. The common position that emerged was that ICTs would allow them to leapfrog over the industrialization of their economies into a post-industrial society. Countries began to launch policies and programmes to acquire a share in international satellite communications and transborder data flow networks. In many countries, however, concern arose that ICTs might entail serious social risks, such as a potential for cultural colonialism, the replacement of jobs by machines, and the erosion of individual privacy and national sovereignty. Towards the end of the 1980s these fears seemed to have abated. A new phase began in the 1990s, characterized by a very strong fear of being left behind and cut off from the emerging global digital highway system.

In many countries, the 'digital rush' is on to ensure connections with the electronic networks for trade, finance, transport and science. This phenomenon has been inspired by the obvious benefits that digital information and communication technologies - at least in principle - seem to offer. Educational facilities can be improved by providing distance learning and on-line library access. Electronic networking has also been used to improve the quality of health services by providing remote access to the best diagnostic and healing practices and cutting costs in the process. Digital technologies for remote resource sensing can provide early warning to areas vulnerable to seismic disturbances or identify land suitable for crop cultivation.

Computer technology can contribute to the development of flexible, decentralized and small-scale industrial production. Thus the competitive position of local manufacturing and service industries can be improved. In Singapore, Brazil and Hong Kong the introduction of computer-aided manufacturing (CAM) technologies has been very successful in small-scale industries. The World Commission on Environment and Development, in its report Our Common Future suggests that 'new technologies in communication, information, and process control allow the establishment of small-scale, decentralized, widely dispersed industries, thus reducing the levels of pollution and other impacts on the local environment'.

The currently available computer-communication technologies make it fairly easy for PC users around the world to create a public sphere in 'cyberspace'. Personal computers, modems and telephone lines are being used to establish new global communities. Organizations in developing countries find it increasingly possible to join these forms of horizontal, non-hierarchical exchange that have already demonstrated their ability to counter censorship and misinformation. Groups of all types, from ecological movements, human rights activists, farmers, senior citizens, to the Zapatistas and the groups attending the Women's summit in Beijing, have made impressive use of the new, fast, reliable and effective networks of communication. The combination of telecommunication technologies with desktop publishing software has created new opportunities for even the smallest action group to disseminate its messages across the globe with relative ease and at minimal expense.

In the late 1980s and early 1990s, various aid projects introduced electronic information systems into rural health services (India), agricultural extension projects (Peru), infrastructural development (Pakistan), or energy management (Malaysia). In some developing countries, special computer training courses have been developed in schools and colleges (Sri Lanka). The growing ICT-demand in developing countries can be seen in the long waiting lists for telephone connections, the increase in cellular systems and the rapidly expanding numbers of Internet users. To meet this demand, more and more developing countries have placed the ICTs at the centre of national agendas for social and economic development. There are plans in many developing nations to enhance telecommunications infrastructures in order to facilitate participation in world markets.

The tendency to use new technologies to meet commercial objectives is problematic for people and regions without the necessary financial resources to attract companies to fulfil their needs. The challenge is made harder by the need for stable telecommunication links and electricity to power nearly all the new technologies. Both are in short supply in the poorest regions. The case of developing countries illustrates the way in which technology evolves and is diffused at different speeds across the world. Whereas new technologies are represented by state-of-the-art digital innovations in the developed world, for parts of the developing world telephones, television or even radio may be the latest technologies. It is in this context that two recent innovations in radio broadcasting represent important advances in the medium. The clockwork (or wind-up) radio is the first.

Communication specialists in development have been aware of the problem faced by isolated communities in obtaining dry-cell batteries to power radio receivers for several decades. Crystal-sets and solar-powered receivers have not proved to be entirely successful. The clockwork radio is powered by a patented power source, which with a few minutes of winding-up will keep a receiver playing for about an hour. It is an exciting invention which has been adapted to work on lap-top computers and other devices, which previously depended on batteries for electrical power.

For the present, the relatively high-costs of these radio sets prevent their extensive diffusion across the developing world. The other innovation is at the broadcaster's end. UNESCO has taken the lead in helping to develop affordable low-power radio transmitters for operating community broadcasting services. These transmitters are assembled from generic components by local technicians, who also assist with maintenance. Such services facilite the decentralization of media control to the community. They help promote participatory communication, which empowers communities, and support the planning and implementation of sustainable development programmes. The main hindrance to the spread of this technology is legislative.

Most developing countries discourage community broadcasting by limiting access to radio frequencies and to a broadcasting licence. A classic example of a new technology converging to support an old predecessor is the technology to stream sound over the Internet. This is the developed world's version of the developing world's evolution towards community broadcasting. The technology is very affordable at both ends. People can receive such Internet radio broadcasts with a relatively low investment while broadcasters can be 'on the air' broadcasting literally to the whole world at very minimal cost. These technologies represent an extremely small fraction of the total number of innovations introduced into the media industry.

The developing world with its highly limited purchasing power has sustained minimal research and development efforts to increase their access to relevant content and channels of mass communication. A study in the Philippines found that where privatization of media has been the norm, programming is not meeting the needs of local populations. This sentiment may extend quite widely across the developing world.

Transmission frequencies are a very valuable resource in some areas of the world where finding a frequency for broadcasting to minority groups is a daunting uphill battle, since regulatory authorities and established media companies have vested interests to protect. The introduction of digital television broadcasting technology with the capacity to place four channels in the same space that one analogue channel used to occupy, will soon make plenty of new broadcasting space available. A significant amount of this newly freed-up space should be reserved for minority interest broadcasting, which is now limited.

Developing countries will probably have to wait for several years before the cost of digital technologies reaches an affordable level. The early users, namely the developed countries, should therefore establish a precedent for safeguarding minority interests and those of disadvantaged groups by reserving such open digital spaces for them. Spaces must be held in trust, not only for minorities, but also for the common good in areas such as education, science and culture, which are not very profitable, but are socially vital.

Use of ICTs in Social Development

Across all industries, there has been a strong growth of investments in ICT applications. Spending on ICT equipment as part of overall spending on business equipment has grown dramatically in most industrial countries. In the United States, for example, such spending rose from less than 5% in 1960 to over 45% by 1996 and if the current trend continues the figure could be over 50% in 2000. According to an estimate of the United States Department of Commerce in 1998, the American ICT-industry generated $683,000 million. In some industrial countries ICT-related activities produce a growing share of the Gross Domestic Product (GDP).

Worldwide investments in telecommunication rose from $115,000 million in 1990 to $152,000 million in 1995. These investments have often been linked to the privatization of public telecommunication operators (PTOs). The privatization schemes introduced in a number of countries have raised considerable funds. The ICT industry encompasses the manufacturing of telecommunications equipment, computers, semiconductors and other electronic equipment, the provision of telecommunications services, computer services and software. It is the world's most important and fastest-growing industry. Of the fifty largest companies in the world, ten are ICT companies. They account for 17.5% of the total revenue of the fifty largest companies, for 23% of the total profits and for 26% of the total number of employees. In 1997, four ICT companies, General Electric, Microsoft, NTT and Intel, were among the ten largest companies in the world in terms of market value. In the same year three ICT companies, General Electric, Intel, and International Business Machines (IBM), were among the ten most profitable companies in the world. Telecommunications, semiconductors and computers are among the high growth industries in the emerging-market economies. Among the 200 top companies in these economies, twenty-two are telecommunications market operators and ten are electronics products manufacturers.

ICTs are affected by a great deal of merger activity. The largest transactions of 1998 include the SBC Communications merger with Ameritech for $272,400 million, AT&T with Telecommunications Inc. (TCI) for $48,000 million, Worldcom with MCI Comm for $37,000 million, Northern Telecom with Bay Networks for $9,000 million, and Alcatel with Digital Service Corporation (DSC) for $4,400 million. There is high degree of concentration in this industry. In the telecommunications equipment market, for example, 50% of all sales are controlled by only five companies. In the market for public telephone switching equipment, five firms (Alcatel, Siemens, Lucent, Ericsson and Nortel) control 76% of all activity.

The ICT market is growing rapidly and expanding globally. The top ten companies in the manufacturing of telecommunication equipment derive an average 61% of their revenues from sales abroad. These are Motorola (United States), Alcatel (France), Lucent (United States), Siemens (Germany), Ericsson (Sweden), NEC (Japan), Nortel (Canada), Nokia (Finland), Fujitsu (Japan), and Bosch (Germany). Most analysts expect a further growth of global sales since the domestic markets in many countries are either too small or already saturated. From various trade figures, it can be estimated that the share of the ICT industry in the world economy ranges from between 10% to 15% of total world trade. In several ICT sectors the world market shows rapid growth rates. The market for computer hardware and software, for example, grew at about 15% annually in the 1990-1995 period. In the same period, the average growth rate for total world trade was 8%. In 1997, worldwide revenues in the telecommunications industry were nearly $600,000 million. Some analysts expect this figure to grow to $1,400,000 million by the year 2000. The value of total imports in the world trade of computer equipment grew by 67% from $87,500 million in 1992 to $145,500 million in 1996. The value of total exports grew by 75% from $73,000 million in 1992 to $127,000 million in 1996 (Comtrade, United Nations Statistics Division). The market for personal computers (PCs) is still growing and may reach a sales figure of over $250,000 million in 2000. There is also rapid growth in the world market for computer software, which in 1996 generated $109 , 3 00 million in revenues.

In the world trade of telecommunication equipment the value of total exports grew by 68% from $65,000 million in 1992 to $108,000 million in 1996. The value of total imports grew by 58% from $66,000 million in 1992 to $104,000 million in 1996. Growth rates in this sector are linked to the worldwide increase in the number of telephone lines. The growth from 519 million lines in 1990 to 693 million lines in 1995 represents an average growth rate of 6.8% per year. In 1995, 45 million new fixed telephone lines were added and 33 million people became new subscribers to mobile communications. In fact, the strongest growth rates are in the mobile communication market, particularly in the United States and Japan. In the OECD countries in 1996-67, the contribution of mobile communications to overall telecommunication services revenues amounted to some 12% and the number of subscribers doubled. In 1990, the worldwide trading of telecommunications services generated some $377,000 million. This figure increased in 1996 to over $600,000 million.

According to data from the International Telecomunications Union (ITU), the developed countries represent some 70% of overall telecommunication equipment exports, showing a $9 billion trade surplus. Particularly striking is the shift from a trade deficit for the USA in 1990 to a trade surplus of $3.2 billion in 1995. Over 100 developing countries produce no exports at all. They are obliged to import and thus show trade deficits that in 1995 exceeded $10,000 million. For most developing countries, the obvious problem is lack of capital for imports, since low overall income means that local telecommunications generate minimal revenues. The profits in national telecommunications operation are, without exception, found in international traffic, but the financial gains from overseas services do not benefit the national telecommunications carrier. For political and other reasons, many countries decide not to reinvest a sufficient share of this income in the expansion and upgrading of telecommunication facilities. Moreover, there is growing competition in the provision of international telecommunications services and strong pressures to lower rates on busy routes. Foreign investments in telecommunications have been stimulated by the privatization of former national public telecommunication operators as part of the worldwide trend toward deregulation that emerged during the 1980s. In the 1984-96 period the 44 PTOs that were privatized raised in total a sum of $159,000 million. Almost one third of the financing came from foreign investments.

Economic Importance of ICTs

The increasing economic importance of ICTs is also linked to the growth of electronic commerce. Although for the moment electronic commerce is still a factor of limited economic significance, with revenues of approximately $26,000 million in 1998, this figure is expected to exceed the trillion dollar mark in the early 21st century. Since it is difficult to measure precisely the economic significance of electronic commerce. Several of its important features, such as easy access to data, cannot be quantified, and reliable and comprehensive statistics are not yet available; this uncertainty leads to widely varying estimates. The OECD definition of electronic commerce refers to commercial transactions that take place through open networks, like the Internet. These transactions are both business to business and business to consumers. The growing number of people around the world connected to the Internet have begun to develop a digital economy.

In cyberspace, consumers can purchase flowers, shirts, jeans, books, compact disks (CDs), tickets, hotel reservations, skin care products, pornography, kitchen equipment and household consumer goods. World Wide Web sales grew approximately from $8,000 million in 1994 to over $45,000 million in 1998. According to various analysts in Business Week, digital trade could grow from $1,200 million in 1998 to $65,000 million over the next three years. Other forecasters propose even higher figures, for instance in the travel industry, book and music sales and financial services. Electronic sales of software also hold enormous growth potential. Whatever the precise significance and validity of the forecasts, the general expectation predicts formidable growth in this sector of the global economy. Most analysts observe that this will be mainly business-to-business trading. Expectations of growth in the business-to-consumer trade are based on the assumption that on-line trading will lower production, and thus distribution, costs by up to 10% of total sales. Some 50% of this reduction of costs may be used to lower consumer prices thus stimulating further purchases by consumers.

Electronic trading via the Internet is in fact the successor to the Electronic Data Interchange (EDI) that is already used by many companies. EDI is the exchange of electronic documents in goods trading and financial services and usually operates within closed Value Added Networks (VANs). EDI is expensive because complicated software applications have to be installed for each new trading partner and flexibility is limited because invoices and orders must be exchanged in fixed standard formats. The Internet facilitates the exchange of electronic data by accepting many different formats. However, many of the big EDI users see EDI as more reliable than current Internet traffic. In the United States at present, the volume of EDI-traffic is some fourteen times greater than that of Internet traffic. Many analysts expect that in the years ahead this ratio will change, first to a more equal distribution between EDI and Internet transactions and later to a definite advance for the Internet. This situation will be reinforced by the rate at which companies begin to share their 'intranets' with more trading partners and thus create 'extranets'.

An increasingly important part of all commercial activity on the digital market is geared toward the control over access to cyberspace. The gates that provide access to the World Wide Web - the so-called web-portals - have become crucial targets in the struggle for dominance in this market. In 1998 a veritable 'portal-fever' emerged as more and more companies sought to secure a piece of the expected profits. In June 1998 the media giant Walt Disney announced it would spend $70 million for the purchase of 43% of the stock in the search engine Infoseek. In 1998, the American National Broadcasting Company (NBC) invested $165 million for the purchase of the online service Snap! from van Cnet Inc. Time-Warner and News Corp. began to develop their own web portals.

Manufacturers of personal computers, vendors of operating systems, producers of browsers, telecommunications operators, Internet Service Providers, search engines, the big producers of information and entertainment are among the many contenders in this field. Recent acquisitions or investments among the various companies involved in cyberspace illustrate the high level of competition in this area. In 1997, Microsoft bought a 5% participation in Apple Computer for $150 million. As part of the deal, Microsoft insisted that Apple Macintosh computers be delivered with the Microsoft 'browser', Explorer. In 1998 Compaq Computer acquired Digital Equipment in a deal valued at $9,600 million. The combined revenues are estimated at around $38,000 million. WorldCom controls 60% of worldwide Internet traffic and can be seen as a major gatekeeper of access to lines and networks. In September 1997, America Online (AOL) acquired Compuserve through a complicated deal that made WorldCom the owner of Compuserve's infrastructure. WorldCom paid $1,200 million to H&R Block (Columbus, Ohio) for the purchase of Compuserve. The subscribers to Compuserve were sold to AOL. Through this deal AOL became the largest ISP on the European market with 1.5 million subscribers. On the world market, AOL has some 12 million subscribers.

The ISPs provide access to the services on the Internet and exercise considerable control over access to cyberspace. Some of them conclude agreements with the search engines. Provider MCI, for example, concluded a deal with Yahoo! in order to guide clients to the Web page of this particular search engine. The world market of ISPs is concentrated. If interest in the Web continues to grow, ISPs are likely to allow certain websites to purchase a right of 'priority'. This would mean that if too many clients browse the Web at one time, customers of the privileged sites will have priority and have to wait less time than others. There is also market concentration in this area and many linkages among the players.

There are indications of a real ICT contribution to overall economic growth, although no definite assessment is possible. In his testimony to Congress, US Federal Reserve Board Chairman Alan Greenspan pointed to increasing growth rates in productivity for the American economy and stated that: 'The dramatic improvements in computing power and communication and information technology appear to have been a major force behind this beneficial trend'. Other analysts raise serious doubts about such a causal link between ICT power and productivity. Of the world's total investment in capital goods, 50% concerns computers and peripherals. Yet expected growth in productivity has not materialized. During the period 1970-90 white collar productivity remained stagnant at around 0.9% per year and improved in the early 1990s to 1.3% - a low figure despite the announcement by Fortune magazine that 'the productivity payoff arrives'. It is not clear at present what factors cause this ICT-paradox. One possible explanation refers to the criteria that are used for the measurement of economic productivity. Another factor may also be the inadequate way in which organizations adapt to the use of ICTs. It could also be that what looks like an unexplainable delay is in fact the normal time lag needed before new technologies can lead to higher levels of productivity.

ICTs are 'synergetic' technologies and their growth therefore leads to growth in other sectors of the economy. They create an infrastructure around their products and services, similar to that of car technology earlier in the century. As with the transition from manual power to mechanization techniques and later to electromechanical innovations, today's shift towards the pervasive application of ICTs has given rise to a range of new industries such as software production, processing services, time-sharing facilities, semiconductor manufacturing, database management or electronic publishing. This potential for new economic productivity requires an educational infrastructure that teaches the knowledge and skills required for ICT-related occupations. Although there has been a considerable increase in ICT teaching in many schools and universities around the world, new multimedia tools are still widely underused or used only to supplement conventional teaching methods. There is also a lack of solid and creative training materials that cater for the specific needs of the developing countries.

The economic benefits that may accrue from the development and the deployment of ICTs are unequally distributed throughout the world. There seems to be general agreement in scientific literature and in public policy statements that the ICT gap between the developed and developing countries is widening and will be a major obstacle to the integration of all countries into the so-called Global Information Society.

The seriousness of the ICT gap is clearly demonstrated by figures on the world distribution of telephones. In 1996 there were 743.66 million main telephone lines in the world. Europe (274.23 million), the United States (170. 5 7 million) and Japan (61.53 million) represent 68% of this total, compared with 1.8% in Africa. The density of telephone lines per 100 inhabitants is also very unequally distributed. Whereas the world average is 12.88 lines per 100 inhabitants, Europe provides 34.6, the United States 63.9, Japan 48.9 and Africa 1.85. In early 1997, some 62% of the world's main telephone lines were installed in 23 affluent countries, which account for only 15% of the world's population. Over 950 million households in the world (65% of the total) were equipped with a telephone. Another indicator of this gap is the revenue from telecommunication services, which reached a world total of $620,000 million in 1996. Europe, the United States and Japan benefited from 77% of these revenues, while Africa received a mere 1.5%. Investments in the telecommunication sector show a similar distribution. In 1996 the world total was worth $166,000 million. Europe, the United States and Japan are responsible for 67% of these investments and Africa for 1.7%.

Total ICT equipment installation reveals highly uneven geographical distribution. The estimated number of PCs in the world in 1996 stood at 234,200,000. The share for Europe (72,864,000), the United States (96,600,000) and Japan (16,100,000) was 79%, while for Africa it was only 1.3%, representing 0. 6 4 computers per 100 inhabitants. The world average for that year was 4.6 computers per 10 0 inhabitants. Far above this average are the figures for Europe, 9.6, the United States, 36.2, and Japan, 12.8. Of all the 47,972,000 fax machines operating in the world in 1996, Europe was using 10,942,500, the United States 17,000,000, and Japan 14,300,000. These figures combined represent 88%, in contrast with the 0.5% in use in Africa. Of the total number of television sets in the world in 1996, Europe, the United States and Japan possessed 47% while Africa possessed only 3%.

At the present time the worldwide distribution of ICT resources is enormously unequal. In terms of availability, accessibility, and affordability of equipment and services as well as the mastery of technical and managerial skills, there are great disparities not only between affluent and developing countries, but also among different social groups within all countries. A very problematic factor is that these disparities, rather than diminishing, are growing throughout the world.

ICTs and Employment Creation

The creation of new employment is often related to various uses of ICT, for example in new service applications in banking, shopping, education, health and business services. The development of networks combined with the lowering of communication costs has stimulated the growth of 'teleworking'. This means that people work from home and use telecommunication services. The fastest growth is generally expected in 'telecommuting' where people work alternately at home and at the office. The Internet could play a major role in creating employment for the design, maintenance and management of sites on the World Wide Web. The growth of electronic commerce initially raised concerns about implications for the labour market, but there is also the expectation that few jobs will really be lost since companies will continue to use traditional forms of commerce along with digital trading. When digital trading finally predominates, some jobs will be lost, but new ones requiring new skills will also have been created. The overall picture is characterized by contradictions. Information-related service jobs are associated with the dislocation of family and community life and threats to the health of workers, especially of women. On the other, new types of employment and modes of work organization can be highly beneficial leading to improved quality of life and greater economic resources.

There is some empirical evidence that automation eliminates jobs, but there is also evidence that automation creates new jobs. What remains uncertain is the eventual balance. The notion of a single standard impact is very inadequate and it is preferable to look at plural impacts. The skills implications of ICTs are varied and are related to differences in socio-economic, cultural and political environments. Different countries will choose different ICT-applications in order to reap different benefits from technological development. It is too early to foresee how all these factors will operate. The observation that in the affluent economies more and more employees use ICT applications in their daily work is generally uncontested.

By and large, ICTs are used by some 50% of the workforce in the industrial nations.

ICTs and Knowledge Development

One essential dimension of human development is knowledge, crucial in enabling people to broaden their choices. ICTs are the basic tools of emerging knowledge-based societies. They represent an important shift from the utilization of natural and material resources to the deployment of data and information and related analytical and processing skills. This development is, however, accompanied by national information and informatics policies through guidelines, workshops and technical assistance. Special consideration is given to 'info-ethical' questions, to achieving a balance between the common good and economic imperatives, and to facilitating the use of information and communication technologies for development purposes by the public sector and the civil society. A strong commitment by the international community is necessary to ensure that commercial interest do not dominate the development of ICTs in the world, more particularly in developing countries.

Governments, public and private institutions have to assume their responsibilities if the gap between information-rich and information-poor is not to continue to widen a strong trend toward the privatization and commercialization of knowledge sources and the concurrent enforcement of legal measures to protect private intellectual property.

The emerging global regime for Intellectual Property Rights (IPR) tends to give more emphasis to the economic aspects of IPR protection than to public interest considerations. There is a dominant economic angle in this regime which gives priority to the interests of large producers over those of small creators and consumers. The central focus is on the misappropriation of corporate property rather than on artistic and literary creativity. The move to give IPR protection to material in the public domain when it has been entered in an electronic database could render access to knowledge more costly - and thus prohibitive - for large numbers of people. In addition, the initiative to extend copyright protection to all forms of digital copying could make the Internet a pay-per-view medium creating obstacles to the access to knowledge for those who cannot pay. Developments in the international regime for intellectual property protection are an attempt to create and maintain a balance between a set of rival claims to the control over knowledge and its dissemination.

The protection of intellectual property rights must provide the incentives, rewards and recognition for individual producers of knowledge in order to stimulate progress. Benefits for the creator, and public access to artistic, literary and scientific works must both be secured. Whereas IPR protection seeks to promote the progress of science, it also restricts access to knowledge, since it defines knowledge as private property and has a tendency to facilitate monopolistic tendencies. It may well be that the current trends in the trade-oriented IPR regime lead to more restricted access rather than better public distribution. Although an absence of legal protection could have adverse effects on intellectual production, the move toward overprotection is 'not conducive to access to the networks by research workers and academics of developing countries'.

ICT developments are more technology driven than user oriented. If the ICT potential for human development is to be successfully exploited, the needs and aspirations of users must be central to the whole process of design, construction and application. The essential requirement of user orientation is hampered by the strong tendency to delegate social responsibility for the governance of the ICT-sector to a global trade regime. In fact, the politics of world communication represent a historical shift from a public service orientation to private competition with a predominantly commercial focus.

ICTs and Cultural Development

The information and communication technologies (ICTs) are advancing with unprecedented speed, particularly in the most economically developed countries, it would be a mistake to regard them as solely responsible for the current changes. This long-heralded momentum, which seemed slow at the beginning but is now well under way, seems likely to continue at a rapid pace and, if some authors are to be believed, will usher in a new information society or information age. It is, however, one thing to note the dynamic development of telecommunications, information technology and the audiovisual media, and quite another to credit them with changes in culture and in other areas of social life. Technical innovation is a by-product - only rarely a driving force - of transformations whose origin lies elsewhere. Technology provides such changes with new areas of opportunity, encouraging activities which would otherwise have been blocked by the dominant organizations in the sector and weakening the barriers set up to defend vested interests or to safeguard specific practices. It is important to look beyond the usual thought patterns, which see the issue as one of adaptation to technological changes, and turn our attention instead to changing trends in cultural production.

ICTs may strengthen cultural production and help it to gain widespread recognition, or conversely, they may cause it to be confined to a restricted area or even to decline. Throughout the world, cultural production tends to be community based. Anthropologists, historians and cultural sociologists rightly emphasize this recurring feature which explains the persistence of locally-rooted and even non-commercial forms of culture, as well as the different ways in which viewers interpret television series, according to their own culture. In other words, despite more than two centuries of industrialized cultural production and despite the aggressive strategies of the increasingly-powerful communications groups, independent forms of entertainment still thrive all over the world. Folk productions are not declining - far from it: books and newspapers are published, films and television series are produced and music is recorded independently of the major companies.

The pessimistic forecasts of the imminent globalization of cultural production heard over the last two decades have been proved wrong - or at least exaggerated. Culture remains an area of social activity in which industrialization meets with resistance and constraints, even though increasingly governed by markets, and despite a growing trend towards the internationalization of production and the transnationalization of subjects, styles and standards. The fact that predictions have not so far been fulfilled is, however, no guarantee for the future. ICTs and the momentum they undoubtedly generate will eventually provide the means to move decisively ahead towards the industrialization and internationalization of cultural production. What in the past was only partly successful is now allegedly resulting directly from ICTs. In other words, what the mass audiovisual media merely launched in the past has now become firmly established and universal through ICTs, which have proven to be more successful at sidestepping the cultural structures of countries and peoples, and certainly more favourable to the worldwide circulation of transnational flows. Individual tools of communi-cation and/or access to data and ready-made programmes are ushering in sweeping transformations in cultural production.

The history of the cultural industries is by no means linear. Until recently, it has progressed unevenly, whenever production techniques were adopted and made widely available, so that works of literature became accessible as books, musical works as records, and films and audiovisual works as screenings in cinemas or as video cassettes. The industrialization of culture has, however, encountered difficulties and setbacks. For producers and publishers, the values attached to culture usually act as 'restrictions', or at any rate as contingencies, for which marketing techniques have yet to be found. It has been more convenient to market the equipment used to deliver cultural works than to introduce successfully on to the market works available either in a physical medium or accessible through projection or broadcasting by the audiovisual media. So the picture of the relationship between culture and industry today presents sharp contrasts. There are striking divergences between:

— developed and developing countries;
— countries which give more or less free rein to market forces, and those in which the public authorities provide impetus and co-ordination;
— countries where the market and industry are the major controlling factors in the cultural sphere, and those where small-scale productions, live entertainment with a popular appeal and non-commercial productions predominate;
— the various art forms: it is very difficult to create added value in dance, poetry and narrative performances, as opposed to filmed enter-tainment, which should be considered an activity straddling art and industry;
— individual access to works and live entertainment;

— cultural productions broadcast through the mass audiovisual media and those which, once published, are bought by consumers.

ICTs are capable of strongly reinforcing trends begun at least two decades ago, thereby giving a decisive boost to the expansion of cultural industries. The areas in which ICTs can make an impact need to be carefully evaluated, however. Contrary to what professionals often claim, it would be wrong to expect multimedia production to create innovative products - apart from games -and important markets in the short term. Innovative products of a truly multimedia type are still too rare and production costs remain too high for rapid progress to be expected. If there is not a rapid change in product design and production methods during the next decade, ICTs will probably not be instrumental in extending the scope of commercial and even industrialized culture, since with the products which are currently available they are increasingly marginalizing certain cultures, standardizing universally accessible products and excluding those who lack the purchasing power to be ICT consumers. The solution to this problem would appear relatively easy and involves speeding up product flow, which is the second major feature of the development of the cultural industries.

Distance-shopping for products hitherto almost e xclusively supplied by specialized end-product distributors or by mass distribution outlets, and downloading products accessible from a distance are two activities that have been made possible by the efficiency of communications networks and the growing sophistication of access terminals. The scope of this new electronic commerce is still difficult to gauge, but there is no doubt that in 1997-98 its growth was such that the major distribution groups all rushed headlong in that direction, preceded by small pioneering firms. This strategic choice was made despite the fact that monetary transactions on the Internet are still not totally safe and that arrangements for remunerating artists and publishers are still under negotiation. Most specialists consider that cultural products are particularly well-suited to this new form of distribution. There are substantial advantages for consumers: real-time access; the opportunity to browse through all available catalogues and products; access to catalogues of foreign firms which used to be accessible only, if at all, with long delays involved. In other words, these new ways of accessing cultural products are of special interest both to the consumers least concerned by mass products, and to specialist publishers and producers.

Paradoxically, the people who are apparently the most critical of this rapid change in the distribution of cultural products ('cultivated' members of society, let us say, who prefer the existing methods of accessing art forms, and also scientists) are those who, for the moment, find it most advantageous to purchase directly via the networks. There is an additional paradoxical aspect to these immediate advantages for the most selective and demanding users. Producers and artists who offer the most distinctive products and who frequently encounter great difficulty in distributing the works they create and publish will obviously be tempted to bypass the large broadcasters and distributors in order to contact consumers directly. This is all the more likely to happen because, throughout the history of the cultural industries, artists and their publishers have tried to eliminate intermediaries with little success. They themselves then joined that enviable group, thus only reinforcing the existing oligopolies.

The current trend consists mainly of users purchasing products after browsing through catalogues on publishers' sites and on the sites of artists acting as producers of their own works. Soon it will be possible to download actual works, meaning that publishers of books and recorded music will no longer need to reproduce and record the work in a physical medium. This is not a utopian prospect; it is already possible to access literary and musical works in this way, or even extracts from them. This phenomenon raises two essential questions about cultural products. Is a work on offer a finished product just because it has been stabilized in a medium? Next, have the forms of monetary payment by consumers, here encouraged to buy works piecemeal, and 'paying-as-they-go', been fully considered? These are not merely technical innovations which, by encouraging a commercial shift, coincide with changes in systems of accessing works. Here technical innovations are changing the very substance of cultural products in various ways, especially by calling into question their finished appearance, an aspect considered fundamental up until now.

In modern societies, the values and images associated with the concepts of leisure, information and culture are still sharply differentiated. Although these concepts are evolving and now sometimes overlap, it would nonetheless hardly be possible to confuse them taken in a strict sense. They have relatively stable definitions: information is more ephemeral than culture, and this idea orients the functioning of those who produce news and information; leisure time is primarily for entertainment, but leisure pursuits encouraging the development of cultural activities are judged as positive. Although the trend began earlier, ICTs are causing these distinctions to grow more and more blurred, and in some cases it is becoming difficult to distinguish between information products and cultural products. Methods of creation (by journalists or artists, with an increasing use of streamlined methods), production structures (more and more often controlled by the same multimedia groups), distribution procedures (via networks or in the form of products accessible on- or off-line), consumption time and conditions of consumer use (use is often individual and involves interactivity with the hardware acting as intermediary in programme communication) are now closely related, not to say identical. These similarities cannot be considered as either secondary or insignificant.

Behind all the confusions and convergences, the question that arises is more than ever that of mass culture, although in forms different from those observed in the 1960s when the phenomenon became evident. As the transmission of standardized and increasingly transnational mass culture boosted by ICTs develops, cultural distinc-tiveness tends to be maintained within an elitist, or at any rate a niche, context. Although distinctive cultural production is not declining, and examples of it which successfully express popular and national identities continue to receive considerable attention, they enter into competition with mass products that are easily distributed on communication networks.

The struggle is to some extent unequal, not because of inadequacy of supply but because the major communications groups are strengthening their hold on the circulation of products. Insofar as future developments can be inferred from the situation today, culture seems to be going the same way as leisure and information. For most people, ICTs have not yet become part of a familiar landscape. They have already led, however, to some fairly radical changes in the functioning and regulation of public services, resulting in considerable hesitation on the part of those responsible for cultural policy. An increase in the supply of commercial products almost inevitably leads to the reduction, if not the disappearance, of non-commercial products (heavily subsidized by public funds) and of semi-commercial products (e.g. small-scale productions and those enjoying tax and customs protection). A movement of this type has recently become apparent in television production. In response to competition from powerful new commercial channels and in order to increase their output of programmes to compete with the commercial channels, with approximately the same resources, the managers of public channels have been obliged to subcontract production, placing it in the hands of new private producers for whom the origin of the orders they handle is of no importance. As a result, production variety in public television programmes has declined sharply, and some types of programme are less available or have actually disappeared since they are not commercially viable in a situation where audience ratings are all-important. Poetry and other literary programmes have disap-peared or been banished from prime-time slots. Even once-popular variety shows have been downsized or incorporated into shows with a wider appeal, since the popularity of a group or singer is no longer sufficient in itself to attract a mass audience. Over the past ten or fifteen years, some national cultural industries have continued to function and have even grown as a result of certain trends in public policy.

In the European Union, community-wide or domestic measures have undoubtedly been beneficial to certain industries in Member States, such as book publishing (the French system of retail price maintenance for books has allowed a network of specialized bookshops to survive), recorded music publishing (radio stations are obliged to play a quota of nationally-produced songs and music), cinema and audiovisual production (a system incorporating various forms of aid to production) and television production. There is, however, no guarantee that these hitherto undeniably advantageous effects will continue in the future. Not only do quota systems run into operational difficulties attracting regular criticism because of their singularity in world commercial transactions, but the fact that programmes can now circulate on the networks and largely escape control from public authorities will tend to reduce the effectiveness of support measures for small- and medium-sized industries operating mainly within a specific cultural or linguistic framework. This does not mean that such measures are unnecessary, but that their effectiveness may become more uncertain, simply because con-sumers will tend to diversify demand, including demand for products from the sphere of high culture.

A number of authors representing different schools of thought have long been predicting a trend towards the individualization of social behaviour, and the emergence of this trend does seem to be reinforced by ICTs, particularly in the developed countries.

ICTs, unlike the media that developed earlier, usually require user-consumers to take active steps not only to access a specific programme but also to interact with it in order to obtain responses tailored to their personal requirements. To this extent, ICTs, more than any other earlier technology, promote a one-to-one correspondence between the content on offer and the user's demands, which are apparently unlike those of anyone else. Where ICTs are involved, cultural consumption is not simply a question of narcissistic contact with works. Likewise, collective forms of consumption are not doomed to disappear, because individualization does not necessarily spell a decline in public performances and other forms of collective entertainment.

Despite predictions to the contrary, the proliferation of individual delivery systems for recorded music has not led to a decline in concerts of all types of music. Complex interactions and processes of mutual i n fluence are observably taking place between different types of music, but it is not to be expected that this will have any practical outcome, although new linkages can be foreseen. ICTs encourage a fragmented, episodic pace of consumption which has little in common with the heyday of collective cultural consumption and this tendency may lead to a number of fundamental cultural changes. One consequence may be for increased cultural consumption to go hand in hand with a decline in discussion and debate focused on cultural productions. It is also possible that performances may become almost exclusively opportunities for the 'promotion' of cultural merchandise, something that would be inevitable if public aid earmarked for live performances were reduced or even abolished, with those responsible taking as their pretext the variety and quantity of commercial products available. This would mark the culmination of the process by which culture becomes a commercial product and, as noted above, is absorbed into the leisure and information sectors.

ICTs have promted American English to the status of an international language. According to a 1998 Euromarketing study, more than one of every two Internet surfers (58%) uses English. Other languages - Spanish (8.7%), German (8.6%), Japanese (7.9%) and French (3.7%) - are much less commonly used. These data, which are obviously difficult to establish, have nevertheless been confirmed by other studies. However, they are difficult to assess because change is so rapid in both hardware and habits. Furthermore, it is not possible, on the basis of data on the preferred language of communication (used for electronic mail and forums), to draw similar conclusions regarding trade in cultural products. For example, after an initial phase when English.. predominated, the satellite channels are now beginning to diversify into other languages. Will automatic translation systems contain applications that will help to reduce misunder-standings between languages and promote genuine multilingualism?

In the past, research has proved disappointing, and researchers are at present cautious, pinning their hopes on the development of computer-assisted translation systems. This indicates recognition of the fact that, in this field, approximations and simplifications are not sufficient, because they undermine languages as vehicles of specific cultural features. Only strong support for translation from producers and from authorities responsible for public policy can help to bring about a more balanced flow of cultural works. If this is not forthcoming, English and probably a few more of the most widely spoken languages will eventually dominate the cultural marketplace. Support for translation and for the development of translation aid systems will not, however, be enough in the absence of systematic efforts to support productions suitable for distribution outside their country or region of origin, and support in distributing them. Recent experience has shown that the successful exportation of films, works for television and sound broadcasting or even literary works, depends as much on international standards being met as on the availability of an appropriate distribution system. It is also important for production costs on national broadcasting networks to have been absorbed in advance, which explains the recent success of Brazilian and Mexican series outside the areas where they were produced. The same factors are likely to be important in the future.

Although in theory the new communications networks guarantee wider distribution, and even distribution that crosses borders and cuts out intermediaries, which may be helpful for niche products that may even be boycotted in their place of origin, it would be illusory to think that world markets will develop on this basis. Direct transactions will leave room for a few new actors, but free flow will probably lead to a rapid jump in production costs and a concentration of distributors. The major communi-cation groups are preparing for this eventuality. Their uncertainties about the future focus on the plans of their direct competitors rather than on the emergence of newcomers or the development of direct commerce that would be beyond their control.

ICTs undeniably complicate a number of issues facing the production of culture in all its diversity. However, the more or less rapid spread of hardware and networks is not the only factor involved in sustaining artistic pluralism within countries and regions and keeping a variety of production methods in place. Blithe and often exaggerated statements to the effect that we are now living in an information society which will impose its ground rules on culture should be viewed sceptically.

For complex reasons that research into technical innovation has already begun to elucidate, technical developments seldom fulfil expert predictions. In other words, ICTs do not contain a blueprint for the future. They will not be the sole factors shaping the future. If, however, those responsible for cultural production worldwide adopt a wait-and-see attitude and fail to grasp the importance of what is at stake, then culture will be increasingly subservient to the norms of mediatized communication and information flows.

Public cultural policies are important and should be reinstated in areas where the field has been left free for the commercial audiovisual media and transborder flows of information. Public action will have little effect, however, if it is confined to protective and defensive measures which are in any case liable to be inefficient, if not impossible, to implement. This issue is likely to give rise to considerable debate and to social movements and even 'resistance' instigated by artists, producers, users and political leaders.

During the 1993 General Agreement on Tariffs and Trade (GATT) negotiations, France strongly supported the idea of 'making an exception of culture' and provisionally won its case, arguing that with the opening of world markets, cultural products should not be treated like other commercial commodities. Since then, the question has been asked worldwide, some counting on a de facto abolition of the 'cultural exception' by technological development, while others are waiting for international organizations and regional bodies to come out in support of cultural pluralism. Another crucial issue being debated is the future of copyright and authors' continuing control over their works in an environment complicated by the emergence of multimedia products. Many developing countries have not yet stated that they are directly concerned by these discussions, which nevertheless do affect them. In order to maintain cultural pluralism, it is pointless to avoid or side-step negotiations on these basic issues. An attempt was made to do this in the case of the Multilateral Agreement on Investment (MAI) by seeking to negotiate behind closed doors within the OECD. What are needed are balanced agreements that acknowledge the distinctive nature of cultural products and do not treat them simply as industrial goods.

Impact of ICTS on Media

The increasingly interconnected nature of the mass media industry has encouraged integration in a complex variety of reciprocal connections. The first set of logical mergers were between different types of media, such as television with radio and the press to create multimedia conglomerates. Mergers of media entities across countries and regions also occurred in order to attain the critical business strength needed to reach global markets. A few hardware manufacturers made strategic moves to purchase media houses producing films, music and other media products. The strategy has paid off in recent years through co-ordinated releases of new generations of hardware, such as Digital Versatile Disk (DVD) players, digital television receivers, and digital music recording devices, together with media products and software to be played back on these new devices. The synergy is mutually beneficial. There would have been no demand for the hardware had there been a lack of attractive media products to play on the devices. Without the devices, the media companies would not have been able to launch a new generation of both old and new releases which help to produce a new stream of revenue for the existing libraries of intellectual properties owned by these media companies. In an interesting new twist to integration and convergence, a major television sports broadcaster has mounted a takeover of one of the most famous soccer teams in the world.

The business strategy is to acquire full control of broadcast and merchandising rights through the outright purchase of the team. If this proves to be a profitable move, it is not impossible that media companies may begin to purchase properties as diverse as universities and restaurants in order to secure publication copyright for scholarly titles and courses, and broadcast licences for cookery programmes. There are two sides to integration and convergence. The case against concentration of ownership can be seen within the printing sector in the United States, where extensive research shows that the twelve largest newspaper conglomerates control almost 50% of all circulation in the largest market for news in the world. In book publishing, nearly every one of the major commercial publishing companies has also been bought and assimilated into larger businesses, while independent bookstores are being forced out of business by a handful of powerful national chains. On the positive side, the sale of some cable television companies, again in the United States, helped raise much-needed financial investment to upgrade distribution systems. The merger of Cable News Network (CNN) with the Time Warner group led to the pooling of extensive complementary intellectual properties, particularly in politics, which has resulted in service on the Internet which offers more depth and data than either company alone could have provided in the print and television media.

The expansionary trends of the media conglomerates, coupled with media technologies which ignore political borders, have forced government-owned media organizations in newly developed and developing countries to respond. Within Asia, the response has generally been to privatize state-owned media in an effort to make them more competitive and attractive to domestic audiences. However, the privatization has been structured in such a way as to protect, preserve and empower traditional cultural values and maintain key government controls at the same time. The Association of South-East Asian Nations (ASEAN) plans to launch a regional direct satellite television broadcast channel, but these plans have been delayed by the financial problems affecting the region. When several large media organizations merge, they create media giants with huge audiences. This is an invaluable asset which helps in maximizing advertising revenue, the lifeblood of media. The merger also pools strategic market information, such as subscriber and advertiser databases which are used to cross-sell media products and advertising across the organizations within the merged group.

Direct selling is probably the showcase innovation of the private sector on the Internet, and Amazon.com is the current undisputed star in this area. Amazon began by selling books over its Internet site and subsequently added music CDs to its virtual bookstore. A strictly e-commerce company, it has captured the imagination of media organizations because it has so far dealt exclusively with media products. Indications are that it will diversify rapidly to include a large variety of consumer products. Every media company with tangible products must at some time have reviewed Amazon's methods for possible emulation. The arithmetic of direct selling to consumers worldwide without having to incur high distribution and sales discounts is an irresistible idea, and an increasing number of media organizations with such product offerings have launched websites to test the feasibility of an Amazon-like sales outlet. Attracting less public attention, but perhaps more exciting in its technological concept, are the direct sales facilities of newspapers, journals, bulletins, and electronic book publishers. Amazon uses the Internet only to promote and process payment for a product before resorting to fairly conventional means for delivering a traditional tangible media product to the consumer. In contrast to this, specialized publishers are offering articles and information from databases for instantaneous downloading over the Internet immediately after a payment has been made at the site. Book publishers will be interested in the mass consumer response to several electronic book devices introduced recently into the market and which approximate the size and feel of a book. They lend themselves to the direct sales of books bought and delivered over e-commerce systems.

The North American book distributor Barnes & Noble has negotiated with various publishers to offer more than 1,000 titles of books for downloading into the devices which have a capacity to store anything from about 1,000 to 500,000 pages at any one time. The e-book is an extremely attractive proposition to book publishers because they do not have to commit expensive print-runs and warehousing expenses up front; the risks are therefore minimum. This may encourage publishers to accept a larger number of manuscripts for publication. It is likely to facilitate the release of traditionally short-run titles, which have been rejected in the past because they were not viable as expensive paper editions. The e-book is a viable alternative to currently available publish-on-demand technology, which deploys high-speed photocopying machines linked to collating and binding machinery. The music industry may be on the verge of making similar direct sales. A new device which downloads and stores audio digital recordings from the Internet for repeated playback by consumers was cleared for public sale, following a court hearing in California (USA) to determine if such a device threatened the preservation of intellectual property rights. The legal endorsement for the device has set the stage for music to be sold directly to consumers, a song or 'cut' at a time, rather than as a compilation on longer-playing discs.

The ICT technologies, with their capacities to move multimedia content anywhere in the world in a matter of seconds, provide the perfect tool for gathering and disseminating news. They have become available at a time when the demand for news is rising rapidly, fuelled by the globalization of trade and national economies. The increasing demand is not only for a greater quantity of news, but also for higher speeds in reporting. This in turn presents developers of technology with demands to increase further the capabilities and speed of technologies creating a powerful iterative spiral, which will lead to even more, exciting technologies.

The demand for news worldwide is obviously not uniform. Television ratings are a good yardstick by which to gauge demand. News dominated the top ten television shows in the United States; soap operas of different origins seem to be the most popular in many other countries such as Brazil, China and South Africa. The demand for news over the Internet appears to be more consistent, with nearly all news sites registering the most number of visitors and Web pages downloaded. Sites operated by newspapers around the world commonly serve millions of page views per month. While most newspapers continue to provide only text and static images on their Web sites, radio, television and other integrated media conglomerates now offer multimedia content which includes text, and sound and video clips of headline news items. Several financial publications operate Web sites with access to constantly updated databases and expert systems·software to work out investment computations and projections.The exponential growth of the Internet as a channel for distributing news can be seen in the meteoric growth of Microsoft National Broadcasting Company (MSNBC), a joint venture between Microsoft and the National Broadcasting Company (NBC) in the United States.

By the first quarter of 1998, the news site served an average of 300,000 users a day with the occasional peak of 900,000 users. Together, they read 200 million pages a month. Measured by reach, it is the fifth largest daily newspaper in the United States. The top four Internet news sites in the country, MSNBC, USA Today, CNN and the American Broadcasting Company, collectively serve up 700 million pages of news every month.Direct satellite broadcast television news channels and the Internet benefit people around the world who want and need to have constantly updated access to news at all times of the day and night. This has caused an insatiable demand for the latest news, which has in turn created the twenty-four-hour news cycle. News operations in the past were governed by deadlines fixed by printing schedules, in the case of newspapers and magazines, and airtimes for conventional radio and television news. Now that the audience is global, every moment of the day and night is the deadline.

All news programming is by definition perpetually incomplete and in a state of being constantly updated. The concept of 'the edition' has been replaced by devices such as 'breaking news' when regular programming is interrupted in television broadcasts, to show raw, unedited, live coverage about a still-evolving news item. On the Internet, a similar device is the 'latest' button, which provides a link to a usually brief write-up of a news event in the making.

The race to be the first on the air or the Internet with the latest news has created an approach to news reporting which concentrates on the immediate, the gathering of eye-witness accounts, and a follow-up of the event as it unfurls and draws to a conclusion. Attention to analytical writing is on the decline. The twenty-four-hour news cycle, and the quickly changing news agenda discourages reflection, research and analysis which take up time, and time is what the editorial departments no longer have to spare. The result is sometimes news reporting which is disconnected from history and the broader geo-political context.

Merrill Brown, editor-in-chief of MSNBC, is mindful of the shortcomings of journalism on the Internet: 'Those of us producing for the Internet haven't always been as thoughtful as we might about putting today's incremental developments into perspective'. Andrew Heyward, the News President of Columbia Broadcasting System (CBS), one of the dominant North American television networks, is equally conscious of television's short-falls. He identified 'the seven daily sins of television news' as imitation, predictability, artificiality, laziness, oversimplification, hype and cynicism. Although not as profitable as the owners would like, the media is now big business. During the con-centration of ownership, large financial investments were made; owners are now eager to recover them. At the same time, profits at many media organizations have shrunk. Together, these considerations have driven media organizations to cut costs and this has harmed the quality and diversity of news services. Among the elements which have been slashed are foreign news bureaus and the amount of original reporting undertaken.

News editors are also less inclined to dispatch their own reporters, photographers and camera crews to cover an event, preferring instead to rewrite wire service stories and tap into news footages from large television news agencies. The impact of this trend is a significantly reduced plurality of perspectives, especially where international news items are concerned. The same television news clips are broadcast by stations around the world, while the same wire service dispatches are carried in the newspapers. This provides the handful of international news agencies which feed the media. organizations around the world with an oligarchic grip on the flow of news and views. This phenomenon is called 'consonance'. Research has shown that the further the geographic origin of a news story from the editorial headquarters of a media organization, the higher the level of consonance. Accuracy of information has also suffered as a result of cost-cutting. Reduced resources to research and confirm facts often lead to the release of not completely accurate news and content. Because of the concentration of media organizations, the effects of these errors are sometimes multiplied across several types of media.

The internet has helped to inject a level of participation in news commentary that did not exist in the past. This has taken the form of on-line polls of audiences and readership using customized software which operate at media Web sites. Although the samples reached in such polls are obviously not always representative, they are nevertheless a good beginning in getting the audience involved in developing opinions about issues. Current methods of polling offer audiences a limited number of choices, identified by the media, which may not always reflect the full spectrum of opinion. Perhaps more useful are facilities at certain Web sites for visitors to post their comments.

The Internet version of a phone-in comment is tremendously popular with interactive radio stations. A few international radio and television broadcasters have also started to use audience postings of comments at Web sites and e-mail, as a channel for the audience to participate in live panel discussions. The low cost of using the Internet by the audience permits this form of live participation at the global level on a sustained basis and, if facilitated effectively, will contribute towards enriching the diversity of perspectives in all types of media. In participation of a different sort, newsmakers now use the Internet to reach out directly to the audience, bypassing the media. Court judgements have been posted directly on to the Internet, as have copious copies of original reports of powerful government-appointed investigating authorities. Such events are being multiplied in a myriad of other events, ranging from the birth of a child to an expedition on Mount Everest.

Quick-thinking editors and their lawyers have found an interesting innovative use of the new technologies in the defence of the freedom of the media. United States media organizations subpoenaed for information in their possession, and faced with prospects of losing the legal challenge when no important information is involved, have been known to publish photographs or broadcast footages so that they can honestly claim that they have not surrendered any unpublished material to the prosecutors. The new technologies allow news stories and pictures to be rushed out into the public domain over the Internet. Television companies, faced with the need to place uninteresting and insignificant footage in the public domain, have been known to broadcast this material in the middle of the night using an idle satellite

Emergence of New Business Models

The evolution of a new generation of media technologies has presented the industry with many possibilities for developing new products and services. One of the key factors, which will help in identifying the final list of possibilities for sustained development, is the parallel evolution of business models applicable to these possibilities. The successful candidates must operate with a business model acceptable to the consumers, and attractive enough to engage media operators. The private sector has long been the primary source for funding of media operations in North America, Europe, Latin America and parts of Asia. With the trend towards the privatization of state-owned media in developing countries, the importance of feasible business models has become critical in the determination of how technologies will be deployed, and what content and software will be offered.

Large audience base models: This type of business model dominate for traditional mass media such as radio, print and television. It has also become one of the most important models for Internet-related operations where 'portal' sites offering search and directory services to the vast World Wide Web have drawn the largest number of users and attracted the keenest interest of investors and entrepreneurs. As with most broadcast organizations, portal sites do not charge for their services but instead derive revenues by selling advertising. In this model, the number of people served by a particular Web site or broadcasting station is crucial in determining the pricing of its advertisements, and eventually its revenue. The same applies to the print media products, which are often priced for the recovery of production and distribution costs only, while profits and creative costs derive from the sale of advertising space. These numbers will take on added importance when members of the audience become customers and shoppers on interactive television and electronic commerce Web sites.

New audience-tracking technologies and sophisticated audience research methodologies enable these numbers to be desegregated into groups with a high propensity to purchase certain goods and services. These advances are a boon to advertisers and will pose a challenge to media operators, who, in the past, were required simply to broadcast advertisements for large groups. The tougher requirements are already apparent in advertising at Web sites where operators are required to broadcast advertisements in the style of banners at the top or bottom of specified Web pages, and the cost of advertising was determined by the number of people accessing the page and seeing the advertisements. This simple formula became a little more complicated when the cost was computed on the basis of the number of people who clicked on the banners and visited the Web site linked to the advertisements. The third formula which is evolving will very likely be based on a sales commission on the actual business transacted as a result of exposure, click-throughs and other services rendered at a particular Web site or page.

E-commerce model: This model has captured the imagination of the industry as the most appropriate for the Internet with Amazon.com as the premier prototype company. Amazon has demonstrated both the potential and the problems of this model. Although it is popularly cited as the most successful electronic commerce company, it has not shown a profit since it started. On the contrary, Amazon consistently incurred losses until the end of 1998. Researchers who have tracked the company's exponential growth blame the losses on high operating costs. Its economics also reveal a staggering scale of business. One study estimated that Amazon must generate $1 billion in annual sales just to break even. The electronic publishing model has been given a boost with the introduction of secure electronic transaction software and systems which permit payments for purchases made over the Internet to be securely debited from credit card accounts. Further progress is expected in the near future when 'smart cards', which enable payment purchases using secure computer codes, are launched worldwide.

Subscription access model: Subscription access was widely thought to be a promising model for the electronic publishing of newspapers, magazines, journals, and newsletters. The typical electronic subscription begins when a person makes a lump sum payment to the publisher, who then provides the subscriber with a unique password, which then permits access to each new edition at a Web site. Although the model was based on very sound logic, it was not well received by people on the Internet. For the present, it appears that the founding principle of the Internet for the free sharing of information still persists. Major content providers have indefinitely postponed plans to charge for access to their sites. To replace this, some providers require visitors to their Web sites to register themselves, or encourage them to click on the advertisement of a corporate sponsor, as a kind of surrogate payment. This has caused extensive revisions in the business plans of media companies started for the exclusive purpose of publishing and selling information over the Internet.

Conventional media, such as television news networks, newspapers, and magazines, which extended their dissemination by recycling selections from their products on the Internet, have enjoyed more prosperity. Their sites regularly clock up millions of visitors each month who in turn each read several Web pages and help to generate a total of many millions more 'page views' for the sites. While people visiting the sites do not pay for their visits, the media organizations running the sites benefit in several ways: firstly, by promoting or cross-selling their flagship on printed or broadcast products via free access to excerpts at the Web site; secondly, by offering archival information such as previously published articles or transcripts of old broadcasts for sale through an automated system of database searches and electronic commerce; and lastly, by exposing people to this new outlet for their products and developing a global audience for future sales of a new generation of products and services.

The Economist and The Wall Street Journal now publish simultaneously on paper and on the Internet. There are many sites on the Internet that provide news. One type are the special Internet news sites, often provided by the Internet Service Providers (ISPs). Others are sites maintained by already-existing newspapers as a complement to the printed product. One can find daily newspapers and news-oriented periodicals from almost every country in the world, representing a mixture of national and regional/local press, as well as news targeting specific groups in terms of language and/or ethnic belonging. One significant result of this development is that, whereas the possibilities of access to traditionally disseminated press were limited, especially concerning regional and local press, news via the Internet means worldwide dissemination.

The former provides subscribers to the printed product and free access to the Internet edition. The latter sells subscription access to both versions. Some newspapers have used their Internet editions to enhance the attractiveness of their classified advertisements by offering package deals, which place such advertisements simultaneously on both printed and Internet editions. As a result of the financial crisis of 1997/98, media organizations throughout Asia, Latin America and Russia are struggling to stay solvent. The media in these regions have been hit by high increases in repayments of bank loans and other forms of business financing, increases in the price of newsprint, and significant drops in advertising revenue, as companies have trimmed their advertising budgets as part of cost-cutting measures. Internet services providers have suffered from the crisis as well, because the values of local currencies have fallen in relation to the US dollar in which the cost of telecommunications connections are calculated. At the same time and for the same reason, the cost of imported networking hardware and soft-ware has also increased.

Challenges of ICTs

The reality of the widening gap in digital capacity raises the serious concern that the poorer countries may not be able to overcome the financial and technical obstacles now limiting their access to the digital technologies. In early 1995 the concern about the ICT-gap inspired many public and private donor institutions to propose plans for the elimination of digital disparity. For example, the World Bank established the Information for Development Program to assist developing countries with their integration into the global information economy. In the same year, the ITU established World Tel, an ambitious project to generate private investments for bridging the telecommunications gap in the world by developing basic infrastructures. WorldTel aims to establish 40 million telephone connections in developing countries over the next ten years, which will require a minimal investment of $1,000 million.

The equitable sharing of communication infrastructures (the electronic highways systems created by carriers such as satellites, cables, fixed lines and mobile transmissions), computing capacity (computers, peripherals, networks), information resources (databases, libraries), and ICT-literacy (intellectual and social capabilities to deploy ICT in beneficial ways) will require an enormous effort from the international community. Massive investments are required for the renovation, upgrading and expansion of networks in developing countries, for programmes to transfer knowledge and for ICT skill training, in particular for women. In 1985, the

Maitland Commission estimated that an annual investment of $12,000 million would be needed to achieve the goal of simple, universal access to a telephone early in the 21st century. To attract private funding, countries will have to liberalize their ICT markets and adopt measures in favour of competition. In this context the World Bank has recommended the creation of investor-friendly business environments, the protection of investments and security for repatriating revenues. When public companies are privatized there may be losses in revenues as a result of the change in service charges or severance payments. The World Bank is therefore proposing to finance the adjustment costs of the adoption of liberalization schemes in individual countries.

The World Bank's policies are characterized by a strong emphasis on economic growth and a key role for the private sector. The expectation is that, in a sufficiently free market, economic growth will also benefit the poorer sector of society. In this context the contribution of the ICTs is to provide the essential infrastructure for economic development. This position bypasses the question raised earlier, as to whether the deployment of ICTs does indeed lead to growth in economic productivity and, if so, whether such growth will be equitably distributed. The governance of ICTs is in fact left to freely operating private entrepreneurs. The basic assumption is that a country's telecommunication infrastructure can be managed by private companies and that, whenever parts of the network are unprofitable, the state will provide the public means to ensure that no citizen is disenfranchised.

There is some debate about the expectation that private funding will create worldwide equity in the access to and use of ICT resources. It appears in any case that the international community and national governments of affluent countries need to bear in mind that problems stem not only from a lack of financial resources but also from a lack of political will. Creating adequate access to ICT resources worldwide should not be a problem in a world economy with income amounting to roughly $22 trillion. The core issue is that expenditures for development assistance represent only $55,000 million and thus a mere 0.25% of this income. The annual costs for all developing countries for adding one thousand million telephone lines, subsidizing over 600 million households that cannot afford basic telephone charges, providing PCs and access to the Internet for schools over a period of ten years could represent from $80,000 to $100,000 million. This is not a prohibitive level of funding. It represents about 11% of the world's annual military expenditure, about 22% of total annual spending on narcotic drugs, and is comparable with the annual expenditure on alcoholic drinks in Europe alone. For a variety of political and economic reasons, many donor governments are presently reducing budgets for financing ICT-development.

Between 1990 and 1995, multilateral lending for telecommunications decreased from $1,253 million to $967 million. Bilateral aid for telecommunications decreased from $1,259 million in 1990 to $800 million in 1995. Financial obstacles are, however, not the only concern. The transfer of ICTs also raises questions about their appropriateness and about the capacity of the recipient countries to make the best use of them. Over the past few decades the prevailing international policies on technology transfer have placed formidable obstacles in the process of reducing North-South technology gaps; the present discussion on the ICT-gap provides no convincing evidence that the technology owners will change their attitudes and policies towards the international transfer of technology.

There is no indication that current restrictive business practices, constraints on the ownership of knowledge, and rules on intellectual property rights that are adverse to developing country interests are radically changing, and there are no realistic prospects that the relations between ICT-rich and ICT-poor countries will change in the near future. The question must be raised as to whether there can be any serious reduction of the ICT disparity, given the realities of the present international economic order. It may well be an illusion to think that the ICT-poor countries could catch up or keep pace with progress among countries in the Northern hemisphere, where the rate of technological development is very high and is supported by considerable resources. This is not to say that poor countries should not try to upgrade their ICT-systems. They should, however, not act with the unrealistic expectation that those who are ahead are planning to wait for them.

In most countries, the problems concerning access to ICTs are handled through public policies based on an already defined technological environment. Developing countries thus find it difficult to assess what digital technologies would be appropriate for their specific development strategies. A problem compounding this situation is that in many cases 'peripheral states seem to have no disinterested non-governmental organizations to advise them on telecommunication technology and the social objectives of regulation that would safeguard those interests that private profit will not meet. Without adequate regulatory intervention to ensure accountability to the general public, market forces that respond to those groups with purchasing power are bound to generate unequal development'. Most developing countries lack the capacity to identify appropriate digital technologies, and, to make matters worse, there is also a critical absence of co-ordination of 'digital' policies among the developing countries themselves.

It is essential to recognize that planning for the adoption and deployment of digital technologies can no longer be a local affair. Global negotiations, such as the recent General Agreement on Tariffs and Trade (GATT) Uruguay Round of Multilateral Trade Negotiations, heavily affect national technology plans, while the processes of globalization. Information and communication technologies and social processes determine the playing field for local actors. As a result, local planning has to take into account the effects of global forces, possible only when planners in the periphery pool resources and mobilize a constituency that counteracts the Northern dominance in global planning. Since today's globalization process is largely determined by Northern forces, 'many developing countries do not obtain a fair share of the benefits of globalization, and some actually suffer net losses'. The North is in control not only due to strength but also because of lack of co-ordination in the South. National technology policies are largely determined by the work of global institutions and their rules and standards. It is vital that developing countries participate more forcefully and effectively in these institutions.

3

World Wide Web as a Communication Tool

Often referred to as WWW or the Web, the World Wide Web usually refers to information available on the Internet that can be easily accessed with software usually called a "browser." Organizations publish their information on the Web in a format known as HTML; this information is usually referred to as their "home page" or "web site". www. The World Wide Web (WWW) emerged from ideas about nonlinear information organization and was developed to meet the information needs of researchers in the high-energy physics community. Today, the WWW offers a system for distributing hypermedia information locally or globally.

The orgin of the Web can be traced back to a project at CERN in 1989 when Tim Berners-Lee and Robert Cailliau built ENQUIRE (*Enquire Within Upon Everything*—a book Berners-Lee recalled from his youth). While it was rather different from the Web we use today, it contained many of the same core ideas. Berners-Lee mentions that much of the motivation behind the project was so that he could access library information that was scattered on several different servers at CERN.

The primary underlying concept of hypertext came from earlier efforts, such as Ted Nelson's Project Xanadu and Douglas Engelbart's oN-Line System (NLS). Both Nelson and Engelbart were in turn inspired by Vannevar Bush's microfilm-based "memex," which was described in the 1945 essay *As We May Think*. Berners-Lee's brilliant breakthrough was to marry hypertext to the Internet. In his book *Weaving The Web,* he explains that he had repeatedly suggested that a marriage between the two technologies was possible to members of *both* technical communities, but when no one took up his invitation, he finally tackled the project himself. In the process, he developed a system of globally unique identifiers for resources on the Web and elsewhere: the Uniform Resource Identifier.

The WWW is made up of three standards: (a) the *Uniform Resource Locator* (URL), which specifies how each page of information is given a unique "address" at which it can be found; *(b) Hyper Text Transfer Protocol* (HTTP), which specifies how the browser and server send the information to each other, and *(c) Hyper Text Markup Language* (HTML), a method of encoding the information so it can be displayed on a variety of devices. Berners-Lee now heads the World Wide Web Consortium, which develops and maintains these standards and others that enable computers on the Web to effectively store and communicate all kinds of information.

The initial "www" program at CERN displayed styled text and images, and it was a WYSIWYG HTML editor as well as the browser. As it ran only on NeXT machines, CERN released a simple, text-only version to the world. Some journalists first encountered the Web through the text browser written by Nicola Pellow and this engendered a myth that the Web was text-only until Mosaic came along. The Web had graphics from the start, at least for NeXT users. However, Mosaic did introduce the ability to combine text and images in a single page. Meanwhile, browsers such as Tony Johnson's "Midas" and Pei-Yuan Wei's Viola added the ability to display graphics also on other Unix machines. Marc Andreessen of NCSA released a browser called "Mosaic for X" in 1993 that sparked a tremendous rise in the popularity of the Web among novice users. Andreesen went on to found Mosaic Communications Corporation. Additional features such as dynamic content, music and animation can be found in modern browsers. Frequently, the technical capability of browsers and servers advances much faster than the standards bodies can keep up with, so it is not uncommon for these newer features not to work properly on all computers, and the web as seen by Netscape or Mozilla Firefox is not quite the same as the web seen by Internet Explorer. The ever-improving technical capability of the WWW has enabled the development of real-time web-based services such as webcasts, web radio and live web cams.

Another significant advance in the technology was Sun Microsystems' Java programming language, which enabled web servers to embed small programs (called applets) directly into the information being served that would run on the user's computer, allowing faster and richer user interaction. JavaScript, however, is a scripting language that was developed for Web pages. While its name is similar to Java it was developed by Netscape and not Sun Microsystems. In conjunction with the Document Object Model, JavaScript has become a much more powerful language than its creators originally envisioned. Sometimes its usage is expressed under the term DHTML, or *Dynamic HTML*, to emphasize a shift away from *static* HTML pages.

The exponential growth of the Internet was primarily attributed to the emergence of the web browser Mosaic, followed by its commercial offspring Netscape Navigator, during the mid-1990s. It brought unprecedented attention to the Internet from media, industries, policy makers, and the general public. Eventually, it led to several visions of how our society might change, although some point out that those visions are not unique to the Internet, but repeated with many new technologies (especially information and communications technologies) of various era. Because the web is global in scale, some suggested that it will nurture mutual understanding on a global scale.

Advantages of Web as a Communication Tool

The range of technologies a Web developer can choose from is now more varied than ever. Besides an array of techniques and tools to shape meaning with HyperText Markup Language (HTML), developers also can use many technologies to add new kinds of multimedia and interactive content to on-line services. New kinds of software to observe Web content are being developed, and the competition for being the provider of Internet software has risen to the highest priority in the personal computer industry. Whereas the view of the Web in 1989 was a text-based browser deployed on an internal network, today the Web is a global medium that encompasses many software and communications systems across many networks. Within just the years 1995-1996, new kinds of system s emerged that enabled new forms of communications over the Web. The Java language, specifically designed for network communications, rose to prominence in 1995 as a new way of communicating on the Web.

Java brought a new way of expressing interactivity on-line and a shift of attention toward write-once, run anywhere, network-distributed software. Java didn't replace the existing systems of the Web that had existed up to 1995, but instead supplemented the Web with new components. Similarly, new technical possibilities expanded regarding the kinds of media a Web page can carry. Although sound, video, and other multimedia effects were possible before 1995-1996, systems emerged during this period that provided high-quality solutions to some of the problems of distributing multimedia on global networks.

Notably, RealAudio emerged as an outstanding solution to providing audio on demand over the Internet. Instead of a click and wait cycle of sound retrieval, RealAudio provides a streaming solution; users can listen to an audio file as it is downloaded instead of having to wait for the whole file to download. This system was a boon to the sound industry; ABC Radio News, CBC Radio, the National Public Radio of the United States, and dozens of radio stations worldwide suddenly could have the Internet as a supplement to the airwaves as a broadcast medium.

Multimedia developers also gained new possibilities for networked communication with Macromedia's Shockwave product. Shockwave provides a set of plugins for its existing Macromedia authorware and enables developers to create multimedia content. The method of distributing RealAudio or Shockwave content to users who obtain freely available viewer software remains a commonplace model for distributing new media on the Web.

Virtual Reality Modeling Language (VRML) is yet another major technology that emerged during 1995-1996 as a component of a Web developer's choices for expression. VRML opens up the possibility for three-dimensional worlds-the creation of a cyberspace more in line with the visions of science fiction writers of the past. Combined with Java, the 3-D worlds of VRML can have behavior—the shapes and structures can respond to a user's presence and input.

The hypertext language of the Web itself-the HyperText Markup Language-also changed. The pressure on the HTML specifications to change to accommodate new ideas was so great that the HTML 3.0 specification was overloaded with new ideas; as a result, it was never finalized. Instead, the HTML 3.2 specification was finalized in 1996. The HTML 3.2 specifications are a scaleback from the original 3.0 draft specifications but are more manageable to implement.

The Web's expansion and change isn't determined by its technical makeup, however. Indeed, technical innovations throughout history often have failed because of their lack of social acceptance and use; witness the picture phone and other technically "good ideas" that people simply never wanted and never used. The Web doesn't seem doomed as yet, however, to the scrap heap. The Web appears to have caught on-at least among the technologically rich people and countries of the world-as part of the communications environment. From Wall Street to Wal-Mart, the Web has become part of the communications culture. In the consumer world, the Web routinely is used to promote everything from Coca-Cola to movies.

Many businesses see the Web now as a key component of their work. As an integral part of future business on the Web, the banking industry gradually is making steps toward serving its customers on-line. Systems of virtual cash are in development that may create not only a widespread promotional market on the Web, but an actual market for trade. With financial payments, the Web is poised to become even a more important part of the global communications and trade systems. According to most demographic gauges, the use of the Internet and Web is fairly extensive. According to researchers at Vanderbilt University, an estimated 28.8 million people in the United States who are 16 and older have potential or actual access to the Internet; 11.5 million of these people use the Web; and 1.51 million have used the Web for a purchase. Although these numbers don't reveal the actual involvement or commitment people have regarding Web communications, they do represent a mass audience that commercial enterprises don't want to ignore.

Presentation and Interaction Technologies of the Web

The Web is a heterogeneous environment where a wide variety of agents provide access to content to users with a wide variety of capabilities. It is good practice for authors to create content that can reach the widest possible audience, including users with graphical desktop computers, hand-held devices and mobile phones, users with disabilities who may require speech synthesizers, and devices not yet imagined. A specification should allow authors to separate content from both presentation and interaction concerns. There are advantages to each approach. For instance when a client (such as a mobile phone) communicates device capabilities to the server (for example, using CC/PP), the server can tailor the delivered content to fit that client. The server can, for example, enable faster downloads by adjusting links to refer to lower resolution images, smaller video or no video at all. Similarly, if the content has been authored with multiple branches, the server can remove unused branches before delivery.

Designing content that that can be recombined on the client also tends to make that content applicable to a wider range of devices. This design also improves caching efficiency and offers users more presentation options. Media-dependent style sheets can be used to tailor the content on the client side to particular groups of target devices. For textual content with a regular and repeating structure, the combined size of the text content plus the style sheet is typically less than that of fully recombined content; the savings improve further if the style sheet is reused by other pages. In practice a combination of both approaches is often used. The design decision about where on this spectrum an application should be placed depends on the power on the client, the power and the load on the server, and the bandwidth of the medium that connects them. If the number of possible clients is unbounded, the application will scale better if more computation is pushed to the client.

Some data formats are designed to describe presentation (including SVG and XSL Formatting Objects). Data formats such as these demonstrate that one can only separate content from presentation (or interaction) so far; at some point it becomes necessary to talk about presentation. Per the principle of orthogonal specifications these data formats should *only* address presentation issues.

HyperText Markup Language (HTML)

HyperText Markup Language (HTML) is a markup language designed for the creation of web pages and other information viewable in a browser. Originally defined as a simple application of SGML, which is used by organizations with complex publishing requirements, HTML is now an international standard (ISO/IEC 15445:2000). The HTML specification is maintained mainly by the World Wide Web Consortium (W3C). The most recent version of HTML is HTML 4.01, although it has been since superseded by XHTML.

HTML is a form of markup that is oriented toward the presentation of single-page text documents with specialized rendering software called an HTML user agent, the most common example of which is a web browser. HTML provides a means by which the document's main content can be annotated with various kinds of metadata and rendering hints. The rendering cues may range from minor text decorations, such as specifying that a certain word be underlined or that an image be inserted, to sophisticated scripts, imagemaps, and form definitions that control web browsers. The metadata may include information about the document's title and author, structural information such as an expression of how the content is segmented into paragraphs, lists, headings, arbitrary divisions, etc., and most importantly, information that allows the document to be linked to other documents. Although most HTML documents contain a main body of text, it is not uncommon to encounter minimal HTML documents that exist only to present visual media in a web browser.

HTML is usually authored in a text editor and stored in a text file with a name usually ending in ".html" or ".htm". Such a file is typically created with the intent that it will be accessed over the World Wide Web, which uses the HTTP network protocol to transfer the files to requesting computers. A request for an HTML document is usually made by a web browser, such as Apple Safari, Mozilla Firefox, or Microsoft Internet Explorer, and upon receipt, the document is rendered and presented to the user. However, HTML can also be transmitted in email messages and rendered by software for email reading, or processed by cellphones that have web browsing capabilities.

Efforts of the web development community have led to a new thinking in the way a web document should be written; XHTML epitomizes this effort. Standards stress using markup which suggests the structure of the document, like headings, paragraphs, block quoted text, and tables, instead of using markup which is written for visual purposes only, like <font>, <b> (bold), and <i> (italics). Such presentational code has been removed from the HTML 4.01 Strict and XHTML specifications in favor of CSS solutions. CSS provides a way to separate the HTML structure from the content's presentation. See separation of style and content. A data format should incorporate hypertext links if hypertext is the expected user interface paradigm. Data formats that do not allow content authors to create hypertext links lead to the creation of "terminal nodes" on the Web.

XML-Based Data Formats

Many data formats are *XML-based*, that is to say they conform to the syntax rules defined in the XML specification

[XML10] or [XML11]. This section discusses issues that are specific to such formats. Anyone seeking guidance in this area is urged to consult the "Guidelines For the Use of XML in IETF Protocols" [IETFXML], which contains a thorough discussion of the considerations that govern whether or not XML ought to be used, as well as specific guidelines on how it ought to be used. While it is directed at Internet applications with specific reference to protocols, the discussion is generally applicable to Web scenarios as well.

XML defines textual data formats that are naturally suited to describing data objects which are hierarchical and processed in a chosen sequence. It is widely, but not universally, applicable for data formats; an audio or video format, for example, is unlikely to be well suited to expression in XML. Design constraints that would suggest the use of XML include: Requirement for a hierarchical structure.

- Need for a wide range of tools on a variety of platforms.
- Need for data that can outlive the applications that currently process it.
- Ability to support internationalization in a self-describing way that makes confusion over coding options unlikely.
- Early detection of encoding errors with no requirement to "work around" such errors.
- A high proportion of human-readable textual content.
- Potential composition of the data format with other XML-encoded formats.
- Desire for data easily parsed by both humans and machines.
- Desire for vocabularies that can be invented in a distributed manner and combined flexibly.

Sophisticated linking mechanisms have been invented for XML formats. XPointer allows links to address content that does not have an explicit, named anchor. [XLink] is an appropriate specification for representing links in hypertext XML applications. XLink allows links to have multiple ends and to be expressed either inline or in "link bases" stored external to any or all of the resources identified by the links it contains. Designers of XML-based formats may consider using XLink and, for defining fragment identifier syntax, using the XPointer framework and XPointer element() Schemes. XLink is not the only linking design that has been proposed for XML, nor is it universally accepted as a good design.

The purpose of an XML namespace (defined in [XMLNS]) is to allow the deployment of XML vocabularies (in which element and attribute names are defined) in a global environment and to reduce the risk of name collisions in a given document when vocabularies are combined. For example, the MathML and SVG specifications both define the set element. Although XML data from different formats such as MathML and SVG can be combined in a single document, in this case there could be ambiguity about which set element was intended. XML namespaces reduce the risk of name collisions by taking advantage of existing systems for allocating globally scoped names: the URI system. When using XML namespaces, each local name in an XML vocabulary is paired with a URI (called the namespace URI) to distinguish the local name from local names in other vocabularies.

The use of URIs confers additional benefits. First, each URI/local name pair can be mapped to another URI, grounding the terms of the vocabulary in the Web. These terms may be important resources and thus it is appropriate to be able to associate URIs with them. [RDFXML] uses simple concatenation of the namespace URI and the local name to create a URI for the identified term. Designers of XML-based data formats who declare namespaces thus make it possible to reuse those data formats and combine them in novel ways not yet imagined. Failure to declare namespaces makes such reuse more difficult, even impractical in some cases.

A specification that establishes an XML vocabulary should place all element names and global attribute names in a namespace. Attributes are always scoped by the element on which they appear. An attribute that is "global," that is, one that might meaningfully appear on elements of many types, including elements in other namespaces, should be explicitly placed in a namespace. Local attributes, ones associated with only a particular element type, need not be included in a namespace since their meaning will always be clear from the context provided by that element.

There are many reasons to provide a namespace document. A person might want to:

— understand the purpose of the namespace,
— learn how to use the markup vocabulary in the namespace,
— find out who controls it and associated policies,
— request authority to access schemas or collateral material about it, or
— report a bug or situation that could be considered an error in some collateral material.

Consider the following fragment of XML: <section name="foo">. Does the section element have what the XML Recommendation refers to as the ID foo (i.e., "foo" must not appear in the surrounding XML document more than once)? One cannot answer this question by examining the element and its attributes alone. In XML, the quality of "being an ID" is associated with the type of an attribute, not its name. Finding the IDs in a document requires additional processing.

Processing the document with a processor that recognizes DTD attribute list declarations (in the external or internal subset) might reveal a declaration that identifies the name attribute as an ID. Note: This processing is not necessarily part of validation. A non-validating, DTD-aware processor can recognize IDs. Processing the document with a W3C XML schema might reveal an element declaration that identifies the name attribute as an W3C XML Schema ID.

In practice, processing the document with another schema language, such as RELAX NG [RELAXNG], might reveal the attributes declared to be of ID in the XML Schema sense. Many modern specifications begin processing XML at the Infoset [INFOSET] level and do not specify normatively how an Infoset is constructed. For those specifications, any process that establishes the ID type in the Infoset (and Post Schema Validation Infoset (PSVI) defined in [XMLSCHEMA]) may usefully identify the attributes of type ID.

Data formats enable the creation of new applications to make use of the information space infrastructure. The Semantic Web is one such application, built on top of RDF [RDFXML]. This document does not discuss the Semantic Web in detail; the TAG expects that future volumes of this document will.

Errors occur in networked information systems. An error condition can be well-characterized (e.g., well-formedness errors in XML or 4xx client errors in HTTP) or arise unpredictably. *Error correction* means that an agent repairs a condition so that within the system, it is as though the error never occurred. One example of error correction involves data retransmission in response to a temporary network failure. *Error recovery* means that an agent does not repair an error condition but continues processing by addressing the fact that the error has occurred.

Agents frequently *correct* errors without user awareness, sparing users the details of complex network communications. On the other hand, it is important that agents *recover* from error in a way that is evident to users, since the agents are acting on their behalf.

An agent is not required to interrupt the user (e.g., by popping up a confirmation box) to obtain consent. The user may indicate consent through pre-selected configuration options, modes, or selectable user interface toggles, with appropriate reporting to the user when the agent detects an error. Agent developers should not ignore usability issues when designing error recovery behavior.

To promote interoperability, specification designers should identify predictable error conditions. Experience has led to the following observations about error-handling approaches.

— Protocol designers should provide enough information about an error condition so that an agent can address the error condition. For instance, an HTTP 404 status code (not found) is useful because it allows user agents to present relevant information to users, enabling them to contact the representation provider in case of problems.

— Experience with the cost of building a user agent to handle the diverse forms of ill-formed HTML content convinced the designers of the XML specification to require that agents fail upon encountering ill-formed content. Because users are unlikely to tolerate such failures, this design choice has pressured all parties into respecting XML's constraints, to the benefit of all.

— An agent that encounters unrecognized content may handle it in a number of ways, including by considering it an error.

— Error behavior that is appropriate for a person may not be appropriate for software. People are capable of exercising judgement in ways that software applications generally cannot. An informal error response may suffice for a person but not for a processor.

The Web follows Internet tradition in that its important interfaces are defined in terms of protocols, by specifying the syntax, semantics, and sequencing constraints of the messages interchanged. Protocols designed to be resilient in the face of widely varying environments have helped the Web scale and have facilitated communication across multiple trust boundaries. Traditional application programming interfaces (APIs) do not always take these constraints into account, nor should they be required to. One effect of protocol-based design is that the technology shared among agents often lasts longer than the agents themselves. It is common for programmers working with the Web to write code that generates and parses these messages directly. It is less common, but not unusual, for end users to have direct exposure to these messages. It is often desirable to provide users with access to format and protocol details: allowing them to "view source," whereby they may gain expertise in the workings of the underlying system.

Future of Web

As the technology of the Web, its social acceptance, and audience expand, the most crucial challenge is to create meaning on-line. Although the Web's widespread use means that it is no longer a novelty to have a Web site, it remains a novelty to develop a Web site well. Web development is extremely easy to start; a novice can put together a Web home page very quickly and announce its existence to the world. What is hard is creating a successful Web site. The challenge for Web developers remains-as it has for almost a decade-to create meaning and value in the on-line medium.

Web developers no doubt have a difficult task. The period 1995-1996 saw the emergence of a Web hangover—a period of disappointment with the truly hard work it takes to develop a Web site well. The massive hype of the mid-1990s about Web communications gave rise to very difficult questions. Professionally developed Web sites involve major investments of talent and resources.

The people funding this work naturally began to ask what kind of return they were getting on their investments. Sites providing a focused service, such as Ticketmaster, succeeded while other on-line ventures that did not involve direct sales floundered. Web publishing remained a serious challenge. Many print publishers developed Web sites. Subsidized by revenue from print sales, sites such as The Wall Street Journal Interactive Edition flourished. Web-based publications scrambled to find advertising money, and many ventures, initially enthusiastically supported, floundered during this period.

The future of the Web will be sure to see more technical innovation and various levels of social acceptance. What remains on the agenda of the World Wide Web Consortium, an industry consortium helping to realize the full potential of the Web, is a long list of activities. The Consortium has planned new developments in the user interface to the Web, technological and social practices, and work on the technical makeup of the Web's systems.

The Internet

The Internet represents one of the most successful examples of the benefits of sustained investment and commitment to research and development of information infrastructure. Beginning with the early research in packet switching, the government, industry and academia have been partners in evolving and deploying this exciting new technology. The Internet today is a widespread information infrastructure, the initial prototype of what is often called the National (or Global or Galactic) Information Infrastructure. Its history is complex and involves many aspects - technological, organizational, and community. And its influence reaches not only to the technical fields of computer communications but throughout society as we move toward increasing use of online tools to accomplish electronic commerce, information acquisition, and community operations.

The first recorded description of the social interactions that could be enabled through networking was a series of memos written by J.C.R. Licklider of MIT in 1962 discussing his "Galactic Network" concept. He envisioned a globally interconnected set of computers through which everyone could quickly access data and programs from any site. In spirit, the concept was very much like the Internet of today. Licklider was the first head of the computer research program at DARPA, 4 starting in 1962. While at DARPA he convinced his successors at DARPA, Ivan Sutherland, Bob Taylor, and MIT researcher Lawrence G. Roberts, of the importance of this networking concept.

In late 1966 Roberts went to DARPA to develop the computer network concept and quickly put together his plan for the "ARPANET", publishing it in 1967. At the conference where he presented the paper, there was also a paper on a packet network concept from the UK by Donald Davies and Roger Scantlebury of NPL. Scantlebury told Roberts about the NPL work as well as that of Paul Baran and others at RAND. The RAND group had written a paper on packet switching networks for secure voice in the military in 1964. It happened that the work at MIT (1961-1967), at RAND (1962-1965), and at NPL (1964-1967) had all proceeded in parallel without any of the researchers knowing about the other work. The word "packet" was adopted from the work at NPL and the proposed line speed to be used in the ARPANET design was upgraded from 2.4 kbps to 50 kbps.

In August 1968, after Roberts and the DARPA funded community had refined the overall structure and specifications for the ARPANET, an RFQ was released by DARPA for the development of one of the key components, the packet switches called Interface Message Processors (IMP's). The RFQ was won in December 1968 by a group headed by Frank Heart at Bolt Beranek and Newman (BBN). As the BBN team worked on the IMP's with Bob Kahn playing a major role in the overall ARPANET architectural design, the network topology and economics were designed and optimized by Roberts working with Howard Frank and his team at Network Analysis Corporation, and the network measurement system was prepared by Kleinrock's team at UCLA.

Due to Kleinrock's early development of packet switching theory and his focus on analysis, design and measurement, his Network Measurement Center at UCLA was selected to be the first node on the ARPANET. All this came together in September 1969 when BBN installed the first IMP at UCLA and the first host computer was connected. Doug Engelbart's project on "Augmentation of Human Intellect" (which included NLS, an early hypertext system) at Stanford Research Institute (SRI) provided a second node. SRI supported the Network Information Center, led by Elizabeth (Jake) Feinler and including functions such as maintaining tables of host name to address mapping as well as a directory of the RFC's.

Computers were added quickly to the ARPANET during the following years, and work proceeded on completing a functionally complete Host-to-Host protocol and other network software. In 1970 the Network Working Group (NWG) working under S. Crocker finished the initial ARPANET Host-to-Host protocol, called the Network Control Protocol (NCP). As the ARPANET sites completed implementing NCP during the period 1971-1972, the network users finally could begin to develop applications.

In 1972 Kahn organized a large, very successful demonstration of the ARPANET at the International Computer Communication Conference (ICCC). This was the first public demonstration of this new network technology to the public. It was also in 1972 that the initial "hot" application, electronic mail, was introduced. In March Ray Tomlinson at BBN wrote the basic email message send and read software, motivated by the need of the ARPANET developers for an easy coordination mechanism. In July, Roberts expanded its utility by writing the first email utility program to list, selectively read, file, forward, and respond to messages. From there email took off as the largest network application for over a decade. This was a harbinger of the kind of activity we see on the World Wide Web today, namely, the enormous growth of all kinds of "people-to-people" traffic.

The original ARPANET grew into the Internet. Internet was based on the idea that there would be multiple independent networks of rather arbitrary design, beginning with the ARPANET as the pioneering packet switching network, but soon to include packet satellite networks, ground-based packet radio networks and other networks. The Internet as we now know it embodies a key underlying technical idea, namely that of open architecture networking. In this approach, the choice of any individual network technology was not dictated by a particular network architecture but rather could be selected freely by a provider and made to interwork with the other networks through a meta-level "Internetworking Architecture".

Up until that time there was only one general method for federating networks. This was the traditional circuit switching method where networks would interconnect at the circuit level, passing individual bits on a synchronous basis along a portion of an end-to-end circuit between a pair of end locations. Recall that Kleinrock had shown in 1961 that packet switching was a more efficient switching method. Along with packet switching, special purpose interconnection arrangements between networks were another possibility. While there were other limited ways to interconnect different networks, they required that one be used as a component of the other, rather than acting as a peer of the other in offering end-to-end service.

In an open-architecture network, the individual networks may be separately designed and developed and each may have its own unique interface which it may offer to users and/or other providers. including other Internet providers. Each network can be designed in accordance with the specific environment and user requirements of that network. There are generally no constraints on the types of network that can be included or on their geographic scope, although certain pragmatic considerations will dictate what makes sense to offer.

The idea of open-architecture networking was first introduced by Kahn shortly after having arrived at DARPA in 1972. This work was originally part of the packet radio program, but subsequently became a separate program in its own right. At the time, the program was called "Internetting". Key to making the packet radio system work was a reliable end-end protocol that could maintain effective communication in the face of jamming and other radio interference, or withstand intermittent blackout such as caused by being in a tunnel or blocked by the local terrain. Kahn first contemplated developing a protocol local only to the packet radio network, since that would avoid having to deal with the multitude of different operating systems, and continuing to use NCP.

However, NCP did not have the ability to address networks (and machines) further downstream than a destination IMP on the ARPANET and thus some change to NCP would also be required. (The assumption was that the ARPANET was not changeable in this regard). NCP relied on ARPANET to provide end-to-end reliability. If any packets were lost, the protocol (and presumably any applications it supported) would come to a grinding halt. In this model NCP had no end-end host error control, since the ARPANET was to be the only network in existence and it would be so reliable that no error control would be required on the part of the hosts.

Thus, Kahn decided to develop a new version of the protocol which could meet the needs of an open-architecture network environment. This protocol would eventually be called the Transmission Control Protocol/Internet Protocol (TCP/IP). While NCP tended to act like a device driver, the new protocol would be more like a communications protocol. Four ground rules were critical to Kahn's early thinking:

— Each distinct network would have to stand on its own and no internal changes could be required to any such network to connect it to the Internet.

— Communications would be on a best effort basis. If a packet didn't make it to the final destination, it would shortly be retransmitted from the source.

— Black boxes would be used to connect the networks; these would later be called gateways and routers. There would be no information retained by the gateways about the individual flows of packets passing through them, thereby keeping them simple and avoiding complicated adaptation and recovery from various failure modes.

— There would be no global control at the operations level.

Other key issues that needed to be addressed were:

— Algorithms to prevent lost packets from permanently disabling communications and enabling them to be successfully retransmitted from the source.

— Providing for host to host "pipelining" so that multiple packets could be enroute from source to destination at the discretion of the participating hosts, if the intermediate networks allowed it.

— Gateway functions to allow it to forward packets appropriately. This included interpreting IP headers for routing, handling interfaces, breaking packets into smaller pieces if necessary, etc.

— The need for end-end checksums, reassembly of packets from fragments and detection of duplicates, if any.

— The need for global addressing

— Techniques for host to host flow control.

— Interfacing with the various operating systems

There were also other concerns, such as implementation efficiency, internetwork performance, but these were secondary considerations at first. Kahn began work on a communications - oriented set of operating system principles while at BBN and documented some of his early thoughts in an internal BBN memorandum entitled "Communications Principles for Operating Systems". At this point he realized it would be necessary to learn the implementation details of each operating system to have a chance to embed any new protocols in an efficient way. Thus, in 1973, after starting the internetting effort, he asked Vint Cerf (then at Stanford) to work with him on the detailed design of the protocol. Cerf had been intimately involved in the original NCP design and development and already had the knowledge about interfacing to existing operating systems. So armed with Kahn's architectural approach to the communications side and with Cerf's NCP experience, they teamed up to spell out the details of what became TCP/IP.

The give and take was highly productive and the first written version of the resulting approach was distributed at a special meeting of the International Network Working Group (INWG) which had been set up at a conference at

Sussex University in September 1973. Cerf had been invited to chair this group and used the occasion to hold a meeting of INWG members who were heavily represented at the Sussex Conference. Some basic approaches emerged from this collaboration between Kahn and Cerf:

— Communication between two processes would logically consist of a very long stream of bytes (they called them octets). The position of any octet in the stream would be used to identify it.

— Flow control would be done by using sliding windows and acknowledgments (acks). The destination could select when to acknowledge and each ack returned would be cumulative for all packets received to that point.

— It was left open as to exactly how the source and destination would agree on the parameters of the windowing to be used. Defaults were used initially.

Although Ethernet was under development at Xerox PARC at that time, the proliferation of LANs were not envisioned at the time, much less PCs and workstations. The original model was national level networks like ARPANET of which only a relatively small number were expected to exist. Thus a 32 bit IP address was used of which the first 8 bits signified the network and the remaining 24 bits designated the host on that network. This assumption, that 256 networks would be sufficient for the foreseeable future, was clearly in need of reconsideration when LANs began to appear in the late 1970s.

The original Cerf/Kahn paper on the Internet described one protocol, called TCP, which provided all the transport and forwarding services in the Internet. Kahn had intended that the TCP protocol support a range of transport services, from the totally reliable sequenced delivery of data (virtual circuit model) to a datagram service in which the application made direct use of the underlying network service, which might imply occasional lost, corrupted or reordered packets.

However, the initial effort to implement TCP resulted in a version that only allowed for virtual circuits. This model worked fine for file transfer and remote login applications, but some of the early work on advanced network applications, in particular packet voice in the 1970s, made clear that in some cases packet losses should not be corrected by TCP, but should be left to the application to deal with. This led to a reorganization of the original TCP into two protocols, the simple IP which provided only for addressing and forwarding of individual packets, and the separate TCP, which was concerned with service features such as flow control and recovery from lost packets. For those applications that did not want the services of TCP, an alternative called the User Datagram Protocol (UDP) was added in order to provide direct access to the basic service of IP.

A major initial motivation for both the ARPANET and the Internet was resource sharing - for example allowing users on the packet radio networks to access the time sharing systems attached to the ARPANET. Connecting the two together was far more economical that duplicating these very expensive computers. However, while file transfer and remote login (Telnet) were very important applications, electronic mail has probably had the most significant impact of the innovations from that era. Email provided a new model of how people could communicate with each other, and changed the nature of collaboration, first in the building of the Internet itself and later for much of society.

There were other applications proposed in the early days of the Internet, including packet based voice communication (the precursor of Internet telephony), various models of file and disk sharing, and early "worm" programs that showed the concept of agents (and, of course, viruses). A key concept of the Internet is that it was not designed for just one application, but as a general infrastructure on which new applications could be conceived, as illustrated later by the emergence of the World Wide Web. It is the general purpose nature of the service provided by TCP and IP that makes this possible.

DARPA let three contracts to Stanford (Cerf), BBN (Ray Tomlinson) and UCL (Peter Kirstein) to implement TCP/IP (it was simply called TCP in the Cerf/Kahn paper but contained both components). The Stanford team, led by Cerf, produced the detailed specification and within about a year there were three independent implementations of TCP that could interoperate. This was the beginning of long term experimentation and development to evolve and mature the Internet concepts and technology. Beginning with the first three networks (ARPANET, Packet Radio, and Packet Satellite) and their initial research communities, the experimental environment has grown to incorporate essentially every form of network and a very broad-based research and development community. With each expansion has come new challenges.

The early implementations of TCP were done for large time sharing systems such as Tenex and TOPS 20. When desktop computers first appeared, it was thought by some that TCP was too big and complex to run on a personal computer. David Clark and his research group at MIT set out to show that a compact and simple implementation of TCP was possible. They produced an implementation, first for the Xerox Alto (the early personal workstation developed at Xerox PARC) and then for the IBM PC. That implementation was fully interoperable with other TCPs, but was tailored to the application suite and performance objectives of the personal computer, and showed that workstations, as well as large time-sharing systems, could be a part of the Internet.

In 1976, Kleinrock published the first book on the ARPANET. It included an emphasis on the complexity of protocols and the pitfalls they often introduce. Widespread development of LANS, PCs and workstations in the 1980s allowed the nascent Internet to flourish. Ethernet technology, developed by Bob Metcalfe at Xerox PARC in 1973, is now probably the dominant network technology in the Internet and PCs and workstations the dominant computers.

This change from having a few networks with a modest number of time-shared hosts (the original ARPANET model) to having many networks has resulted in a number of new concepts and changes to the underlying technology. First, it resulted in the definition of three network classes (A, B, and C) to accommodate the range of networks. Class A represented large national scale networks (small number of networks with large numbers of hosts); Class B represented regional scale networks; and Class C represented local area networks (large number of networks with relatively few hosts).

A major shift occurred as a result of the increase in scale of the Internet and its associated management issues. To make it easy for people to use the network, hosts were assigned names, so that it was not necessary to remember the numeric addresses. Originally, there were a fairly limited number of hosts, so it was feasible to maintain a single table of all the hosts and their associated names and addresses. The shift to having a large number of independently managed networks (e.g., LANs) meant that having a single table of hosts was no longer feasible, and the Domain Name System (DNS) was invented by Paul Mockapetris of USC/ISI. The DNS permitted a scalable distributed mechanism for resolving hierarchical host names into an Internet address.

The increase in the size of the Internet also challenged the capabilities of the routers. Originally, there was a single distributed algorithm for routing that was implemented uniformly by all the routers in the Internet. As the number of networks in the Internet exploded, this initial design could not expand as necessary, so it was replaced by a hierarchical model of routing, with an Interior Gateway Protocol (IGP) used inside each region of the Internet, and an Exterior Gateway Protocol (EGP) used to tie the regions together. This design permitted different regions to use a different IGP, so that different requirements for cost, rapid reconfiguration, robustness and scale could be accommodated. Not only the routing algorithm, but the size of the addressing tables, stressed the capacity of the routers. New approaches for address aggregation, in particular classless inter-domain routing (CIDR), have recently been introduced to control the size of router tables.

As the Internet evolved, one of the major challenges was how to propagate the changes to the software, particularly the host software. DARPA supported UC Berkeley to investigate modifications to the Unix operating system, including incorporating TCP/IP developed at BBN. Although Berkeley later rewrote the BBN code to more efficiently fit into the Unix system and kernel, the incorporation of TCP/IP into the Unix BSD system releases proved to be a critical element in dispersion of the protocols to the research community. Much of the CS research community began to use Unix BSD for their day-to-day computing environment. Looking back, the strategy of incorporating Internet protocols into a supported operating system for the research community was one of the key elements in the successful widespread adoption of the Internet.

One of the more interesting challenges was the transition of the ARPANET host protocol from NCP to TCP/IP in 1983. This was a "flag-day" style transition, requiring all hosts to convert simultaneously or be left having to communicate via rather ad-hoc mechanisms. This transition was carefully planned within the community over several years before it actually took place and went surprisingly smoothly. TCP/IP was adopted as a defense standard three years earlier in 1980. This enabled defense to begin sharing in the DARPA Internet technology base and led directly to the eventual partitioning of the military and non- military communities.

By 1983, ARPANET was being used by a significant number of defense R&D and operational organizations. The transition of ARPANET from NCP to TCP/IP permitted it to be split into a MILNET supporting operational requirements and an ARPANET supporting research needs. Thus, by 1985, Internet was already well established as a technology supporting a broad community of researchers and developers, and was beginning to be used by other communities for daily computer communications. Electronic mail was being used broadly across several communities, often with different systems, but interconnection between different mail systems was demonstrating the utility of broad based electronic communications between people.

At the same time that the Internet technology was being experimentally validated and widely used amongst a subset of computer science researchers, other networks and networking technologies were being pursued. The usefulness of computer networking - especially electronic mail - demonstrated by DARPA and Department of Defense contractors on the ARPANET was not lost on other communities and disciplines, so that by the mid-1970s computer networks had begun to spring up wherever funding could be found for the purpose.

AT&T's free-wheeling dissemination of the UNIX computer operating system spawned USENET, based on UNIX' built-in UUCP communication protocols, and in 1981 Ira Fuchs and Greydon Freeman devised BITNET, which linked academic mainframe computers in an "email as card images" paradigm. With the exception of BITNET and USENET, these early networks (including ARPANET) were purpose-built - i.e., they were intended for, and largely restricted to, closed communities of scholars; there was hence little pressure for the individual networks to be compatible and, indeed, they largely were not. In addition, alternate technologies were being pursued in the commercial sector, including XNS from Xerox, DECNet, and IBM's SNA. It remained for the British JANET and U.S. NSFNET programs to explicitly announce their intent to serve the entire higher education community, regardless of discipline. Indeed, a condition for a U.S. university to receive NSF funding for an Internet connection was that "... the connection must be made available to ALL qualified users on campus." NSF also elected to support DARPA's existing Internet organizational infrastructure, hierarchically arranged under the (then) Internet Activities Board (IAB). The public declaration of this choice was the joint authorship by the IAB's Internet Engineering and Architecture Task Forces and by NSF's Network Technical Advisory Group of RFC 985 (Requirements for Internet Gateways), which formally ensured interoperability of DARPA's and NSF's pieces of the Internet.

A key to the rapid growth of the Internet has been the free and open access to the basic documents, especially the specifications of the protocols. In 1969 a key step was taken by S. Crocker (then at UCLA) in establishing the Request for Comments (or RFC) series of notes. These memos were intended to be an informal fast distribution way to share ideas with other network researchers. At first the RFCs were printed on paper and distributed via snail mail. As the File Transfer Protocol (FTP) came into use, the RFCs were prepared as online files and accessed via FTP. Now, of course, the RFCs are easily accessed via the World Wide Web at dozens of sites around the world. SRI, in its role as Network Information Center, maintained the online directories.

The effect of the RFCs was to create a positive feedback loop, with ideas or proposals presented in one RFC triggering another RFC with additional ideas, and so on. When some consensus (or a least a consistent set of ideas) had come together a specification document would be prepared. Such a specification would then be used as the base for implementations by the various research teams. Over time, the RFCs have become more focused on protocol standards (the "official" specifications), though there are still informational RFCs that describe alternate approaches, or provide background information on protocols and engineering issues. The RFCs are now viewed as the "documents of record" in the Internet engineering and standards community.

The open access to the RFCs promotes the growth of the Internet because it allows the actual specifications to be used for examples in college classes and by entrepreneurs developing new systems. Email has been a significant factor in all areas of the Internet, and that is certainly true in the development of protocol specifications, technical standards, and Internet engineering. The very early RFCs often presented a set of ideas developed by the researchers at one location to the rest of the community. After email came into use, the authorship pattern changed - RFCs were presented by joint authors with common view independent of their locations.

The use of specialized email mailing lists has been long used in the development of protocol specifications, and continues to be an important tool. As the current rapid expansion of the Internet is fueled by the realization of its capability to promote information sharing, we should understand that the network's first role in information sharing was sharing the information about it's own design and operation through the RFC documents. This unique method for evolving new capabilities in the network will continue to be critical to future evolution of the Internet.

The Internet is as much a collection of communities as a collection of technologies, and its success is largely attributable to both satisfying basic community needs as well as utilizing the community in an effective way to push the infrastructure forward. This community spirit has a long history beginning with the early ARPANET.

The early ARPANET researchers worked as a close-knit community to accomplish the initial demonstrations of packet switching technology described earlier. Likewise, the Packet Satellite, Packet Radio and several other DARPA computer science research programs were multi-contractor collaborative activities that heavily used whatever available mechanisms there were to coordinate their efforts, starting with electronic mail and adding file sharing, remote access, and eventually World Wide Web capabilities.

In the late 1970's, recognizing that the growth of the Internet was accompanied by a growth in the size of the interested research community and therefore an increased need for coordination mechanisms, Vint Cerf, then manager of the Internet Program at DARPA, formed several coordination bodies - an International Cooperation Board (ICB), chaired by Peter Kirstein of UCL, to coordinate activities with some cooperating European countries centered on Packet Satellite research, an Internet Research Group which was an inclusive group providing an environment for general exchange of information, and an Internet Configuration Control Board (ICCB), chaired by Clark. The ICCB was an invitational body to assist Cerf in managing the burgeoning Internet activity.

In 1983, when Barry Leiner took over management of the Internet research program at DARPA, he and Clark recognized that the continuing growth of the Internet community demanded a restructuring of the coordination mechanisms. The ICCB was disbanded and in its place a structure of Task Forces was formed, each focused on a particular area of the technology (e.g. routers, end-to-end protocols, etc.). The Internet Activities Board (IAB) was formed from the chairs of the Task Forces. It of course was only a coincidence that the chairs of the Task Forces were the same people as the members of the old ICCB, and Dave Clark continued to act as chair.

In 1985 there was a tremendous growth in the more practical/engineering side of the Internet. This growth resulted in an explosion in the attendance at the IETF meetings, and Gross was compelled to create substructure to the IETF in the form of working groups. This growth was complemented by a major expansion in the community. No longer was DARPA the only major player in the funding of the Internet. In addition to NSFNet and the various US and international government-funded activities, interest in the commercial sector was beginning to grow. Also in 1985, both Kahn and Leiner left DARPA and there was a significant decrease in Internet activity at DARPA. As a result, the IAB was left without a primary sponsor and increasingly assumed the mantle of leadership.

The growth continued, resulting in even further substructure within both the IAB and IETF. The IETF combined Working Groups into Areas, and designated Area Directors. An Internet Engineering Steering Group (IESG) was formed of the Area Directors. The IAB recognized the increasing importance of the IETF, and restructured the standards process to explicitly recognize the IESG as the major review body for standards. The IAB also restructured so that the rest of the Task Forces (other than the IETF) were combined into an Internet Research Task Force (IRTF) chaired by Postel, with the old task forces renamed as research groups.

The growth in the commercial sector brought with it increased concern regarding the standards process itself. Starting in the early 1980's and continuing to this day, the Internet grew beyond its primarily research roots to include both a broad user community and increased commercial activity. Increased attention was paid to making the process open and fair. This coupled with a recognized need for community support of the Internet eventually led to the formation of the Internet Society in 1991, under the auspices of Kahn's Corporation for National Research Initiatives (CNRI) and the leadership of Cerf, then with CNRI. In 1992, yet another reorganization took place. In 1992, the Internet Activities Board was re-organized and re-named the Internet Architecture Board operating under the auspices of the Internet Society. A more "peer" relationship was defined between the new IAB and IESG, with the IETF and IESG taking a larger responsibility for the approval of standards.

Ultimately, a cooperative and mutually supportive relationship was formed between the IAB, IETF, and Internet Society, with the Internet Society taking on as a goal the provision of service and other measures which would facilitate the work of the IETF. The recent deveiopment and widespread deployment of the World Wide Web has brought with it a new community, as many of the people working on the WWW have not thought of themselves as primarily network researchers and developers.

A new coordination organization was formed, the World Wide Web Consortium (W3C). Through the over two decades of Internet activity, we have seen a steady evolution of organizational structures designed to support and facilitate an ever-increasing community working collaboratively on Internet issues.

Commercialization

Commercialization of the Internet involved not only the development of competitive, private network services, but also the development of commercial products implementing the Internet technology. In the early 1980s, dozens of vendors were incorporating TCP/IP into their products because they saw buyers for that approach to networking. Unfortunately they lacked both real information about how the technology was supposed to work and how the customers planned on using this approach to networking.

Many saw it as a nuisance add-on that had to be glued on to their own proprietary networking solutions: SNA, DECNet, Netware, NetBios. The DoD had mandated the use of TCP/IP in many of its purchases but gave little help to the vendors regarding how to build useful TCP/IP products.

Network management provides an example of the interplay between the research and commercial communities. In the beginning of the Internet, the emphasis was on defining and implementing protocols that achieved interoperation. As the network grew larger, it became clear that the sometime ad hoc procedures used to manage the network would not scale. Manual configuration of tables was replaced by distributed automated algorithms, and better tools were devised to isolate faults.

In 1987 it became clear that a protocol was needed that would permit the elements of the network, such as the routers, to be remotely managed in a uniform way. Several protocols for this purpose were proposed, including Simple Network Management Protocol or SNMP (designed, as its name would suggest, for simplicity, and derived from an earlier proposal called SGMP), HEMS (a more complex design from the research community) and CMIP (from the OSI community).

A series of meeting led to the decisions that HEMS would be withdrawn as a candidate for standardization, in order to help resolve the contention, but that work on both SNMP and CMIP would go forward, with the idea that the SNMP could be a more near-term solution and CMIP a longer-term approach. The market could choose the one it found more suitable. SNMP is now used almost universally for network based management.

In the last few years, we have seen a new phase of commercialization. Originally, commercial efforts mainly comprised vendors providing the basic networking products, and service providers offering the connectivity and basic Internet services. The Internet has now become aimost a "commodity" service, and much of the latest attention has been on the use of this global information infrastructure for support of other commercial services. This has been tremendously accelerated by the widespread and rapid adoption of browsers and the World Wide Web technology, allowing users easy access to information linked throughout the globe. Products are available to facilitate the provisioning of that information and many of the latest developments in technology have been aimed at providing increasingly sophisticated information services on top of the basic Internet data communications.

The Internet has changed much in the two decades since it came into existence. It was conceived in the era of time-sharing, but has survived into the era of personal computers, client-server and peer-to-peer computing, and the network computer. It was designed before LANs existed, but has accommodated that new network technology, as well as the more recent ATM and frame switched services. It was envisioned as supporting a range of functions from file sharing and remote login to resource sharing and collaboration, and has spawned electronic mail and more recently the World Wide Web. But most important, it started as the creation of a small band of dedicated researchers, and has grown to be a commercial success with billions of dollars of annual investment.

The Internet, although a network in name and geography, is a creature of the computer, not the traditional network of the telephone or television industry. It will, indeed it must, continue to change and evolve at the speed of the computer industry if it is to remain relevant. It is now changing to provide such new services as real time transport, in order to support, for example, audio and video streams. The availability of pervasive networking (i.e., the Internet) along with powerful affordable computing and communications in portable form (i.e., laptop computers, two-way pagers, PDAs, cellular phones), is making possible a new paradigm of nomadic computing and communications. This evolution will bring us new applications - Internet telephone and, slightly further out, Internet television. It is evolving to permit more sophisticated forms of pricing and cost recovery, a perhaps painful requirement in this commercial world. It is changing to accommodate yet another generation of underlying network technologies with different characteristics and requirements, from broadband residential access to satellites. New modes of access and new forms of service will spawn new applications, which in turn will drive further evolution of the net itself. The most pressing question for the future of the Internet is not how the technology will change, but how the process of change and evolution itself will be managed. The architecture of the Internet has always been driven by a core group of designers, but the form of that group has changed as the number of interested parties has grown. With the success of the Internet has come a proliferation of stakeholders - stakeholders now with an economic as well as an intellectual investment in the network.

4

Digital Communication

The information and communication technologies have generally been referred to as 'new' or 'high' technologies - they are highly visible, and have not yet, despite their pervasiveness, become part of the natural infrastructure of society which, according to Borgman is invisible when it functions adequately and only becomes visible upon breakdown. The influence of new technologies on future developments is often wildly miscalculated, and human ingenuity is such that tools are often employed for purposes other than those for which they were designed.

With the digital revolution, data and information can now be transmitted to all corners of the world, and that is significant for almost all humanity, and it is significant for libraries. But though many predict that we are reaching a halcyon period of cheap access for all, there are still political, cultural and financial issues that prevent this in many strata of society and many parts of the world. The digital divide exists and could further disadvantage the poor, the under-educated and those in developing countries as the better-off, the better educated and the economically developed race ahead into the digital future. Views on the democratizing nature of electronic networks vary wildly and we need to be cautious in our evaluation of these: for some we are on the verge of global utopia, an 'age of optimism', for others the internet 'continues to remain an expensive western toy' in a world where less than 2% of the population is connected to it and where 80% of the population has never even made a telephone call.

In order to understand the changes taking place in our information activities, it is vital to understand some of the underlying structures and principles of the digital world. All digital data, from whatever original it derives, has the same underlying structure, that of the 'bit' or the Binary digit. A bit is an electronic impulse that can be represented by two states, 'on' or 'off', also written as '1' or '0'. A 'byte' consists of eight bits, and one byte represents one alphanumeric character. A ten-letter word, for example, would be ten bytes. Bits and bytes are linked together in chains of millions of electronic impulses; this is known as the 'bit stream'. A 'kilobyte' is 1024 bytes, and a 'megabyte' 1024 kilobytes.

Digital images are represented by 'pixels' or picture elements - dots on the computer screen or printed on paper. Pixels can carry a range of values, but at the simplest level, one pixel equals one bit, and is represented in binary form as 'black' (off) or 'white' (on). Images captured at this level are 'bi-tonal' - pure black and white. Images can also be represented as eight-bit images, which have 256 shades of either grey or colour, and 24-bit images, which have millions of colours - more than the eye can distinguish. The number of bits chosen to represent each pixel is known as the 'bit depth', and devices capable of displaying and printing images at high bit depths (36 or 48 bits) are now emerging.

Bit depth is the number of bits per pixel, 'resolution' is the number of pixels (or printed dots) per inch, known as ppi or dpi. The higher the resolution, the finer the texture of a digital image. The resolution of most computer screens is generally in the range of 75 to 150 pixels per inch. This is adequate for display purposes, but visual content at this resolution is inadequate for printing (especially in colour), though images of black and white printed text or line art are often acceptable. Highdensity images of library originals (manuscripts, photographs, etc.) need to be captured in the range 300-600 ppi for print-quality output. Almost any kind of information can be represented in these seemingly simple structures, as patterns of the most intricate complexity can be built up. Most primary sources held in libraries and other cultural institutions are capable of digital representation (anything that can be photographed can be digitized, though there are issues with the faithful representation of 3-D objects). When digital they are susceptible to manipulation, interrogation, transmission and cross-linking in ways that are beyond the capacity of analogue media. Creating an electronic photocopy of a plain page of text is not a sophisticated process compared with analogue technologies, but being able to then automatically recognize all the alphanumeric characters it contains, plus the structural layout and metadata elements, is sophisticated, and is only achievable in a digital environment.

Alphanumeric symbols are the easiest objects to represent in digital form, and digital text has been around for as long as there have been stored-program computers. These symbols are also the most compact to store, an important factor at a time when capacity was limited and expensive. Early computers were good at processing symbols rapidly, but input, output and display of data were difficult. Input was via punched cards or tapes, output through printers or plotters with limited capabilities, and display was limited to ASCII symbols, displayed line by line, often with only upper case available. Special fonts and characters were fearsomely difficult to represent, though some early pioneers made creative use of graph plotters for non-Roman character sets.

Early digital character representations were sparse in their storage needs, and early computer programs economical in their need for processing power. Storage and power have been increasing steadily over the past three decades, with the capacity of the processor chip doubling approximately every 24 months, much to the surprise of many experts, and although this trend cannot continue indefinitely for physical reasons, the immediate future will see further startling increases in computing speed. Increases in network capacity (also known as bandwidth) have also been huge, but rather less linear and predictable than increases in power because there are different factors that come into play here.

Bandwidth is delivered through copper wiring which has a relatively low capacity, through optical fibre cables, which have almost infinite capacity, and through wireless transmission, which has variable capacity, given that portions of the airwaves have to be assigned with care to avoid interference of signals. Adding bandwidth can mean a process of digging up roads and laying cables to replace earlier wiring, a hugely expensive procedure, which must be funded by many different commercial and public bodies in most countries.

Storage capabilities for digital data have also been growing exponentially: in the mid-1980s a 20Mb hard drive was regarded as massive storage, and 256Kb of RAM as sufficient memory. Now even laptop computers come supplied with 20Gb hard drives and 256Mb of RAM, which is 1000 times the capacity of machines of less than 20 years ago. But we need all this power and capacity to deal with the data that is coming our way in many media formats, as digital text, digital images, digital video and digital sound.

An average page of digital text takes around 20Kb of storage space, which means that there can be 32,500 pages stored on an average 650Mb CD-ROM. High-quality professional digital cameras and scanners can potentially capture digital reproductions of the original in such detail as to require at least 300Mb of storage space, allowing just two images to be stored on an average CD-ROM, and moving images and sound are even more hungry of space and power, though there are advantages in data compression that are helping to reduce the load.

Data compression comes in two forms: 'lossless', which means that the compressed file loses no information in the compression and decompression processes, and 'lossy', where there is data loss in the processes. Lossy compression gives more compact results than lossless, resulting in smaller files to store or transport, but the derived images are of a lower quality - which may not matter if the files are for web delivery, but which is unacceptable for high-quality printing or long-term storage.

Increase of capacity and power in any of the component areas of digital processing and transmission are not just linear benefits: the relationship between demand and supply is complex and paradoxical. For example, a desktop computer would probably give excellent service for eight to ten years, but is likely to be replaced in most professional or even personal environments in two to four years.

The resale value is likely to be very low, if there is any value left in the machine at all. This is because new developments render hardware and software obsolete so rapidly. Compare this with other everyday machinery, the car for instance. There are people who change their cars every couple of years, for a variety of reasons to do with reliability, economy or prestige, but rarely because a particular model has become obsolete and will not run on certain roads, and there is certainly considerable resale value left in most cars. In the world of information supply, it is difficult to know whether the advances are driven by user demand or by the commercial imperatives of the suppliers of information and the suppliers of technology. Libraries are caught in the middle, having to purchase and provide ever more expensive and technologically demanding content to a wider range of users across a greater demographic and geographic area.

Media Technologies

Changes in media brought about by digitization and the Internet are much more fundamental and transformative. Yet ironically many of these fundamental changes will not be immediately apparent to the average media consumer. People will still watch movies and television; will still read books, magazines, and newspapers; and will still want to listen to music. For many people it will not matter that a song was created, produced, and even distributed digitally. A useful analogy in comparing the state of digital and analog media today is to picture an iceberg floating in the ocean. Just as only a small percentage of the whole iceberg is visible above the water, in today's media world the primarily analog media products we see, such as books or videotapes, are only a small part of the overall media creation process. Most mass media today already utilize digitization in some way, even if the final product is still predominantly analog. But this will change over time as consumers get more of their media content digitally. Four key concepts of digital media are;

Multimedia: Combining video, audio, and text is not unique to digital media-everyday television is just such an example of multimedia-but digital media allow for easier creation of multimedia than in analog media and provide for greater opportunities in fully integrating media types to complement each of their strengths.

Interactivity: The ability to interact with media content and obtain unique, personalized, or localized information is a powerful force in changing how the public uses and perceives media. It greatly shifts the balance of power from passive media consumers to active media consumers and creators.

Automation: By creating various programs and automated functions such as search tools, collaborative filtering (automatically determining likely interests based on previously viewed or purchased material and comparing that to what others who have purchased the same material also bought or viewed), and updating content, computers greatly reduce the amount of work humans must do and, increasingly, can supplant some human roles in the media production workflow process.

Ethereal quality: Digital media are not actually physical products, like books, photographs or CDs, although they usually are eventually represented in some kind of physical product.

But even as far-reaching as these elements are in changing the media landscape, they are still incomplete without one important element: a network that connects computers or media devices to each other so they can communicate. There are many kinds of networks, but we will concentrate primarily on the Internet and the World Wide Web. Because all data that pass through the various networks-telephone, cable, or satellite-are at one or more stages digital, we will use the term "digital media" to mean not only digital but networked, or online, media as well.

Out of all modern media, the Internet/World Wide Web reached 50 percent of U.S. households faster than any other media technology. 58 percent of U.S. households, or 166 million persons, went onto the Web. The Internet is more complex in its requirements for adoption than all other media. One can't simply go out and "buy an Internet" as one could for most other media, such as radio or TV. Instead, one must first have a computer and a means of connecting it to the Internet, plus a higher level of technical media literacy to use the computer than is required for a television or even VCR. What Is Online Communication?

The broader topic of online communications, of which the Internet is a vital part, must be clarified. Although many may consider the term online as synonymous with the Internet, online is in fact a term with a larger meaning. Online refers to the interconnected, networked media that permit the direct, electronic exchange of information, data, and other communications. Everything from local area networks to wide area networks, such as the Internet, are part of the online world. (Local area networks allow communication in limited environments, such as inside an organization.) In other words, the Internet and the World Wide Web are part of the online communications world; they are not the entire online world. However, the Internet and the Web are among the most important parts of the online world for mass communication, because they are where much digital, online media content resides and is available to the public.

Digital media of course plays a role in every communication function that analog media plays, ranging from surveillance to entertainment. Whether democracy and society ultimately will be better served by an Internet-connected society is impossible to say. However, there is no doubt digitization and online media are changing and will continue to change mass communication and the public that receives almost all of its entertainment and information from mass media.

A 24/7 media environment is quickly emerging, if not already here. Newspapers have had to create policies so their online versions do not scoop their printed morning edition the next day-as much so they do not tip off their competitors as for not wanting to hurt their own newspaper sales. With cable TV there is of course 24-hour entertainment and news, and the always-on nature of the Internet has taught the public that they can obtain specific media content on demand as long as they are connected to the Internet.

Even media that we are accustomed to thinking of as "set" once created, such as magazines or books, can easily be updated at any time if they are distributed in digital form. A nonstop media environment, although increasing the opportunities for news, information, and entertainment, also has its negative side. With new messages being delivered all the time and a huge choice of media to interact with, it can be very easy to become distracted with flashy entertainment or essentially "drown" in information.

The pervasiveness of the media system means that wherever one goes, there is likely to be unprecedented access to mass communication. A new media pioneer who works as a civilian researcher in a naval research lab once remarked that he was leaving for a week's vacation in the Caribbean on an island where there was no Internet, no phone service, and no communication services of any kind. He had to escape. Unfortunately, with today's global satellite communications, it's not possible to truly "escape" anywhere on the planet.

Increasingly portable media devices and flat-panel screen technology improvements also mean that we have a growing ability to take our media with us and access it (or have it thrust upon us) in places where we previously did not encounter media. Displays in elevators are one example of how advertisers are using technology to reach a captive audience. Pervasive mass communication means better access to entertainment, commercial information, and news. Such access means there is at least the potential for a better-functioning democracy, because more information is available. Of course, better access may not come evenly to all or allow everyone to benefit equally from that access.

Simply providing more information into the media system may often result in a widening, rather than a narrowing, of the gap in knowledge between those in high and low socioeconomic groups.Personal Information Space The convergence of digital media is leading to the development of a personal information space. A personal information space is a virtual location assembled and accessed online where an individual keeps data, or information. It is more than just a digital personal library, however. In a personal information space, one can process private voice, fax, and e-mail communications, and create, access, and store Web-based media content, including multimedia, all from any location around the world.

No longer is one's personal information space limited by geography, time, or culture. One can access a personal information space when mobile computing and communications devices are connected to global, wired, and wireless telecommunications networks. Increasingly, the personal information space is being integrated with public information space (i.e., the content generated by media organizations and others). Unfortunately, the personal information space is also subject to various threats and dangers, such as erosion of privacy, computer hackers, or technical failures.

Internet Technologies

Prior to the era of the Internet, institutions or organizations that had computers had no simple way for the computers to communicate with each other, even if they were connected by a wire, as computers ran machine-specific languages and programs that could not be understood by other computers. In 1969, the foundations for the Internet were laid when the Defense Advanced Research Projects Agency (DARPA) launched the Advanced Research Projects Agency network, or ARPAnet. ARPAnet was the first national computer network, connecting many universities around the country for advanced, high-speed computing applications and research. It was not yet the Internet, but it was the beginning of online communications. But there was still no "common language," or protocol, that computers could use to easily transmit information via the network.

Although it is difficult to pin down an exact date when the Internet officially started, in 1982 the Defense Department adopted TCP/IP as the basis for the ARPAnet. Moreover, at this time researchers began defining an "internet" (lower case i) as a connected set of networks using

TCP/IP, and the "Internet" as a set of connected TCP/IP internets.Creating the World Wide Web For the first decade of the Internet's existence, its usage was limited largely to researchers. Use of the Internet required knowledge of a variety of arcane commands and terminology. The limited, specialized nature of the Internet underwent a fundamental change in 1991 when Tim Berners-Lee, an MIT researcher at a physics laboratory in Switzerland, invented the World Wide Web and began to open the use of the Internet to a much wider set of users. The advent of the Web as a global publishing medium made possible the most fundamental shift in human communication since the advent of the printing press five centuries earlier. The Web enabled easy many-to-many communication over distance and time.

In addition, in contrast to traditional media of mass communication, anyone can create and publish on the Web for very little cost or expertise. The World Wide Web (WWW) is a subset of the Internet and is perhaps best described as a global electronic publishing medium accessed through the Internet. Technically speaking, the Web is made up of an interconnected set of computer servers on the Internet that subscribe to a set of TCP/IP network interface protocols. These technical protocols include assigning to a Web site a Uniform Resource Locator (URL) based on its TCP/IP Internet address, which is the Web site address that Web users are familiar with. URLs include the instructions that are read by a Web browser, a navigational tool to travel the Web.

A Web page is any document, or collection of content, that resides on a Web site. The content can take any form, including text, graphics, photographs, audio, video, or interactive features, such as surveys or discussion forums. A Web site can consist of one page of content or many such pages and can include hyperlinks to other Web sites. Content on a Web page is tagged, or marked up, using what is known as hypertext markup language, or HTML, to format the content so it displays correctly on a screen. In addition, each document uses hypertext transfer protocol (HTTP), which enables the standardized transfer of text, audio, and video files, as well as e-mail from one address to another.

Another huge gain in making the Internet accessible to even more people was the creation in 1993 of Mosaic by Marc Andreeson, then at the National Center for SuperComputing Applications (NCSA) at the University of Illinois at Champaign-Urbana. Mosaic, which eventually became Netscape, provided a graphical user interface with the Web that computer users who had Macs or Windows PCs could quickly understand and use. Although GUI browsers Viola and Erwise were also created in 1992, by the end of the year Mosaic was being written about in mainstream media and became the most well-known Web browser.

Microsoft created their own graphical browser, Internet Explorer (IE), in 1996 to compete with Netscape's browser, then called Netscape Navigator. By offering Internet Explorer free and eventually bundling it with the Windows operating system, IE was able to become the dominant Web browser in only four years, with 75 percent usage compared to Netscape's 25 percent. In 1999 Netscape was bought by AOL, a year before AOL acquired Time Warner. As any regular Web user can attest, Web sites and text size often look different not only on different browsers but on different versions of the same browser. More advanced functions or codes on Web sites may not show up on earlier browser versions, thus making it difficult for Web designers and content companies to create Web sites that are consistent across the online audience.

Reflecting the continued dramatic, almost exponential growth of the Web, by 2001 millions of individuals and organizations had published "home pages" on the Web. With the cost barriers to entry in the global publishing arena removed or dramatically lowered, the Web for the first time brought press freedom to virtually any citizen with access to a computer and a phone line. Of course, more than half the world lack either or both of these, so we're still a long way off from realizing the dream of fully democratic communications.

In some Scandinavian countries Internet penetration has reached 75 percent. So even traditional mass media aren't by any means necessarily universal relative to the Internet and the Web. Yet, when one considers the fact that only a tiny fraction of the U.S. or world's population has its own printing press, television, or radio station, the Web has dramatically increased the diversity of media voices available. Of course many of these voices are lost in the global cacophony of the Web, but that is a different issue.

In its broadest sense, the Internet encompasses virtually all other media, as well as a broad cross-section of human culture, commerce, and creation. Virtually anything one can think of almost certainly exists in some form on the Internet, from information in the Library of Congress to deliberately misleading information created by hate groups or individuals. As distinguished communications scholar Fred Williams once observed, "Going on the Internet is like going through someone else's trash."

The Internet as we know it now is not controlled by any one person or organization. It is a medium of multimodal (i.e., it involves the various senses) content and interactive communications, in particular e-mail, where users (and organizations) send and receive text and increasingly audio, video, photos, graphics, and hyperlinks. Although much of the content on the Internet is available free to users, there is a growing trend among media and technology companies to start charging consumers, especially after advertising dropped off sharply after the dot-com meltdown in 2000. Content or services that were previously free, such as a given amount of disk space or the ability to check remote e-mail accounts through Web e-mail accounts such as Hotmail, for example, were starting to be offered only to paying consumers. This trend of partially free services or content and payment for what is considered "premium" content can also be seen among media companies online, and it is still too early to tell whether these strategies will be successful in generating revenues.

Online media companies are also experimenting with increasingly obtrusive online advertising, such as larger pop-up ad windows or automatic pop-under ads that are changing the look and experience of the Web for users. In the early 1990s there were many debates among users of online discussion groups about whether any advertising should even be allowed on the Internet, considering the fact that it was created by using taxpayers' money.

Computer-based Networks

Networks have long been a fundamental part of mass communication, especially broadcasting. Networks, or systems of interconnected communication vehicles, can take many forms. In broadcasting, networks of affiliated local stations provide a means of distributing shared programming to audiences across large geographic regions, most typically the entire country. Traditionally, these networks have been linked through analog technology. Today's networks are increasingly digital. This offers several advantages in mass communication, most importantly the ability to transmit multiple streams of information, including audio and video content, text, or other types of data. In addition, computer-based networks permit the distribution of content to be more flexible, so if one route of the network is unavailable, the network can automatically and efficiently reassemble through a different route.

Digital networks permit compression of data, which enables a mass communicator to send more information in the same amount of space on the network. Finally, a computer network easily permits downstream and upstream communications (from the source to the receiver, and vice versa), whereas traditional networks were largely one way and relatively expensive.

A modem (a foreshortening of modulate-demodulate) is used to convert the digital information in a computer to analog signals for transmission over a phone or cable TV line and to convert analog signals to digital information for a computer. Modems can also operate wirelessly by converting data into radio signals. Modems were invented in the 1960s, before the days of the personal computer, as a means of letting "dumb terminals" (i.e., electronic machines where users typed information on keyboards) dial into a remote computer.

These early modems converted the typed characters into audio tones that were sent over the telephone line and then were converted back on the other end of the line where they were received by the computer, which processed the information received. Today's modems operate in a much more efficient and faster fashion. Whereas early modems were hard-pressed to convert and transmit 300 bits per second, today's modems can convert and send millions of bits per second. This allows them to rapidly send or receive not just text but also audio and video.

Bandwidth is a crucial element for online communication to reach its full potential to be a mass medium. Without what is called high-speed, high-bandwidth, or broadband connections to the Internet, most people online are unable to receive audio or video in real time or at the same quality as they are used to from television or radio. Narrowband is the term used for low bandwidth communications, such as dial-up phone modems. Bandwidth available for Internet service has traditionally been narrowband via dial-up modems, typically delivering anywhere from 28 kilobits to 56 kilobits per second. Video at these narrowband rates is very limited, usually a small window of jerky motion, of low-resolution imagery and only marginally better sound. In a technical sense, bandwidth refers to the electromagnetic frequency or spectrum available for delivering content. Bell Labs scientist Claude E. Shannon in 1948 provided a precise mathematical definition of bandwidth, defining the capacity of a communications channel in terms of bits per second. A voice phone call, for example, uses about 3000 hertz (Hz) bandwidth, whereas a telephone modem operating at about 33.6 kilobits per second requires a little more bandwidth, or about 3200 Hz.

Think of bandwidth not so much as electromagnetic frequency, however, but more in terms of how large a pipe is that comes to your home delivering data rather than a physical thing like water. Someone who is able to tap the large "data pipe" directly can access the flow of data at equally high speeds. Sometimes this is called a "fat pipe." However, if the pipe that accesses the main pipes is very thin, data will come at only a trickle, no matter how fast his or her personal computer is. As of 2002, the Internet was relatively limited in terms of available bandwidth. It varied depending on how a user connected to the Internet, such as a telephone modem or a cable modem, although a second generation of the Internet known as Internet 2 brought 45,000 times more bandwidth. At that time the Internet 2 was already providing a very high-speed connection among 170 universities. It promises in the future to bring such high-speed connectivity to a broader portion of society.

One of the great challenges that cable and telephone providers have begun to solve in the past decade is the so-called "last mile" obstacle (not always literally the last mile, but somewhere from a few hundred yards to more than a mile or so). For more than a decade, many cable and telephone companies have had considerable bandwidth available in their backbone or trunk lines but have run into a problem connecting these broadband facilities over the "last mile" to the end consumer. The cost of making these final connections has been prohibitive. But as the cost of the technology has fallen and various technological innovations have occurred, it has become increasingly feasible to provide the last-mile connections. When this is completed, it means that consumers will have the same broadband access that currently only large organizations have.

Telecommunication Technologies

In the world of telephony, development of the digital subscriber line (DSL) has made it possible to use standard telephone wire, the twisted-pair copper wire in most homes, to provide relatively low-cost broadband capabilities in the home. Other emerging network technologies, such as aDSL (asymmetric DSL, which means high-speed downstream, much slower upstream), are also being deployed by the phone companies. Telephone companies have lagged somewhat behind in their delivery of highspeed Internet and broadband digital video services to the home, with DSL available in only a handful of markets.

Many customers have complained bitterly about late or no installation, technical troubles with little customer support, and lack of communication between the telephone companies and the Internet Service Providers (ISPs) that have hampered easy installation of DSL services. In the cable TV world, the cable modem and the set-top box have made it practical for many cable systems to begin rolling out digital cable services that not only provide digital TV program services to the home but also permit highspeed Internet access and telephone service. Broadband content delivery via already existing coaxial cable systems mean that cable modems are roughly 174 times faster than 56k modems. One problem of the cable modem is that the network is not switched; the network bandwidth is shared by the users within each local geographic area, or node. In other words, the more users on a given cable modem node, the slower the network becomes. Cable companies can put fewer users on nodes by increasing the number of nodes, but this of course increases their costs. TCI has already indicated that movies on demand or video on demand will be limited in its cable modem service to about 15 minutes in duration.

Bandwidth availability is gradually increasing as low-cost bandwidth rolls out nationwide in the first years of the twenty-first century and low-cost digital consumer access devices enter the marketplace. The importance of broadband capability to usage patterns on the Internet may be profound.Research shows that Internet users with broadband access already have substantially different behaviors than when they used dial-up connections. One trend that has been noted is that they are more likely to create and distribute media content than dial-up users. Online expenditures more than double for users of broadband services.

David Clark says that broadband Internet could bring "Real-time high-fidelity music, telephone, video-conferencing, television and radio programs.... There will be new entertainment options, such as movies-on-demand, and new features, such as the ability to call up information about a movie's director or its actors as they appear on screen. Users will be able to play online games-live-against many contestants scattered around the globe."Of course, the data on high-bandwidth users are hard to interpret, because those who have access to broadband capabilities in 2002 are, in general, what are called "early adopters." They tend to have more income, are more educated, and are likely to be two-parent households. They are different by nature than the late adopters, and it may be in part these differences that account for the differences in how they connect to the Internet. In a sense, talking about online mass communication means talking about all of mass communication. Today, countless offline mass communication products, whether print or electronic, also exist in some form online, whether for free or fee. The American Journalism Review counts 4925 online newspaper sites, and all of the top-50 magazines by circulation have Web sites, as do thousands of specialized periodicals. Some use their Web sites mainly to showcase their printed material, but others publish original material online as well. As bandwidth increases, most television stations will place more of their content online, just as an increasing number of radio stations do already. Similarly, more of the cinema and recording arts will become available online as connectivity and bandwidth continue to increase. Many mass communication sites originally created solely online are also available, from one-person operations to major endeavors by large companies such as Microsoft in their creation of the online magazine Slate. Even companies not traditionally involved with mass communication have found that maintaining their own Web sites is an excellent way to communicate directly to a large audience.

Digital Newspapers

Newspapers are among the leading providers of online news. Online newspaper sites also face direct competition on a number of other fronts in the online arena, including to some degree the general public, who can put online eyewitness accounts of events. Matt Drudge's site was ranked twentieth in August 2002 of top news sites. News services such as AP or Reuters offer their breaking news content online on news aggregator/portal sites such as Yahoo! News, which was in third place. Newspaper Web sites have the potential to take back some of the ground in breaking news coverage that they lost to television, but this can create an odd situation of a newspaper Web site "scooping" its more established print version, which comes out on a set schedule.

The competition online newspapers face with cable and broadcast television news channels shows in part the complexity of the online mass communication world. For example, there is nothing stopping a newspaper from training some of their journalists to shoot and edit video footage, which could then be webcast on the newspaper's site. The same could apply to audio recording. This is exactly what some newspapers have been doing, such as the Tribune Company, whose flagship newspaper the Chicago Tribune and flagship television station WGN are part of a converged news operation providing considerable quality online video news.

Advertising is another big area in which newspaper companies are threatened by the Internet, especially classified ads. Classified ads make up a large portion of advertising revenues for most newspapers, but online classified ads aggregators can allow people to search far more ads than are usually covered in a newspaper's circulation area. If a consumer wants to look for an item in a region that is covered by four or five different newspapers, there is no reason for that person to go to each newspaper's Web site to look at classifieds when he or she can see them all on one Web site. Likewise, a consumer can visit an online auction site like eBay and reach a nationwide group of potential sellers or buyers.

Digital Books

Digital books offer a variety of advantages over printed books, including permitting the reader not only to read the text but to make electronic annotations and bookmarks, access the content of the book via an interactive table of contents, and keyword search the entire text. Digital books and their sale online also point to a fundamental issue in the future of how mass communication industries will derive much if not most of their revenue: from online transactions, or what is called e-commerce. Although few people still may want to read a book on a standard computer screen, the Internet has brought a growing number of books online and made them available universally. Much of the content of these online books may be most valuable as a research tool, but many may also find them a potentially viable way to read for pleasure. Segments of a book can be printed out, for example, saving weight and space when traveling, and as computer screen technology gets better and creates sharper images, reading on-screen will not be as tiring as it can be today.

In the late 1990s, major publishers prepared for a growing surge in consumer demand for electronic books, and many experimented with the online sale and distribution of digital books. However, after the economic slowdown in 2000, which hit technology and Internet companies particularly hard, and a subsequent slowdown in sales of digital books, publishers started to adopt a slower, more cautious approach. However, many believe that just as young people powered the paperback revolution, the young are showing a voracious appetite for digital books. Dennis Dillon, a librarian at the University of Texas, was initially surprised at the popularity of electronic books.

"No one was sure whether anyone was going to read any digital books," said Dillon, the university's head of collections and information resources. "We were somewhat skeptical." After minimal promotion of the University of Texas's newly purchased electronic books, with titles from Euthanasia: A Reference Handbook to From Barbie to Mortal Kombat: Gender and Computer Games, they are suddenly the most popular titles in the library. "Usually a book has a one-third chance of being checked out. So to have some titles checked out 25 times in two months-that's shocking."Some of the leading online book publishers and distributors conduct their business exclusively online. Among the leaders are netLibrary, peanutpress, 1stBooks and Xlibris. NetLibrary and peanutpress sell and distribute exclusively digital books online. They carry large numbers of titles, ranging from books published by university presses to trade books. Xlibris and 1stBooks are print-on-demand (POD) publishers who specialize in helping authors publish their own books, but they also offer digital books for online distribution.

Digital Magazines

Despite the low bandwidth requirements for online text, online magazines have not been very successful to date. There are very few purely online magazines, Slate.com and Salon.com being two of the most prominent ones, but even these two online magazines have not been profitable despite publishing articles from world-class writers. Print-based magazines have done little original online content, preferring to use online versions of their magazines mainly for promoting print stories or archiving past issues. There are several likely reasons that online magazines have fared poorly, despite the apparent benefits the online world would seem to bring to magazines and long-form nonfiction writing in particular because of the lack of space limitations.

One of the main reasons is technological; reading long blocks of text on computer monitors becomes tiresome because the resolution of computer monitors has not reached the same quality as text on a printed page. Even once computer monitors do achieve higher resolutions, there is still the issue of portability. In other words, unless monitors can compete with a printed magazine in terms of clarity and portability (and to some extent disposability), there is likely to be a barrier among people in reading anything of any length in a digital format. This of course is not unique to magazines, as digital books and newspapers face the same issues. E-ink or some other digital form of paper may solve this problem, but this will not reach consumers for a few years yet. Changing behavior among the public in how they consume media is another factor weighing against long-form, text-based narratives like those found in The New Yorker or The Atlantic Monthly.

With greater competition for their attention during the day, the public seems less willing to spend the time necessary to read long articles. In an online environment, readers are also more likely to click on hyperlinks to get more information rather than wait for the author to fully explain a point. Likewise, an article may be a starting point for a much more robust discussion among Web users in the form of online discussion groups. However, there could be an important niche for magazines to provide a measure of distance and perspective on issues and to thereby be a voice of authority in their specialized area. If a magazine is perceived as having suitable authority and is respected highly enough by its readers, it seems that the public is willing to pay for online subscriptions. Consumer Reports Online is one of the few success stories in the online magazine world, with over 580,000 subscribers who can access archived articles and reviews on various products.

Digital Radio

Thousands of radio stations offer live webcasts of their regular over-the-air transmissions, although there are unsettled issues regarding royalty payments for webcasts of recorded music. In 2002, the U.S. Copyright Office decided that webcasters must pay 70 cents per song heard by 1000 listeners, half of what a government panel recommended they pay in a decision in February 2000 but still less than what the recording industry was asking. Webcasters also have to pay royalties retroactively from 1998, and many of them said the rates and retroactive payments would cost them hundreds of thousands of dollars and force them to shut down. Traditional radio stations are exempt from this new royalty payment method, successfully arguing in 1998 that they are helping promote the music. The term radio is itself somewnat meaningless in an online digital world in which music is not broadcast over the air but retrieved by users on demand over the Internet. In that way, online "radio" is technically audio programming, and in some ways will seem much closer to the current state of on-demand online music downloads, even though the term radio may stay with us or change its meaning.

Regardless of the technical approach, online-only radio stations such as spinner. com are free of many FCC regulations and don't require a license to operate. Moreover, they reach a global audience, and there's no potential for signal interference. As a result, there are hundreds, possibly thousands of online radio stations. Many of these stations operate independently of any broadcast parent, although legislation is being drafted that will bring them under some of the same rules broadcasters face.

Online radio stations must abide by the Digital Millennium Copyright Act, however, which prohibits the advance posting of playlists, which would permit users to plan in advance when to copy songs. Even before the 2002 rulings on royalty payments for webcasts, some online radio stations paid royalties to one of the two music licensers in the United States, the American Society of Composers, Authors and Publishers (ASCAP), or Broadcast Music Inc. (BMI). Live transmissions of sports events have emerged as an important part of online radio. In the case of major league baseball, Internet users must pay a fee to listen to live audio webcasts of professional baseball games. Some other professional sports, such as the National Football League (NFL), make the audiocasts of their games available for free online. One of the challenges of listening to online radio is finding stations that are available. One list with more than 10,000 Internet radio stations from all around the world was created by WMBR-FM at the Massachusetts Institute of Technology. It allows for searches by country or region, call letters, format, or frequency.

Digital Music

The MP3 file format represents an interesting example to illustrate how the new networked digital marketplace works. It's indicative how the recording industry is likely to sell much of its music in the future. The $5 billion recording industry is faced with a dramatic shift as users embrace digital audio and all the flexibility and power it affords them. The MP3 file format is used to compress near-CD-quality audio of music, which then lets the files, which generally range between 2 and 4 MB in size, be distributed easily over the Internet. There is nothing inherently illegal in the MP3 file format itself; it is simply the technology used to compress audio files. The problems with the recording industry arise because consumers can copy, download, and distribute music largely for free through file-swapping services such as KaZaA. The recording industry has long held that it is acceptable for an individual who purchases an album, cassette, or CD to make a copy for personal use, and it is of course not uncommon for friends to exchange copies of music among themselves.

File-sharing of online music takes these exchanges to completely new levels, how-ever. At any given time during the day, it is not unusual for 1.8 million users to be on a service such as KaZaA, exchanging close to 300 million files. These are not simply audio, of course, and can include video, text, and images as well, but it would be safe to say most of the files being shared are music files. KaZaA, Morpheus, Grokster, the now-defunct Napster, and many other online peer-to-peer file sharing systems have been at the core of this phenomenon. For now, suffice it to say that the major labels and everyone else in the recording industry value chain are enormously threatened by this development. They lose significant control and, they say, their profits and investments are being reduced along with the piracy of their intellectual property.

In 2001, the major record labels finally began getting into the online music business themselves even as they maintained their lawsuits against file-swapping services. Warner Brothers, BMG, EMI, Arista, Virgin, Jive/Zomba, and others teamed up to launch MusicNet.com, a for-profit online music distribution service. Consumers pay $9.95 a month to RealOne, which uses Real Networks to enable music downloads. Even as the labels become more involved in digital distribution of their music-belatedly, many would say-other industries within the current music distribution industry will also be faced with drastic changes, such as those in the plastics industry, distributors, and retailers.

Finding new songs and artists that you may like may become more difficult than ever in the digital age. As production and distribution costs decrease, more people can create their own professional-sounding (although not necessarily good) recordings and distribute them digitally. One solution that is emerging is the use of intelligent agent-based collaborative filtering, a sort of music club for the digital age. Amazon.com and other e-commerce organizations already are making use of collaborative filtering to alert their customers to new books and music that they would be likely to find appealing, based on previous purchases and the purchasing patterns of people with similar buying tastes.

Digital Film

The Internet has proven a valuable means of distribution for film, especially independent and short films, which have traditionally found distribution to be the most vexing bottleneck in becoming successful. Because independent and short films vary widely in quality and style and are produced outside the mainstream of Hollywood, few theaters, or theater chains, have been interested in showing them. Because of the low cost of online distribution and the potential to build audiences over time and space, a growing number of Web sites provide extensive independent and short films online, typically for free viewing. Two of the leading independent film sites are Indie Films and ifilm. These advertising and e-commerce-supported sites feature hundreds of independent films and film trailers for free viewing. BMW Films is another interesting example of an online film site, in this case funding the production of independent short films-as long as all funded and shown films feature BMW cars. As commercially oriented as this may sound, the films produced have been of very high quality and not too crass in their commercialism. The quality of the online films available on the site, some done by famous directors, have been praised widely by leading independent critics.

Digital Television

There is a wide variety of sources of video content online. Most television stations and all major networks maintain Web sites. A small but growing number of them provide at least some of their programming via the Web. An even smaller but growing number of these and other programmers provide near-broadcastquality video programming via the Web, some of it on demand. Viewers can go to the station's Web site and select from a variety of news and information options, including stories reported in text, audio, or video format. These various formats help add depth to the stories that video-only formats simply are not able to do because of the need for interesting visuals, sometimes at the expense of exploring related issues to a story.

For established broadcast or cable stations, changing to a digital format that allows them to take full advantage of the capabilities of online video can be expensive. Jim Topping, former general manager of KGO-TV (KRON's ABC-owned competition in San Francisco) and then senior vice president (now retired) at ABC-owned TV stations, notes that the installation of a powerful video server cost KGO-TV $9 million. Other technology to help the station become digital cost another $12 to 14 million. This investment gives KGO-TV the capability of delivering any of its programming at high quality and on-demand via the Internet or other broadband media. However, the investment KGO-TV made is prohibitive for the majority of stations, especially those in smaller markets.

Of course, a $9 million investment is not necessary to start transmitting digital video on the Internet. One small-market station has found a way around the high price tag. In Kingsport, Tennessee, DMA 93, WKPT got a digital signal on air for just $125,000. George DeVault, president of Holston Valley Broadcasting Corp., owner of the ABC-affiliated station, decided to forego HDTV initially and bought and installed a digital system to put a standard definition television signal on air. This low-cost approach is what has opened the door to many independent producers who are now transmitting television-like programming on the Internet. Public television stations are also converting to digital television.

A June 1999 Arbitron NewMedia Internet study showed that at that time almost three-quarters of Internet users in the United States spent up to 30 minutes a week watching streaming video. Nearly half planned to watch more streaming video in the future. The development of television programming on the Internet has given rise to at least two main types of online video programming: that which has been transferred from off-line television and original Internet video programming. Because so much of online video or television is still in its infancy and still largely constrained by technological issues such as bandwidth, computer storage capacity, and screen resolution, it is likely that these two types will morph or change in ways that we cannot foresee and create some kind of as yet uninvented form of online programming.

An early example of the type of hybrid that may develop is Alternative Entertainment Network TV (AENTV), which combines original Internet video programming and aggregates digital video originally aired on television. AENTV was named one of the "10 Great Video Sites on the Internet" by Broadcasting & Cable magazine and has collected hundreds of hours of programming from a variety of TV shows, all available on-demand and for free. This type of programming, which simply serves up programming originally produced for television, is still perhaps most common, although there is no definitive study yet available to prove this. Although there are examples from virtually every type of programming category, most "television" programming of this type is simply promotional.

Trailers, soap opera clips, and sit-com excerpts are put online to generate viewer interest in an upcoming show that will appear on television. One exception is Comedy Central, which provides much of its television programming online on-demand. The most common type of nonpromotional programming thus far from overthe-air television stations is news and public affairs. CNN.com, MSNBC.com, CBS News, ABC News, Fox News, and NBC News are among the leaders in providing online video news. The CBS Boston affiliate WBZ provides exceptional regional online video news, as do Seattle CBS affiliate KIRO and NBC San Francisco affiliate KRON.

A leading provider of international video news online is the BBC World, which provides live video news feeds online. Viacom's 2000 acquisition of CBS has begun opening up greater opportunities for television, or video, on the Internet. With its new Internet division, MTVi, including both MTV and VH1, as well as its recently acquired SonicNet, Viacom CBS is positioned well to provide not only online music but also online music video. Combined with CBS video news strength, the Viacom CBS empire is poised to take a leadership position on many online television fronts. DTV can be interactive, which opens the door to more participation and interest in shows among viewers.

ABC's Enhanced TV synchronizes customized interactive content over the Web during many of its programs, such as Who Wants to be a Millionaire and Monday Night Football, which offers an interactive play-along synchronized game as well as live statistics and facts about the players and teams. ABC has initially focused on the "two-screen" platform whereby viewers have an Internet-connected computer in the same room as their television, so it's not truly interactive television. There are more than 40 million homes that today are capable of such TV-Internet convergence, which is closer to a critical mass than the current set-top box installation numbers. Currently several companies are trying to make the convergence complete, either as a PC-turned-TV or a TV-turned-PC.

Television programming typically has been provided to the public by a limited set of program providers. They have made their programming available on a scheduled basis, packaged for mass audiences and broadcast according to a controlled schedule. Just as online music distribution opens the music recording industry to potentially thousands of new artists (i.e., program providers), the Internet opens the TV business to thousands, perhaps millions, of new TV program providers. Internet-original programming began with web cams, tiny cameras that attach to a computer that have enjoyed enormous popularity around the world.

Web cams have provided typically live feeds of everything from a coffee pot at Oxford University to a seemingly endless series of individuals inviting the public to pay to watch their uncensored private lives. This early experimentation among amateurs has given rise to much more serious original online video programming, however. Some of the most interesting are web cams set up by researchers to allow viewers from around the world to observe important, unusual, or simply interesting experiments or other research in action. Universities and not-for-profit organizations have also used online video to show lectures from famous guest speakers, panel discussions, or to highlight on-the-scene video footage shot elsewhere in the world that does not make it to mainstream media.

Online programming guides, also known as electronic program guides (EPGs) in digital television or video, are becoming a necessity as Liberty Media chairman John Malone's outdated notion of a "500-channel universe" is replaced by a "million-channel universe." Leading the way in the online program guides today is tvguide.com, the online version of TV Guide, with 50 million subscribers. Tvguide.com offers viewers a fully interactive and keyword-searchable guide to the coming week's television programming from terrestrial broadcast to cable, satellite, and the Internet. The site also features daily news about television and other media, a database on more than 40,000 movies, and digital video.

The same developments that have challenged the recording industry will start to emerge in the television industry as digital television enters the marketplace and broadband use increases, allowing for fast downloads of large files. Digital video files are much larger than what most people can accommodate in downloads, which has hampered the popularity of video file-swapping online. Fixed media, such as videotapes or DVDs, are still primarily used for on-demand, repeated viewing, although new technologies could easily change this as well and make fixed media obsolete.

The television industry has been closely watching what the recording industry is doing with the hope that they will not repeat the same mistakes. However, concerns about intellectual property theft and unwanted competition have limited some programmers' forays online. Large television companies, broadcasters, and cable companies generally see the Internet and digital video as threatening their loss of control and their existing franchises, and whether they learn from the experiences of the recording industry or follow them in litigation and political lobbying to stop potential threats to their control remains to be seen. So far, attempts at creating secure digital media have not been successful. They have either been extremely clumsy and overly restricted consumers' ability to play media such as a CD on a variety of devices, have been foiled by low-tech mechanisms such as using a black marker pen to mask digital encoding, or have been extremely unpopular with consumers and thus failed, such as what hap- pened with the DIVX format that forced consumers to pay per use of a digital video they "bought."

Traditionally, media enterprises, like other industrial-age businesses, required heavy capital investment. Capital was required to build the transmission towers for television and radio stations. It was required to buy printing presses and to build cable systems. Not only was the infrastructure expensive, but it created enormous barriers to entry for prospective competition. In the digital age, these rules are changing. Some of the most significant barriers to entry are shrinking. Capital costs are reduced, as anyone can go online and create a Web site and potentially compete with established media companies. It's part of why relative newcomers such as AOL, Yahoo!, and eBay have been so successful. Of course, the cost of producing quality original content is still relatively high, especially for video but less so for text or audio. Moreover, few media enterprises have found a formula for making profits in the online world, as most people seem unwilling to pay for content and advertising does not seem to be very effective. Most large online media outlets have the backing of traditional media companies behind them, such as MSNBC.com, a joint venture between NBC and Microsoft, or CNBC.com. With advertising and other revenues being generated from the parent companies, these online endeavors can afford to take losses for a while as online revenue models can be tried and tested. Many smaller, independent media dot-com companies were not so fortunate, especially after the economy and stock market spiralled downward from spring 2000. Some severely scaled back their business plans, and others, such as award-winning online crime news Web site APBNews.com, went out of business. Other online media enterprises such as Salon.com, which are still creating quality original content, are now charging for what used to be free.

Digital Libraries

Every library is different, every digital library is different, and different players are advancing many definitions for the digital library. Arms, for instance, defines a digital library as: a managed collection of information, with associated services, where the information is stored in digital formats and accessible over a network. A crucial part of this definition is that the information is managed. For the Digital Library Federation in the USA: Digital libraries are organizations that provide the resources, including the specialized staff, to select, structure, offer intellectual access to, interpret, distribute, preserve the integrity of, and ensure the persistence over time of collections of digital works so that they are readily and economically available for use by a defined community or set of communities.

Some prefer to work with the concept of the 'hybrid' library, as they believe that this more closely describes the reality of libraries, which have always been hybrid. The digital is one more (albeit very different) format that librarians have to deal with in a multi-format environment, where for many years non-documentary mixed-media objects, both analogue and digital, have been growing in importance, and where technology for access has had to be provided. Most libraries can supply microfilm and microfiche readers, video players, audio tape and CD players, as well as terminals for access to digital resources. However, there are often strategic reasons for defining activities as coming under a digital libraries heading - the possibility of securing funding, for instance, from programmes which are defined as digital library initiatives.

Hybrid libraries are designed to bring a range of technologies from different sources together in the context of a working library, and also to begin to explore integrated systems and services in both the electronic and print environments. They exist 'on the continuum between the conventional and digital library, where electronic and paper-based information sources are used alongside each other'. The concepts of virtual libraries or libraries without walls reflect the integrative possibilities inherent in the digital: if significant library collections are digital, then the confines of space no longer define boundaries upon information.

Virtual collections from many different sources can be assembled and accessed from anywhere, without the user even knowing where the sources reside, and personal virtual collections can be built to serve many purposes. Hence a virtual library could potentially be enormous, linking huge collections from all around the world together, or it could be very small, being the personal digital collection of one individual. Digital libraries are, like any so-called revolutionary change, a development of a whole range of underlying theories and technologies that have come together to create a paradigm shift.

The speed of recent developments has taken some librarians by surprise, especially the exponential growth of the amount of digital data available, but they are understandable if we look at some of the precursors that have led to the current trends: new developments rarely spring fully formed from the ether. There are many different kinds of digital libraries creating, delivering and preserving digital objects that derive from many different formats of underlying data, and it is very difficult to formulate a definition that encapsulates all these. Some principles are:

— A digital library is a managed collection of digital objects.

— The digital objects are created or collected according to principles of collection development.

— The digital objects are made available in a cohesive manner, supported by services necessary to allow users to retrieve and exploit the resources just as they would any other library materials.

— The digital objects are treated as long-term stable resources and appropriate processes are applied to them to ensure their quality and survivability.

Vannevar Bush, one of Roosevelt's advisers in World War II is generally credited with being the first thinker to suggest mechanical and electronic means of dealing with complex information, and of finding paths through information universes that could be marked for others to follow. Bush was grappling with the problem that has beset humanity since the invention of printing, and possibly before. How, when so much information is available, does one remember what has been read, make connections between facts and ideas, and store and retrieve personal data? Pre-literate humanity was capable of prodigious feats of memory, but the total amount of knowledge it was necessary to absorb was orders of magnitude smaller than it is now. When writing became widespread, personal notebooks and handbooks were used as aides-memoires, but these could handle only a fraction of the data that even one individual had to cope with by the 1940s.

Emanuel Goldberg developed very high-resolution microfilm, and also the technology underlying microdots, in the 1920s. In 1932, he wrote a paper describing the design of a microfilm selector using a photoelectric cell, which Buckland sees as 'the first paper on electronic document retrieval'. Paul Otlet saw huge possibilities in new forms of information recording and transmission: he was aware of the information and communication possibilities of telegraph, telephone, radio, television, cinema and sound recordings.

Paul Otlet visualized new kinds of work desks where there would be no documents, only a screen and a telephone with access to documents on film which could be called up at will. Otlet also formulated some new organizational principles which would hold all the documents in a linked relationship: a Universal Network for Information and Documentation which would connect centres of production, distribution and use regardless of subject matter or place - a development that uncannily presages the world wide web.

Though Otlet and Goldberg may have formulated the underlying theories upon which hypertext and information retrieval, and therefore digital library developments, came to be based, it was Bush's legacy that inspired later thinkers and developers. In 1962 Douglas Engelbart started work on the Augment project, which aimed to produce tools to aid human capabilities and productivity. He also was concerned that the information explosion meant that workers were having problems dealing with all the knowledge they needed to perform even relatively simple tasks, and Augment aimed to increase human capacity by the sharing of knowledge and information. His NLS (oN-Line System) allowed researchers on the project access to all stored working papers in a shared 'journal', which eventually had over 100,000 items in it, and was one of the largest early digital library systems. Engelbart is also credited with the invention of pointing devices, in particular the mouse in 1968.

The mid-1960s saw other pioneers conceiving of grand schemes that at the time seemed so innovative as to be impossible, but now are coming to realization. Ted Nelson designed his Xanadu system in 1965, in which all the books in all the world would be 'deeply intertwingled' (in his words - Nelson incidentally coined the word hypertext). Nelson also tackled the problems of copyrights and payments by proposing that there should be electronic copyright management systems that would keep track of what everyone everywhere was accessing, and charge accordingly through micro-payments. Impossible to implement at the time, these ideas are now commonplace, but it took Tim Berners-Lee to put them all together in the late 1980s.

Creation of Digital Data

Despite the difficulties of the early technology, some scholars recognized the value of the computational manipulation of textual materials immediately. Text had to be painstakingly entered on punched cards or tape, but the benefits appeared so great in terms of retrieval and analysis that they persisted. Father Roberto Busa, for instance, formulated the idea of automated linguistic analysis of text in the years 1942-6, and started working with IBM in New York in 1947. He produced more than six million punched cards for his edition of the works of Thomas Aquinas, and in 1992 the first edition of his CD-ROM was published.

In the 1980s a new technology appeared in the form of the Kurzweil Data Entry Machine (KDEM), which was developed to provide texts for the blind. It used optical character recognition (OCR) to create electronic text for printing on Braille printers or (eventually) conversion to sound using text-to-speech processing. The KDEM was extremely expensive (in the tens of thousands of dollars), but it could be trained to recognize different typefaces and fonts, and it was relatively accurate - probably as accurate as modern OCR packages. Other text conversion needs could, of course, be satisfied using the KDEM, and large corpora of digital text were created for many purposes.

The Oxford Text Archive, for instance, gathered many of the texts that it still supplies as output from the KDEM service operated nationally by Oxford University until the early 1990s, and these have been used all over the world as the basis for digital text collections, at the Universities of Michigan and Virginia in the USA, for instance. Digital text is now everywhere, as output from word-processors, publishers and OCR engines. Interestingly, OCR is faster and cheaper than it was in the 1980s, but it is still not as accurate as it needs to be to replace rekeying and typesetting, especially if the materials are pre-20th century. Many library projects use OCR to capture bodies of printed text; others, where the text is too difficult or a higher level of accuracy is needed, use rekeying. However, there are some new developments in the processing of text that greatly improve retrieval from inaccurate OCR. For maximum usefulness, digital text needs more than representations of alphanumeric symbols on the printed page; it also needs metadata to record other information about the textual object from which it derived. Markup languages such as the Standard Generalized Markup Language (SGML), define textual metadata and specify complex schemas of standard metadata tags to inform all the processes to which digital text might be subject: description, retrieval, preservation, print output, and so on.

While early document-processing technologies generally operated on strings of linear text, the possibilities of hypertextual linking within documents were recognized too, though this was initially difficult to implement on a computer. Despite the claims of many modern gurus of cybernetic hypertext theory, written text is not linear but can be interlinked, interwoven and annotated on the printed page in highly complex structures not susceptible of computational representation by the first generations of hardware and software. From the mid-1980s, better screen technology, more processing power, the development of the mouse and the advent of the Graphical User Interface (GUI) have transformed the ability of the computer to represent and link documentary objects.

In the last five years, digital camera technology has developed to the extent that digital images can be captured that equal or even exceed largeformat analogue photographic reproductions. These have disadvantages, however: the cameras are expensive, and the file sizes huge, which causes problems for storage and delivery. However, from valuable originals, large archive images can be captured and stored for the long term, with lowerquality derivatives being delivered for viewing and printing. This is acceptable for most uses, and means that good-quality images can be integrated with other media for a more complete user experience.

As of 2001, the British Library has produced a high-quality digital facsimile of the 15th-century Sherborne Missal that is on display in its galleries on the largest touch screen in the UK. The unique feature of this resource is that the pages can be turned by hand, and it is possible to zoom in at any point on the page at the touch of a finger on the screen. High-quality sound reproduction accompanies the images, allowing users to hear the religious offices that make up the text being sung by a monastic choir. Now documents can be represented by high-quality images, with underlying searchable text, and with annotations in text, sound or video.

Cameras are being developed that can capture 3-D images, and there are sophisticated capture devices for digital sound and video, deriving in part from the huge growth in these formats in the entertainment industry. It is, of course, possible to treat the printed page as an image. Capturing digital images from printed pages has the advantage that the page will appear on the screen exactly as it was in the original. The disadvantage of this presentation is that the search and retrieval functions are lost, but a combination of both image and text representation means that documents can be represented by images, with underlying searchable text and with annotations.

There is a rhetoric that suggests that we are moving rapidly from print to digital media: this is not borne out by evidence from the publishing industry and from copyright libraries. The death of the book has been predicted with every new communication or entertainment technology, the telegraph, recorded speech, film, television and the internet, but the book seems to be thriving. At the beginning of the 21st century, the UK copyright libraries, for instance, are receiving more print material than ever before (in 1999 the figure was around 105,000 items for the British Library alone), and this is without the materials that they purchase.

Production of digital data is certainly on the increase, but it does not seem to be accompanied by a concomitant diminution in the printed output, though it is changing both the publishing industry and the world of libraries. In the 15th century, the introduction of the printing press industrialized the production of books, but did not do away with handwriting. What it did do was change book production from a cottage industry carried out in monasteries to a commercial industry, and incidentally resulted in a huge loss of authority on the part of the Christian Church in Europe.

Johannes Gutenberg, born sometime in the last decade of the 14th century, and trained as a goldsmith, produced the first book in Europe printed from movable cast type, the so-called 42-line Bible. Despite popular misconceptions, Gutenberg did not invent this method of printing, which was known in China and Korea from around the 11th century. What he did was to combine the technology of the goldsmith's punch with that of the winepress. The result was the printing press - a machine that combined flexibility, rapidity, and economy to allow the production of books that the increasingly literate, increasingly numerous European city dwellers could afford to buy and read. The 42-line Bible was produced in around 1455.

Hand-set movable type not only produced books faster than handwriting, it produced them in multiple copies. While with early printed books it is not quite true to say that every copy is the same, the differences are small compared with the differences between manuscript copies. And printed books can be produced in the hundreds and thousands, even millions, which is the significant advance. Evidence for the instant huge potential market for multiple copies can be found, according to Kilgour, in the estimates of the numbers of books printed in the last third of the 15th century, that is in the 30 years after the death of Gutenberg in 1568. These estimates suggest that there were some 12 to 20 million books printed - more than the number of all manuscripts produced in medieval Europe up to that time.

More books call for more readers, and so literacy rates rose rapidly in the next three centuries. Paper was made from linen rag during this period, but in the Napoleonic Wars rag was needed to make bandages, so wood-pulp paper processes were developed. Wood was plentiful and the process cheap, which meant that print output could increase. This happened in several ways: more publications were printed, and works were often longer, hence the growth in the multi-volume work of fiction in the 19th century. Periodical publications were produced which appeared monthly, then weekly, then daily and the mass media were born.

Early printing presses were wooden and were hand-operated, and the type was hand-set. This remained the case until the beginning of the 19th century, when things changed rapidly with one of those 'paradigm shifts'. Printing-press technology moved to iron presses, operated by steam, to mechanical type, to hotmetal type to phototypesetting and then to computer typesetting by the 1970s. Publishing began to become a separate industry from printing in the 18th century, and grew rapidly throughout the 19th century with the increasing mechanization of the processes, and the further growth of literacy rates and the demands of a reading public. 'The total book production of the nineteenth century exceeded that of the eighteenth by 440%', and many of the publishing giants that still control the industry (though in very different configurations) came into being during this period.

Computer typesetting brought an unanticipated by-product: electronic text. This was not always kept initially, and when it was, the typesetting codes used for marking up the text rendered it largely unusable for any other process. However, standardization of markup languages has meant that it is now possible to use electronic text for purposes other than printing, and many publishers have embraced electronic publishing in the last five years, especially in the production of journals.

With the revolution in printing and the birth of the publishing industry came new developments in libraries. In the Middle Ages in Europe, libraries were either monastic institutions holding relatively few, very valuable books or belonged to private individuals. Many of the great libraries of today are based upon some of the collections of these monasteries and individuals. When the British army invaded the city of Washington in 1814 and burned the Capitol, including the 3000-volume Library of Congress, Thomas Jefferson sold his personal library to the Congress to 'recommence' its library. The purchase of Jefferson's 6487 volumes for $23,940 was approved in 1815. In the 18th century, circulation libraries and subscription libraries started to appear to satisfy the demands of the larger reading public for cheap access to print, and the 19th century saw the rise of the great public libraries.

Librarians have always sought to mechanize routine processes as much as possible, and so were early adopters of computer technologies. Database programs were developed early in the history of computing for use in stock control, payroll systems and other commercial activities. The adoption of administrative systems for catalogue record creation was an early example of the use of computerized processes in libraries. This started as merely a means of producing, for manual filing, printed catalogue cards or slips, which would be referred to by library staff and users as a means of finding library resources. To extend the duplication of catalogues and thus the number of user access points to the catalogue, microformats were used, 'enabling multiple copies of the catalogue to be distributed for the first time and new sequences, such as title catalogues, to be introduced'.

Alongside this new capability to share catalogues, there started co-operative efforts to share the cataloguing load and to benefit from aggregating cataloguing effort across multiple libraries. Because bibliographic description is such a highly structured construct, the computerization of the catalogue was a significant and inevitable next step from these early mechanization initiatives. This was not the computerized catalogue as we know it now in the guise of the OPAC (Online Public Access Catalogue), but a straightforward listing of the library's resources with no links to borrower records or to external resources.

In tandem with the development of the computerized catalogue came the move to automate circulation functions. Initially, this was no more than associating a borrower number with a book accession number while the full records of each were kept on separate computer database or paper systems. Even these most basic functions were only available to the largest libraries because of the great expense involved. However, this was to change as computing technology became more widespread and software developed the capability to create connections between different parts of databases and to integrate functions in a primitive fashion.

As soon as it was possible to get the circulation system to 'talk' to the catalogue, it was possible to automate some library functions, such as overdue notices. As important as the mechanization of routine staff-intensive functions, was the means it gave library managers to measure and assess borrower activity in great detail for the first time through reports generated from the computer logs and databases. This knowledge greatly enhanced acquisitions and stock management strategies and has helped librarians to cope proactively with changes in funding structures, bor- rower requirements and the user community, and with the accelerating expansion in information resources.

Electronic Data Interchange (EDI)

EDI refers to the computer exchange of business information using a standardized data format. Standardized EDI messages are based on common business documents such as purchase orders, invoices and delivery notes, which are interchanged between computer systems without human intervention or interpretation. It has been in use since the 1970s, but it was not until the late 1980s and early 1990s that any attempt was made to move away from proprietary systems to open standards. Adopting EDI can eliminate the mailing of paper documentation and the manual processing of quotations, purchase orders, invoices, shipping documents, customs documents, and other business transactions. Because the data is processed and stored automatically, tasks such as re-keying data and printing purchase orders and invoices are eliminated.

The use of EDI has been as significant a development for libraries as for the business world. The integration of the cataloguing and ordering process, plus the ability to chase orders that have not arrived on time automatically, speeds up acquisitions and gets resources to the user more quickly on their arrival. Automated financial controls can be pre-set to generate purchase orders and fiscal reports, and also to limit certain types of expenditure to defined budgetary plans. Librarians, as early adopters of EDI, have been among the first to partake in e-commerce and thus understand e-commerce's trials and tribulations but also its great advantages to the management of library services.

As far back as 1902 we can trace how basic technology was used and the results shared by libraries in a co-operative way. In that year the Library of Congress began selling printed cards that in effect 'made that library the centralized cataloguing agency for thousands of American libraries'. In computing terms we have to wait until 1971 for the same level of resource sharing and economy, when OCLC introduced an online shared cataloguing system for libraries. Today this co-operative catalogue is available to libraries in 76 countries and territories around the world, with over 46 million cataloguing records available, as well as associated interlibrary loan and reference database services.

In the UK, the Birmingham Libraries Co-operative Mechanization Project (BLCMP) was established in 1969 as a joint venture between libraries in Birmingham. BLCMP was created to realize the benefits of a shared approach to library computing and built a large shared database of over 19 million bibliographic records. The Research Libraries Group (RLG) also provides extensive shared resources through a set of online catalogues that offer millions of records describing materials created around the world.

In many areas, libraries are showing intensive co-operation and sharing of the fruits of computing technology. NORDINFO (the Nordic Council for Scientific Information), which celebrated its 25th anniversary in 2001, was founded as a bridge between Nordic research libraries and the growing information and documentation sector. The general objective set for the coming years is to work towards what has been called 'The Nordic Electronic Research Library'.

Another significant example of sharing for mutual benefit is the important realm of interlibrary loans. No single library holds all published information and most cannot hold even a sizeable sliver of it, but the librarian's role is clearly to provide access to the complete body. The only sensible solution is to share access to the resources through interlibrary loan. All the above co-operatives support this and local cooperatives for interlending exist all over the world at regional and national levels. Most of this is now being managed or documents delivered via electronic means. The British Library Document Supply Centre, for instance, received 34% of requests by postal means in 1993-4 but now receives less than 13% by post and the remainder by electronic means.

Challenges of Digital Communication

One of the most significant challenges all online media properties face is building a revenue stream not only to cover costs but to return a profit. As of this writing, few content sites had found a way to produce a substantial revenue stream, and, with the tightening economy of 2001-2002 and a substantial drop in venture capital and advertising revenues, the situation is even more difficult. There are several ways online media companies can generate revenues-at least in theory. These include traditional methods such as advertising, subscriptions, and syndication, as well as methods that are either unique or feasible in an online environment, such as e-commerce and micropayments.

However, none so far have proven to be inherently better than other method, and dot-com companies as well as online media companies are still experimenting with methods to earn profits. It is likely that more advanced technology will open the door to creative revenue generating models that are unavailable today. For the time being, the revenue streams that appear most viable for content sites involve a combination of advertising, subscription, and micropayments. AOL produces substantial revenues, but mostly from its monthly subscription fees, which are actually charges for online service rather than content per se. AOL does produce some revenue from online transactions in the form of online shopping. This may grow significantly in the future as more consumers become used to buying online.

Advertising has proved disappointing in generating revenues for all but the largest portal or content sites, such as Yahoo! or MSNBC.com, which attract millions of visitors. Media companies both offline and online charge advertisers for the cost per thousand (CPM) of audience members. This means a magazine with a circulation of 100,000 can receive more for carrying ads than a magazine with a circulation of 10,000. In the online media environment, technology allows Web site owners not only to see exactly how many people have visited a given page on the site but to track whether people clicked on the advertisement on that page or not.

Because the average numbers of click throughs on ads are generally extremely low (ranging between 0.75 percent for standard banner ads to 1.5 percent for large oversize ads in the center of the screen), advertisers have become more cautious about placing their ads online based simply on the numbers of visitors to a site. It may well be that ads are similarly ineffective in the analog world, but there is of course no way to measure that in the concrete terms that the online world can provide.

Online companies have tried a number of things to improve click-through rates on ads and thereby increase revenues. Larger ads, animated ads, pop-up and pop-under ads have all been tried, but with minimal success. In fact, most computer users seem much less patient with advertising than they are on television probably overhyped in the late 1990s, it could be argued that it has likewise been looked at overly skeptically in the post-dot-com boom era. Yet, e-commerce presents an interesting opportunity in the long run for media businesses operating in the digital age.

The online arena is an environment in which consumers can not only get information about products on demand, but, conversely, media and other organizations can deliver promotional messages specifi-cally targeted to individuals based on their online profiles. In many cases consumers can also purchase those products or services and even have them delivered digitally via the Internet, as is the case for music, computer software, digital books, videogames, and some other products. For those that can't be delivered electronically, most are shipped via commercial delivery services anywhere in the world. A major issue for online media organizations is how to provide a secure environment for payments for online transactions. Many consumers are concerned about the safety of providing a credit card number via the Internet and thus are afraid of venturing online to make a purchase of any type. Another issue that online media organizations must consider when venturing into e-commerce is maintaining viewer trust in their content and disclosing potential conflicts of interest or even the appearance of conflicts of interest.

Broadband digital media present both an opportunity and a threat for those in the media and communication industries. On the one hand, long-standing corporations, institutions, and entire industries are being turned upside down by the digital revolution. Businesses built on analog technologies of production and distribution are trying to figure out how to adapt in the digital age. New efficiencies of creating and delivering content in a digital, networked environment are emerging throughout the world. Long-held, highly profitable business models based on the analog world are less viable in a digital marketplace. Yet, uncertainty prevails in the largely digital world. Dot-com stocks have plummeted. Converting to digital production and distribution costs a lot of money, and the returns are not guaranteed. No wonder so many executives in the media business are nervous about digitization choice and change. Nevertheless, the new digital world means new business opportunities. It means opening new markets that formerly were restricted by political, economic, and geographic boundaries. It means new storytelling formats that bring true interactivity to television and radio. It means creating immersive audio and video on demand for consumers who want their media, in all its forms, customized according not only to their preferences but also to their current geographic location and many other factors.

Overall, the digitization of television and radio means an expansion of the business pie. In other words, the size of the marketplace is growing, which means extraordinary business opportunities for those brave enough, talented enough, and persistent enough to enter the fray in a creative manner. Established businesses face the additional hurdle of having to deal with their own corporate culture that insists on placing a priority on protecting their existing business interests. This shortsighted thinking opens new opportunities for entrepreneurial startups nimble enough to adapt to an uncertain and rapidly changing marketplace.

5

Communication in Cyberspace

Cyberspace is a virtual reality within the world's computers and computer networks. Cyberspace is a common theme in science fiction. The word "cyberspace" was coined by William Gibson, the Canadian science fiction writer, in his novelette "Burning Chrome" and was subsequently popularized in his novel Neuromancer. While cyberspace should not be confused with the real Internet, the term is often used simply to refer to objects and identities that exist largely within the computing network itself, so that a web site, for example, might be metaphorically said to "exist in cyberspace." According to this interpretation, events taking place on the Internet are not therefore happening in the countries where the participants or the servers are physically located, but "in cyberspace". This becomes a reasonable viewpoint once distributed services become widespread, and the physical identity and location of the participants become impossible to determine due to anonymous or pseudonymous communication. The laws of any particular nation state would therefore not apply.

The internet tools now allow remote, virtual collaboration in ways that were not possible just a few years ago. To use these tools successfully, product development teams must have a complementary IT infrastructure, matching tools, and the appropriate leadership, as well as the incentives and discipline to work together in a new way. These virtual teams - not "collocated" but "co-wired" - offer distinct advantages. Most virtual collaboration software allows for automatic recording and tracking of the proceedings of meetings. Action items are written down and indexed. Repositories of knowledge are available that make the inventory of knowledge much more visible.

Most virtual project teams have a knowledge manager position to care for this inventory. Collocated teams could take advantage of these same techniques, but few have the discipline to do so. For example, it is difficult to record and index coffeepot conversations. Partners and suppliers may be in different regions and time zones. The project can carry on through non-real time threaded discussions and overlap meetings. Shopping the world for design expertise and manufacturing capacity allows you to concentrate your design capacity on the areas where you add the greatest value. Many of these outside designers are willing to share the risks and rewards of your product, giving them high incentives for successful delivery. If managed correctly, this method of collaboration can significantly shorten time to market and time to volume manufacturing. Companies can gain a market advantage by improving their ability to do co-wired innovation faster than their competitors. The shift from a collocated to a co-wired environment requires a strategy for a Collaboration layer and a Control layer of infrastructure, the formation and training of distributed, collaborative teams, and the ability to change the way these teams are motivated and managed.

A co-wired product development team requires a communication infrastructure of two layers - a collaboration layer and a control layer. The collaboration environment includes areas for four levels of communication: project management, real-time design sharing, structured discussion and social and brainstorming spaces. The control layer builds and stores the knowledge inventory. The various design tools should smoothly connect these two layers. If they are properly organized and managed co-wired teams can develop products faster than collocated teams. Some types of communications, such as team building meetings, should be face-to-face or via video-conferencing, whereas other types such as technical exchanges can happen in real time or virtual time over the Internet, or by email. The meetings and communications should be "bandwidth-matched" to the needs at the time. Co-wired, virtual teams can take advantage of global expertise and diversity with very flexible capacity.

The infrastructure and leadership of co-wired teams must provide for fast acknowledgement of communications, mutual understanding of each communication and a path for commitment and actions. The leader of a virtual, collaborative team should invest significant time in achieving the trust and social inclusion of all team members. The leader's goal is to align goals, processes, skills and tools across the team. Remote team members should be treated with the same respect and given the same promotional opportunities as collocated team members.

Computer-Mediated Colonization in Cyberspace

Frits Grotenhuis analyzes how cultural differences between the Dutch and Americans issue in mis-communication in Computer-mediated Colonization (CMC) environments. This not only frustrates the goals of business mergers, it further documents important ways in which CMC technologies of themselves cannot overcome cultural differences. Dineh Davis turns attention to a much broader sense of culture—the culture of the Internet and its technologies as favoring the extraverted, the busy, and the noisy, in contrast with the personal and cultural preferences of much of the world for ways of being and becoming human that stress humility, quiet, and reflection.

Grotenhuis and Davis thus complement one another as Grotenhuis demonstrates cultural conflicts external to CMC technologies, while Davis documents cultural conflicts embedded in these technologies and their implementations in a global Internet culture. Finally, Alexander Voiskounsky's research suggests an interesting and creative middle ground, i.e., multiple uses of the Net and the Web that utilize Russian as a lingua franca and thus helping people from diverse countries sustain and foster important cultural activities.

As Grotenuis makes clear, culture plays an ongoing role in the "nuts-and-bolts" elements of international business—first of all, in efforts to merge companies from diverse cultural settings. In particular, contra the assumption that CMC technologies will somehow ease these processes, culture rather complicates the use and efficacy of CMC technologies. This brings to the foreground a crucial lesson: some problems such as "communication failures" or "lack of teamwork" are better understood as breakdowns in intercultural communication. At the same time, of course, success for managers in a global society depends on their ability "to communicate successfully with managers and employees from other cultures."

Grotenhuis explores the impact of culture on two Dutch-American mergers by way of focusing on "cultural collisions" related to CMC practices, using a case study approach. Some fascinating differences emerge here between the two cultures in terms of business. Americans tend to be short-term oriented and result-driven. Americans are in a "permanent process of moving, of instability", which is perhaps not surprising in a country with few unions, in contrast with the trade unions and working councils in the Netherlands.

Grotenhuis further notes that the brevity of e-mails, while favored by the medium and "netiquette", contributes to culturally-based miscommunication. Americans tend not to provide context, which makes Dutch recipients feel ill-informed. Contrary to cherished American emphases on equality, informality, and direct communication, the Dutch regard their US colleagues as more hierarchical and less honest. As well, the Americans are perceived as more ethnocentric: "Generally they think that what works in the US, that will be good for Europe as well, instead of adapting to a different situation. What is good for the USA, that is not always necessarily good for Europe too." Finally, as these comments suggest, stereotyping occurred that hindered communication.

In particular, Grotenhuis notes that "despite all advantages of computer-mediated communication, still, face-to-face meetings remain necessary to prevent clashes in the long run." In this way, Grotenhuis' study stands as one more piece of evidence in the larger turn towards embodiment as an essential feature of human identity, one that is not easily abandoned for whatever advantages and freedoms may enjoy in cyberspace.

On the contrary, the risk is precisely that, in the face of the diversity of aptitudes, attitudes and values that make of "happiness" or "optimal experience" for individuals and cultures, when begin to base an entire culture on a single technological platform, are bound to create constraints on some subset of the population. When such a platform is installed cross-culturally and globally, dissent and dissonance become inevitable."

This dissent and dissonance is apparent first of all on the level of human identity, i.e., in the conflict between the tendency of the media to privilege publicity, self-promotion, busy-ness, indeed "noise," and those cultures and individuals that instead endorse humility, privacy, patience, and deliberation. As well, the role of English as a lingua franca means that the Web and the Net are limited by the limits of this particular language. Like all languages, English is good for specific kinds of expressions and thought, and less capable of expressing, or even allowing, others.

Davis further characterizes cyberspace as the equivalent of the "tyranny of the majority" over a voiceless minority - "... those whose biological, cultural, or behavioral upbringing precludes them from embracing the exhibitionist, impatient mentality of the other half of the human race," as this latter is at work in the technoculture of cyberspace. Indeed, the very term "cosmopolitan" - contra its claim to universality - excludes a significant portion of humanity:

> The very concept of cosmopolitanism can have tremendous appeal to some, while it may not serve the emotional needs of others who have led happy, albeit sheltered and "provincial" lives, in isolated communities. Though a culture of consumerism may appeal to some, it has brought others closer to an understanding of how obvious disparities can become across the producer-consumer divide. If colonization and invasion are inevitable then, she hopes, the colonizers will learn the lessons their predecessors - i.e., that conquest is more secure and stable when elements of the old culture are preserved in the new culture, if in albeit transformed guise.

Davis' initial summary of the presumed values and orientations of technoculture include: "all humans have the same intrinsic interests and value system based on a Protestant work ethic, a need for higher challenges and matching skills, a desire to move from physical to mental labor, an affinity for abstraction and compartmentalization of life affairs, and a peak pleasure experience in an intellectual, disembodied state." Again, this critique of disembodiment in cyberspace vis-à-vis embodiment and "non-mediated interpersonal relationships" contributes to the central debate and recent turn in CMC literature.

National and Cross-cultural Realities

Contra utopian hopes that cyberspace would prove to be "gender-blind" and thus a space in which women could enjoy greater equality and acceptance, an extensive body of research has now made it clear that carry gender with us into cyberspace - sometimes with terrifying results, including the famous "virtual rape" in cyberspaceand other forms of discrimination and violence towards women.

Gender, of course, is a central element of the worldview defining specific cultures, i.e., the roles played by males and females, their relationship to one another (hierarchical, egalitarian), etc. It is hence perhaps not surprising, except for those holding to the more utopian view, that gender differences pervade attitudes towards and uses of CMC technologies, even in cross-cultural comparisons. Nai Li and Gill Kirkup's study of British and Chinese students' use of and attitudes towards the Internet. Despite the considerable differences between British and Chinese cultures, they share similar patterns of gender differences, ones that work to the disadvantage of women.

Ann Willis makes clear that these patterns of gender discrimination are at the heart of North American Internet culture as well - at least as that culture is represented by Wired magazine, the putative voice of the "digital revolution." Here again, despite ostensible commitment to radical equality as a primary goal of the digital revolution - indeed, a goal and value that function as crucial arguments justifying or legitimating the revolution - Wired instead works to "re-power" the familiar elites of earlier epochs, i.e., white males in the middle and upper classes.

Li and Kirkup begin with a helpful review of the pertinent research on gender vis-à-vis information technology. The findings are not encouraging for those committed to gender equality: women have more negative attitudes regarding computers and greater computer anxiety; women use these technologies less, and are less likely to take computer courses or pursue computer-based careers. These differences extend to attitudes towards and use of the Internet in numerous ways, and this, despite the fact that women now form the majority of Internet users. As Li and Kirkup point out, much of the research on gender and the Internet has been done in Western countries, but it is also clear that attitudes towards computers and CMC technologies depend in some measure on culture.

Willis notes that the hype surrounding the 1990s "digital revolution" - more carefully, the utopian, specifically libertarian vision of individual liberation in cyberspace as free market— is dying down, in part as it is overshadowed by more familiar stories of "old and new media mergers, deals and machinations as companies re-shuffle to position themselves within an on-line services communication context."

In this context, perennial questions remain regarding access, identity, power, etc., in sharp contrast with the utopian promises of radical equality and democracy. In Willis' view, this is not surprising as these issues were raised by what might think of as the flagship journal of the digital revolution, Wired. Simply, while Wired professed to be the "voice of the digital revolution"- one as ostensibly radical as the industrial revolution - Willis' analysis makes clear that this version of the revolution was always only for the elite, i.e., white males, college educated, at the top of the income scales and prominent institutions in the United States. This argument is extended later on in her matter as she observes that in the period between 1993 to 1996, only one African-American was pictured on the cover — and that, to illustrate not individual success in an ideal free cyber-market, but to image the hacker who inhabits the margins of a predominantly white world of success and power.

In particular, Wired emerges as the bully pulpit for laissez-faire capitalism and privatization - what Willis calls "techno-libertarian" ideology. In dramatic tension with its democratic claims, the world of Wired is first of all a gated one. By focusing on ostensibly technological solutions to political issues — e.g., increasing bandwidth as eliminating information scarcity and inequalities — this ideology sidesteps and suspends genuine issues of power, as participation in Wired's vision of the future clearly depends on social and financial status, knowledge, and education.

Indeed, as its laissez-faire credentials suggest, the magazine - consciously or not - invokes an equally 19th century Social Darwinism: "This is the digital revolution, you are either part of the steam roller or part of the road." This Social Darwinism at work in the competition of the marketplace, Willis later points out, hence provides techno-libertarians with a handy response to concerns about the digital divide, the gap between information haves and have-nots. In a Social Darwinist world, winners and losers are a given, a necessary outcome of competition, not a problem of justice or reason for concern.

This intrinsically hierarchical worldview is further consistent with Willis' observations of the marginalization of women and people of color in the world of Wired. This marginalization, Willis notes, squares with the more general observations of how such publications replicate sexist discourse despite their overt claims regarding egalitarianism as an inevitable and desirable outcome of the digital revolution. As Willis sees it, Wired instead "re-powers the binary 1950s gender ideologies of women positioned in the domestic private sphere with men in the public sphere of work and business." This occurs in numerous ways, perhaps most prominently through the metaphor of "frontier" for online culture - i.e., "a wild, dangerous, out of control place," one where only tough guys survive and women appear, if at all, in the role of whores or good girls.

Perhaps the greatest disjunction between the revolutionary rhetoric of liberation through technology and the realities of online praxis is in the central legitimation claim for the digital revolution - namely, that it will inevitably democratize. The libertarian version of democracy, as Wired makes clear, however, is rather the (limited) plebiscite notion of "clicking For or Against" - i.e., responding to ostensible choices, absent dialogue, debate, and the hard slow work of building consensus among diverse perspectives. This latter view, however, makes sense in the ideological framework of Wired because it coheres and resonates with the free market of commerce as the primary model of human interaction. Behaviors and choices as producers and consumers, as negotiators in a marketplace, are thereby conflated with "democracy". Consumer trading is equated with public participation - one participates in "democracy" by behaving as a consumer.

This commodification of democracy, one that morphs it into a primary free market model, is part of a larger pattern of commodification that Willis calls "über-consumption." Willis cites here Solnit, who finds PacMan to be the symbolic metaphor of such über-consumption - its sole purpose, after all, as a disembodied head-mouth "was to devour what is in its path as it proceeds through an invisible maze". In the face of this analysis, Willis then asks the sensible question, "...what exactly is revolutionary about Wired's digital projection?" — especially when it appears that Wired rather works to reinscribe "older, feudalistic and laissez-fair, ideals and practices, thus inhibiting possibilities of the participatory potential for modes of communication like CMC."

In broader terms, contra the postmodern claims of the 1980s and 1990s that new means of communication automatically mean revolutionary changes in social, political, and cultural practices. Willis makes clear, rather, that culture is conservative —it is much rather the case that older patterns of belief, values, and practices will express themselves in new forms made possible by new technologies, instead of the case that new technologies will reshape those older patterns.

Willis' discussion of Wired, much has been made of "electronic democracy" as one of the specific ways in which CMC technology would fulfill utopian hopes for liberation via technology - whether in modernist or postmodernist guise. In particular, Jürgen Habermas's theory of communicative reason and correlative concept of the public sphere has provided a central theoretical foundation for explorations of how far CMC technologies might indeed serve democratic hopes. While Habermas is critical of especially libertarian views of democracy, libertarianism predominated Net ideologies in the 1990s. Tim Jordan's essay provides an extensive justification of such Net libertarianism as part of his analysis of "cyberpower."

Unlike earlier enthusiasms for life online that emphasized radical discontinuities between embodied and disembodied identity, Jordan's treatment of identity and renovated hierarchies recognizes a number of important connections between online and offline experience. So, for example, while acknowledging that certain aspects of offline identity - e.g., gender, race, geographical location, etc. - may be hidden online, Jordan claims that it would be a mistake "to assume that the powers that flow around offline identity...are absent online...." Instead, he argues, identify the particular forms of identity that emerge in cyberspace and what kinds of power attaches to them.

On this basis, moreover, he attends to the ways in which "offline hierarchies are reinvented online", precisely on the basis of online identities as still implicating offline identity. This means, in different terms, that in contrast with the either/or's characteristic of 1980s and 1990s emphases on the radical differences between online and offline, Jordan's account of cyberspace is something of a middle ground. This middle ground recognizes the both/and - the ways in which cyberspace is both different from and similar to ordinary lives as embodied human beings in real spaces. So, for example, Jordan reiterates some of the familiar claims regarding the difference between online and offline - e.g., that hierarchies will be flattened by more egalitarian forms of communication that emerge in cyberspace, and that the Net, in the famous phrase, interprets censorship as damage and simply routes messages along different pathways, thus undermining governmental efforts at control.

At the same time, however, identities in the real world, and the relative power or lack thereof that we enjoy, accompany us into cyberspace. By the same token, Jordan points out this same interrelationship between the individual and the technologies of CMC: "individual powers in cyberspace will be defined by the technology we are using and the capabilities this technology offers." This is so, moreover, because the technology embeds social and/or ethical values - an aspect of what Jordan calls "technopower," the conjunction of seemingly dead technology with living social values that "constitute the very possibility that cyberspace exists in the first place."

This technopower, more broadly, has a trajectory. Contra the liberationist theme characteristic of 1980s and 1990s postmodern enthusiasm for cyberspace, Jordan claims that "The direction of technopower in cyberspace is toward greater elaboration of technological tools to more people who have less ability to understand the nature of those tools." Instead of the technology delivering greater power and control to the users —the promise of all modern technologies—control is rather delivered "to those with expertise in the increasingly complex software and hardware needed to constitute the tools that allow individual users to create lives and societies."

This process involves information overload, as moving information from the costly and time-consuming production processes of print into cheap and quick electronic forms contributes to the explosion of information. The solution to this, of course, is more technology to organize, filter, and dispose of information. However, this only adds to the problem of information overload, according to Jordan, leaving only an elite of real experts to enjoy any putative freedom in cyberspace. Contra a "hopeful form of power" for the individual, "...cyberpower of the social is pessimistic because it reveals networks of interactions that increase the ability to act of an expertise-based elite."

Jordan's third layer of cyberpower is the imaginary, the layer that includes sense of urgency to either jump on the bandwagon of new possibilities just around the corner and/or to flee the imagined disasters of dystopian futures. Jordan nicely summarizes the various forms of utopias imagined for cyberspace, including hopes for personal immortality, virtual "heavens" in which perfect equality is achieved, and the cyborg as overcoming binary oppositions that found oppression. Favorite dystopias, by contrast, turn on cyberspace qua panopticon, i.e., the space in which the individual becomes perfectly transparent to complete surveillance. Jordan makes the important point that both these hopes and fears rest on the belief that "everything can now be manipulated through information codes," i.e., there is no resistance, nothing that cannot be reduced to information.

For Jordan, finally, the future is up for grabs. While he argues that libertarianism - the ideological conjunction of individual liberty and free markets - is best suited to cyberspace, he sees it as contested ground, a battleground between the individual and the social, including the possibility of dominance by elites.

Holmes begins with a review of some of the most important voices regarding democratization in cyberspace, including Mark Poster's seminal analysis of the Internet as facilitating especially postmodernist conceptions of democracy, before turning to Habermas's conception of the public sphere proper. He points out that the public/private distinction presumed in this conception becomes problematic, first of all, as broadcast media override geographic and kinship foundations of one's sense of the public sphere.

As well, as the Internet and other electronic media introduce interactivity - a point stressed by Poster as marking out "the second media age" - the question arises as to whether broadcast and network forms of communication make a new kind of public sphere possible. In contrast with the enthusiasts who find network communication thus redemptive, Holmes examines what kinds of interactivity are indeed made possible with CMC technologies. While he finds important mismatches between the Habermasian requirements for the public sphere and the kinds of dialogical reciprocity that may take place in CMC, Holmes likewise finds that the postmodern alternatives are also lacking - first of all, because they fall into an overly simple technological determinism.

Holmes comes to a complex middle ground, claiming first that as individuals engage in a variety of communicative media, they participate not so much in a "pre-given public sphere" but rather "in the process of constructing publicness across a range of mediums." Hence it is less the case that, as postmodernists tend to argue, "...the contemporary public sphere is breaking down and becoming fragmented as is the fact that it is sustained across increasingly more complex, dynamic and global kinds of communication environments."

In sharp contrast with the euphoric enthusiasm for the digital revolution of the 1990s, contributors thus raise a range of critical concerns. CMC technologies do not serve as a culturally transparent medium that somehow eliminates cultural differences and culturally-based obstacles to communication On the contrary, CMC technologies embed specific communicative preferences that work against effective cross-cultural communication.

Indeed, CMC technologies may embed preferences for the public, the busy, the noisy, the unreflective and the self-promoting that runs directly at odds with individual and cultural preferences for privacy, silence, reflection, and humility.

In fact, both cross-culturally and at the heart of the North American self-promotion of CMC technologies, find a variety of clear biases against women. These biases, indeed, are consistent with more libertarian understandings of the sorts of freedom and democracy facilitated by the Net and the Web. Even such an articulate defender of Net libertarianism as Tim Jordan recognizes that in the competition for multiple forms of power available in cyberspace, traditional elites and hierarchies may win out once again, despite justifications to the contrary that claim greater equality and democracy will inevitably emerged in a Wired world. Indeed, the problem of realizing any form of electronic democracy is complex. The strong theoretical foundations provided by Habermas are fundamentally challenged by Luhmann, who, as taken up by Moeller, argues instead that participation in cyberspace is the end of "individuality," much less "democracy."

It would thus seem safe to say that the bloom is indeed off the revolution. But this is by no means to argue that the revolution has failed. On the contrary, that it is precisely through recognizing these critical limitations and dangers in CMC technologies that are thus able to make use of them in informed ways that are more likely to succeed in their goals. In other words, precisely by recognizing the role of culture in communication above and beyond what CMC technologies can - and cannot - accomplish, are better able to teach and train people to use these technologies in culturally-informed ways that are more likely to facilitate rather than frustrate cross-cultural communication. Similarly, by recognizing how far CMC technologies may favor male ways of knowing and communicating, women and men who are interested in more egalitarian relationships and communication can use these technologies in ways more likely to foster rather than hinder such equality. Finally, by refining theoretical understanding of what democracy might mean, and determining - through both theoretical debate and reflection on what happens in praxis as diverse users take up CMC technologies in diverse cultural settings - how far these technologies might indeed encourage more democratic forms of polity are better prepared to make effective use of these technologies for the sake of genuine democracy rather than its counterfeits.

In all these moments, in fact, it appears that if wish to realize at least some of the goals of the "digital revolution" - greater gender equality, greater democracy, etc. return to a broader understanding of how lives online rest on and interact with lives offline, i.e., as embodied human beings inextricably implicated in multiple webs of relationships with other human beings in diverse communities, traditions, histories, cultures, and, indeed, with a larger ecological system. Such a (re)turn, will include attention to the social context of use of CMC technologies as a way of shaping their design and use in light of the values and bias they can embed, and in order to avoid various forms of computer-mediated colonization, i.e., the imposition of unwanted and alien cultural values and communicative preferences that otherwise is likely to result from the naïve assumption that these technologies are culturally neutral. While there are, unfortunately, a range of examples of such colonization—there are also examples of utilizing CMC technologies in ways that avoid colonization, however inadvertent, while sustaining both local cultural values and preferences alongside communication with those beyond the boundaries of one's immediate community and culture.

Attractiveness of Cyberspace

The Internet is obviously international and transnational. Since it first came into life in the USA, the majority of the

Internet "aborigines" - beginning with the times of ARPANet - reside in North America. Moreover, the great majority of the WWW content information is located on the US/Canadian web-servers; userful data are often mirrored elsewhere. The cyberculture - whatever that means - originated in the USA. The majority of surfers and site-visitors, e-consumers, Listserv and Usenet subscribers, online chatters and players, fans of club-like web activities, discussants at webforums, etc. used to also belong to the North American culture. The newly emerged global influential Cyberculture used to be strongly dependent on a good command of English language, and on the willingness to share cultural norms established by native English speakers.

Parallel to a global view on evolving virtual communities, a culture-specific approach seems to be no less needed. "The Internet and local cultures both determine each other". The dialectic idea of interdependence between a global cyberculture and local network subcultures is principal and worth discussing. Since the global influence is quite obvious, it is time to stress the impact of local cultures on the evolving world-wide Internet culture. At first, might restrict ourselves to purely ethnic subcultures - Far Eastern, Latin American, Eastern/Central European, Southern/Central/Western/Northern African, Southern Asian, etc. At the moment, some of them can hardly be called influential, but times change.

The advance of the new millennium marked the time period when the proportion of North Americans and native English speakers on the Net decreased to only less than the half of the global Internet population. By the end of 2000 "the US share of global Internet users dropped from 40 percent to 36 percent ... while 12 percent live in the world's other English-speaking countries. Thus, the total proportion of native English speakers decreased to less than 50 per cent: even if add New Zealand, the same would be true now in 2002.

This news is sort of a challenge for the Internet aborigines. The same source stresses that "in every global region where English in not the main language spoken, nine-in-ten Internet users prefer to get local information in their local language". Of no less importance are customers' orientations: "Web users are up to four times more likely to purchase from a site that communicates in the customer's language. Are the North American high-tech producing, consulting, and/or trading companies going to save their once-privileged positions in the rapidly changing market? If local markets are important, the companies' CEOs should pay special attention to multinational communication, to advertisements, to precise and culturally adequate translation of news, products and services presented on websites.

Thus, the Internet is now multilingual and multifocused. Taking into consideration non-English-speaking language-specific ethnic groups, one should mention that some of them have developed web sources that look attractive for both residents and foreigners. The volume of content based on the use of the Spanish language seems to be quite sufficient not to bother with English-based web content. Even for bilinguals familiar with the English language, non-English web-based chats and information sources oppose or substitute the global Internet.

Some countries pursue protective policies towards the integrity of national culture and ethnic language in Cyberspace, for example France or China. Sometimes ethnic segments of the Internet originated from abroad. The initial Arabian newsgroups and listservs, for example, were organized by emigrants from different Arabian states. More often representatives of diaspora communities participated in web activities initiated in metropolias. This is highly characteristic for the USA. The Global Internet Statistics are estimated that "there are some 16 million Americans who are more likely to access the Internet at home in their own language, rather than in English", while in the office they are more likely to access the Internet in English. The leading languages opposing English in the USA as a medium of home use of the Internet are, in descending order, Spanish, Chinese, Italian, German, Korean, Polish, Japanese, Portugal, and Greek. The real numbers are, at most, estimates or qualified guesses. Besides, the real numbers reflect both the proportion of native speakers of these languages residing in the USA, and the level of attractiveness of the Internet segment referring to their mother tongue. In 2002, the idea of accessing the Internet in a mother tongue does not seem too attractive to old or new emigrants from Vietnam or Indonesia who reside in the USA, even if some of them might have problems mastering English. Thus, the local segment of the Internet is called "attractive" if it really attracts visitors from outside the local community. To simplify the definion, might call "local" every non-English-based segment of the Internet, however large the proportion is of the world population. Probably not all of these segments are attractive, as tried to show earlier.

Of course, each website, and/or group of closely connected websites, is designed to attract outsiders, and the number of hits, clicks, visits, sessions, or the target audience reached, are very important measures. But the segments based on ethnic languages usually include every type of website which advertises itself, and yet the segment itself has or lacks qualities that might make it attractive. Thus we save the term "attractiveness" for the most broad - based on ethnic languages other than English- segments of the Internet.

The Internet related culture in Russia is very young, it has been developing since 1990 - the year when the Russian computer network established a connection with Western European. The Internet population in Russia is not numerous and the WWW content is modest in its quantity.

Chronologically, the first published estimates of the number of networkers in Russia were made by an American and refer to 1994. Globally, actual approximations of the Russian Internet population and the WWW content are as follows.

About 5,000,000 high-quality PCs with modern software are in service in Russia. About the same number of older PCs are in service and are not likely to be connected to the Internet. The Russian segment of the Internet includes approximately 700,000 connected computers and more than 350,000 unique IP-addresses. The computers with access to the Internet are rather innumerous; that is, users most often access from office/school/university, and less often from home. Sociological data confirm that this is true. Statistics of web traffic suggests that weekend traffic is less tense than work-time traffic. This might be partly shadowed by the fact that there are so many time zones in Russia due to its huge area.

There are more than 140,000 domains in Russia, and among those there are more than 75,000 second-level domains. One should take into account that, usually, only .RU and .SU domains are counted. It is known that some Russian sites belong to .ORG, .NET or .COM, but they are probably innumerous, and webcrawlers can hardly identify them. At the same time, some servers within the .RU or .SU area are physically located outside Russia.

The annual increase of Russian-language content is over 200%. In January, 2002, it contained about 60,000,000 indexed documents, which are well rubricated and fully searchable. The global volume of information is estimated as close to 1Tb, and an average web-server contains as much as 2.5Mb information.

Hundreds of Russian-language newsgroups are active; FIDONet users participate in over 2,000 moderated echo-conferences. The most universally used search engines are Rambler and Yandex which were originally Russian productions. Lycos started business in Russia in 2001 and organized its Russian service. Major world-wide search engines, such as Google and AltaVista, operate with Cyrillics.

One need not know Russian or read Cyrillic to search through Russian web content using originally Russian search engines, since the queries are automatically translated. A complicated morphology of the Russian language is handled and sentence parsing is performed. All the advanced products support major alternative Cyrillic charsets.

Estimates of the number of Internet users in Russia are being made by several sociological agencies. The agencies are mostly Russian, but agencies from abroad are active as well. Research data has been available since 1996, when the first representative research was performed. Sadly, since that time, the number of Internet users in Russia has been the subject of strong disagreement among the few agencies that are systematically carrying out fieldwork in the area.

The number of actual Internet users in Russia were 3,300,000 (3.6% of adult population), of whom 60% are men and 40% are female, more than 20% are teenagers, 40% are aged between 20 and 29, about 20% are aged between 30 and 39, and only 6% of Internet users in Russia are over 50 years of age. These data refer to November, 2000. Since that time no reliable data have been published, and it is only reasonable to assume that the number of users have increased and exceed 4,000,000. The Russian Ministry of Communications estimates the number of permanent Internet users as 2,500,000 to 3,000,000 and the number of casual users as about 5,000,000. Residents of Russia comprise approximately 1% of the world-wide Internet population.

Economically and politically, the Internet means a lot to all those who identify themselves with the Russian segment of the Internet. The previous tense links between the residents of the newly independent states that have formed after the collapse of the USSR, show a tendency to be called, at best, virtual. Personal contacts are severely reduced both in quantity and quality due to ever-increasing travel, phone and postal tariffs, customs emerging at previously transparent frontiers, decrease in the exchange of TV programs and in the circulation of newspapers, problems with the exchange of the unequally "weak" national currencies, acts of brutality and/or expectations of hostility towards the representatives of minority ethnic groups, etc. In addition to inefficient personal contacts, and in many ways due to the same reasons, economical and industrial ties have reduced too.

Only political extremists and/or marginal nationalists would deny that the huge territory - one sixth part of the globe surface (with the exception of oceans and seas) - is possibly open for re-establishing traditional forms of links and for maintaining those working and personal contacts that have happily survived - on the new information technologies basis. Global telecommunications seem to emerge just in time to mediate processes of filling in the "inefficient communication" gap.

Telecommunications are heavily used on an organization-to-organization level. But this is not enough. The Internet, mobile phones, videoconferencing systems, etc. bring a new potential to solve the problem of keeping contacts among people who were born and got to know each other in their common country, lived there a life-long period of time, spent leisure time together and paid visits, but recently found themselves residing in diverse states and facing severe problems when they make attempts to engage personal or social contacts.

For the purposes of mediation in establishing contacts and in the formation of distant communities the WWW content is of special importance. The tendency is that Russian web content is widely used by members of Russian language communities outside Russia. Non-residents of

Russia are very active in newsgroups, including both ethnic Russians and ethnic non-Russians. The latter speak Russian fluently, they are often born and bred within the Russian culture and usually are educated in Russia and/or in the Russian language. The majority of this special Internet community population found themselves outside Russia when the Soviet Union collapsed in 1991. They now reside in the former Soviet republics - now independent states.

A minority of the community members are permanent or temporary residents of diverse countries (usually, but not exclusively, Germany, the USA, and Israel), and they feel themselves closely connected with the Russian culture. Global Internet Statistics estimates the number of Americans who regularly access the Russian segment of the Internet is 100,000. The migrants represent what is often called the Russian diaspora: they continue to speak Russian, and they support websites with the content devoted exclusively to Russian culture. One of the most important web sites of this type is Little Russia in San Antonio, Texas - it has already attracted interests of communication researchers.

The diaspora consists mostly of "new" migrants, and partly of "old" emigrants from Russia, including those who were born abroad. One should take into account that in the twentieth century there were at least four periods of massive migration from Russia to the West and/or East, and respectively four waves of migrants can be differentiated depending on the time of their escape from the Soviet regime.

The other source is the webservice SpyLog which traces most of the navigation within the Russian segment of the Internet. The SpyLog tracker presents data that approximately 40% of navigations are systematically made from outside Russia. Among the visitors from abroad there are native Russian speakers and those who speak Russian fluently, as well as foreigners meeting certain problems when they read Russian sources. The browser interfaces are in Russian for the majority of navigators from the former Soviet states, with the exception of representatives of the three Baltic States, who use browsers with English or local language interfaces. Almost all visitors from Western Europe, Israel, or the USA use the browsers with an interface in the local language. Thus, browsers give some hint about visitors to the Russian Internet segment and the degree of their closeness towards the Russian Internet culture.

The reasons have been deduced from discussions with colleagues, personal friends, or acquaintances residing outside Russia. These discussions have been held over several years, beginning approximately in 1994. The discussions have never taken place in a laboratory setting, and have never taken the status of a formal interview. No formal procedure of handling the results was used, but for classification. More sophisticated procedures would require discussions to be recorded. The number of respondents are approximately 70 non-Russian residents. The above-mentioned statements should prove that Russian content on the Internet, though incomparable to the English-based content in quantity and quality, is nevertheless one of the attractions of the Net for non-residents. It is noteworthy that modern residents of Russia are about 60% of the overall population of the former USSR. The reasons for former Soviets from outside Russia being attracted with Russian-based content are mainly as follows:

— Lack or shortage of attractive web site content in their ethnic languages. The majority of post-Soviet states (with the single exception, perhaps, of Estonia) are far behind Russia in the rate of people's access to the Internet and in the number of web sites.

— Poor (if any) command of official ethnic languages of post-Soviet states by ethnic Russians residing there.

— Poor literacy skills in their mother-tongues of numerous non-Russians in the post-Soviet states. Often

> they speak their ethnic languages fluently but have problems with writing and reading, i.e. with composition and comprehension of scholarly texts due to the fact that when acquiring formal education they used Russian solely.

Political and/or religious leaders of some ethnic groups who used Arabic or Mongolian alphabets in the pre-Soviet period feel pressure to return to cultural origins. It seems only natural for some of them to cease using the now-actual alphabetical systems that are based mostly on a slightly modified Cyrillic and to make a change to the historically proven way of writing and reading. These decisions result in a peculiar sociolinguistic situation when different generations speaking the same language might soon have no common literacy to exchange written texts, including private letters. Happily this process is slow and the situation of cross-generational misunderstanding is perhaps a futurist one.

In less populated countries it is impractical to originate and support newsgroups and to compose valuable websites content in ethnic languages, except for purely official information and for data of exclusively local interest. Even if ethnic language newsgroups and websites are available, more diverse views are expressed and more valuable information displayed might be found in Russian-based newsgroups and websites. Usually, in post-Soviet states, educated people have some command of English, but their command of Russian is in most cases much better. This fact explains, at least partly, the reasons for their attraction to the Russian language segment of the Internet. Individuals might feel nostalgia towards older times when all the citizens of newly independent states stayed closely united in the USSR; they maintain interest in news from the former parent state and in contacts with former compatriots.

Media in some post-Soviet states are less independent compared to the Russian media. Residents of these countries may find it convenient and reasonable to get access to less censured news via login to the network versions of Russian news agencies. Usually they would try to know more about internal/external politics in their own states — this is a continuation of an old tradition of Soviet times to learn internal news through media from abroad. Politically-minded people from the former USSR - both within and outside Russia - tend to keep group discussions of numerous political issues; some of them blame the former communist regime, and some of them blame the modern ones.

Some representatives of Russian-speaking diaspora residing outside the territory of the former USSR find it attractive to take part in newsgroups and/or to originate/construct/support websites in the Russian language. Their motivations differ: they give consultations on diverse aspects of foreign life; being competent in web-related issues they share knowledge with subscribers to Russian newsgroups; they consult and support originators of network-related projects in Russia; they try to find people they used to know earlier in order to keep personal contacts; they try to find ways to share their hobbies with those speaking their mother tongue; they originate and support websites containing diverse collections.

Russian Internet experts are often believed to be more advanced, experienced and competent than their colleagues from many other post-Soviet states. The outside-Russia networkers, trying to enlarge their competence in the information technology related news and to follow discussions of the principal hard/software decisions, find it worthy to subscribe to the Russian language newsgroups and to surf the updated reviews published on Russian websites. Usually they find in this way much more valuable information compared to the quantity and quality of information available in the ethnic languages of the states in which they reside. These are some of seemingly important reasons which partly explain the attractiveness of the Russian segment of the Internet for the Russian speaking foreigners.

The modes of Internet usage are largely dependent on the level of command of English and on the competence in behavioral patterns peculiar to North American culture. Like many other activities, especially those dependent on the technologies' usage, Internet-based communication and cognition relies on a heavy use of English. Few ethnic languages claim to be attractive for foreigners participating in online discussions and/or visiting websites. It is stated that the Russian segment of the Internet is such a cluster of attraction.

The qualitative and quantitative parameters of the Russian segment of the Internet are described briefly and give evidence that these parameters are developing rapidly. Some probable reasons that might explain the foreigners' interest to Russian-language web sites, discussion lists, or web-forums are proposed. These foreigners are partly ethnic Russians residing in the former Soviet states outside Russia, and partly non-Russians who feel themselves connected to the Russian culture; a much smaller but influential part constitute former Soviets who have emigrated to the Western/Eastern states outside the borders of the former Soviet Union.

Do's and Don'ts of Online Communication

There are distinct advantages to E-mail and the phenomenon of electronic communication. A large amount of paper is saved on a global scale, with reduced amounts of paperwork flying between businesses and internal departments. Speed of delivery is an undisputed plus, as your message can be delivered in minutes to anywhere around the world. It can be easier to get to 'the top', as E-mail addresses of those executives friendly enough to open their Inboxes to the masses are often available. In addition, E-mail is perceived by many to be less intrusive than a phone call, as it offers the luxury of being dealt with whenever the recipient has the time, although that obviously favours the person being contacted, and not anyone who needs an immediate response. A diverse group of people learning how to browse the Internet . However, as use of this medium increases, with a diverse group of people of various religions, nationalities, genders, age groups and experiences learning how to browse the Internet, the question of netiquette arises.

A quick guide to some of the do's and don'ts of online communication

- When it comes to E-mails, it is a good idea to know your mailbox's limit. You should even choose them according to their capacity if you think you will be getting big files that could clog up your Inbox. Rinaldi suggests that you check E-mail daily, delete unwanted or used messages immediately, keep stored messages to a minimum, and remember that you can download or copy text to a word processing package, or even to a floppy disk, for storage there. This will reduce the pressure on your account's storage space, and generally make your Inbox easier to use.
- Form a habit of frequently virus-checking your system, especially after a bout of downloading from other systems or over the Internet.
- Do remember that your files may be accessible to others, so refrain from maintaining anything personal on your hard disk.
- An argumentative or belligerent E-mail message is called a 'flame', and the general rule is that you should not send any, even if you receive one yourself. Should this happen, go make a coffee and calm down before replying.

— Be professional and careful what you say about other people. E-mail is easily forwarded without your knowledge.

— Today, it is easy to copy, or 'cc', practically anyone on your mail. And we sometimes find ourselves copying people almost out of habit. In general, this is rude. People have less time than ever today, precisely because they have so much information to absorb. Before you copy people on your messages, ask yourself whether they really need to know. If the answer is no, don't waste their time.

— Consider the difference in time zones. If you require an immediate response, remember that the person you are writing to might be asleep while you're just finishing your lunch, so be patient and log onto a time zone Web site.

— Ensure your E-mail messages are succinct. Because E-mail is so easy to use, everybody's using it, and your message will certainly be one of many that day. When replying to previous correspondence, include relevant information from the original text but no more. Do not return the whole message back to its creator, simply select the appropriate parts in order to clarify the emphasis of your response.

— Your mail should have a concise subject title that reflects the content, that way the user can locate the message quickly and easily. However, look out for the tricks that Spammers use, as they will often put subject titles such as 'The Information You Requested' or 'My Reply' to engage your curiosity.

— A signature is a good idea, as it renders you credible and accessible. Around four lines is a reasonable length. Your signature footer should include your name, position, affiliation and Internet address.

— Should you receive an important E-mail that warrants a considered response, send a short reply to indicate that you have received the message and will reply shortly. This is professional and most useful to the individual biting their nails at the other end.

There are a plethora of do's and don'ts to consider when writing and managing e-mails, but the important thing to remember is that none of this is enforceable, merely desirable. Arlene Rinaldi writes that "netiquette is just a set of guidelines," to be ignored or followed as people see fit. Following the guidelines, however, can prevent you from annoying people and raise your profile with associates across the world with whom the only contact you might ever have is an E-mail. At the very least, following netiquette can make your messages be welcomed, treated with a higher priority and above all, more enjoyable to read.

Each organization on the Internet should provide and inform its users on expected standards of conduct when using its network and when accessing other networks while using Internet resources. The punitive measures for not adhering to the organizations policies should also be provided.

Technology is supposed to be our friend: it is meant to improve our lives, make things easier for us and assist us in doing many complicated things quicker and all at once. "How did we ever do 'this' before our ever-helpful technological device was invented?" is what we supposedly all ask ourselves whilst shaking our heads in wonderment. However, according to new research there is a fine line between using PCs and software devices that is often slipped off to violent effect.

A recent survey conducted by Massachusetts-based Concord Communications showed that 83 percent of 150 respondents from the US have witnessed physical attacks upon computer equipment as a result of a growing trend.Another investigation by Symantec Corp., which worked with the UK's National Opinion Poll organisation, discovered that over 40% of British PC users have sworn at, kicked and physically abused their computer equipment. The London-based international research company MORI completed a survey, aptly named Rage Against The Machine, which showed how 40% of 1,250 UK workers surveyed have witnessed colleagues abusing their computer machinery both physically and verbally. The same results also indicate that almost half of all those who work with computers suffer from frustration or stress because of IT difficulties. According to the MORI poll it's not just the machine itself that causes such an extreme reaction, as aggravation can also be aroused by the time taken to fix a problem and the jargon sometimes used by the support personnel. Crashing software and uncooperative mice are also triggers for bouts of computer rage. Pulling cables out to cause the system to crash is apparently a popular method for taking revenge upon a troublesome machine.

The costs of machine or software failure are expensive to say the least. The Confederation of British Industry claims that £25,000 per person per year is the price of one hour lost everyday at work. But when it comes to having these problems fixed, a massive 75% of those questioned said their IT support staff were unable to fix the problem. Over a fifth experience the same problem again as the symptom was dealt with, but not the root cause. According to MORI's statistics, one in eight people have seen staff from the IT department being bullied by office workers after their technology crashes. The real issue here, of course, is stress caused as a result of technological failure. MORI's poll claims that almost one in five people within the manufacturing industry say they feel stupid as a result of their computer problems. A third of people who suffer regular computer crashes have to work late or take work home as a result, which will probably lead to higher stress levels and is not healthy for the individual's morale.

PC manufacturer Compaq says that many IT problems are easy to fix. Around half of all calls to its help line, for example, are from individuals who have forgotten their password and are locked out of their machines. As well as choosing a more memorable password, using good quality reliable equipment, insisting upon a high standard of cabling for your office network, using reliable methods of backing up data, deleting unused files to keep your system clear and keeping your virus checking software up-to-date will all help to minimize computer failures and keep your staff happier.

Full and proper PC training is another simple premise that is very often overlooked by companies, but one that can de-mystify and simplify the whole computing process and maintain harmony in the long run.Within the next 15 years, the steady progress in producing faster, cheaper, and more powerful computer chips will be unavoidably impeded by the laws of physics. It all started 37 years ago. "Integrated circuits will lead to such wonders as home computers, "wrote Gordon Moore, a young researcher at Shockley Semiconducter,"...automatic controls for automobiles, and personal portable communications equipment." The year was 1965, three years before he would co-found the largest silicon chip manufacturer now in existence.

Gordon Moore inadvertently set a precedent with his paper, which Electronics magazine asked him to write for their 35th anniversary edition. His submission entitled,"Cramming more components onto integrated circuits" presented the idea---a new idea at the time---that the development of smaller transistors at lower unit production costs would translate into exponential progress in silicon chip complexity at minimum cost. In other words, performance would double each year. In 1965, chips could hold 60 transistors. Moore predicted that by 1975 as many as 65,000 transistors could be crammed onto a single chip. In perspective, Intel's Pentium 4 chips now hold over 42 million transistors. The ability to fit more transistors on a silicon chip simply means that information can be processed faster.

The press dubbed the observation"Moore's Law", and it has become a widely accepted and universally acknowledged precept that has come to account for not only chip complexity but also faster performance, translating into computer performance that doubles every 18 to 24 months. In an interview with Dori Jones Yang in 2000, Moore admitted he used to cringe every time someone used the term, and stated about his original ten year prediction that,"Really, that's as far ahead as I've ever been able to see." Moore's predicted rate of progress has been embraced by the industry, becoming somewhat of a self-fulfilling prophecy. If a company progresses faster, fabrication and development costs become prohibitive. If it progresses slower, components may be less expensive but the company falls behind the competition.

In the late 90's, the digital world started becoming increasingly anxious about the supposedly inevitable demise of Moore's Law. Chip manufacturers had two major problems: physical barriers blocking the continued diminution of transistor size, and financial barriers in fabrication costs.

While computing power was doubling every two years, fabrication costs were doubling every three years. This situation would inevitably lead to the slowing or stop of chip manufacturer's progress. If Moore's Law holds true, manufacturers will need to individually place atoms to manufacture silicon chips throughout the 2010's. At the 0.10-micron stage (each transistor would be composed of less than 100 atoms), small silicon chips containing millions or billions of transistors would no longer be able to control the flow of electrons.

With each generation of increased performance, the size of computer-based products becomes smaller. If manufacturers simply made larger chips to fit more transistors on them, the products would also have to become larger to accommodate them, or our smallest electronic products and applications would not be able to be improved upon.

What do we want when we buy a new computer or other electronic gadget? We want it to be fast, reasonably priced, and as small as possible. This has been the trend maintained by the progress of companies such as Intel and AMD, making the new products we see on the shelves of electronics stores available and affordable. Moore's Law is why our computers become obsolete so quickly. By the time Intel or another chip manufacturer can work out the kinks of doubling performance, again, the cycle of Moore's Law has taken us through another two years or so, and current products are half as powerful as the next generation of technology.

Communication and Culture of Cyberspace

Power is a complex notion in social theory and discussion of it will be necessarily short. Here will be taken to mean the various ways in which different individuals have different possible actions they may be able to take. Such an interpretation is open to a voluntarist reading and a structuralist reading; it is also open to different interpretations of the moral or ethical meaning of power around the two poles of power as the name for that which creates social order and power as a form of domination.

This interpretation of power is derived principally from theories developed by Max Weber, Barry Barnes and Michel Foucault. The legitimacy of this interpretation rests on this matters aim of defining power in cyberspace, not the nature of power itself. Having taken a definition of power from a broad reading of social theory, it is the utility of this definition in helping to define cyberpower that is most important and not an answer to the complex question 'what is power?'

In front of a computer screen, reading the glowing words we confront singularity before building a sense of others in the electronic world. There is a double sense of individuality here. First, people must simply connect to cyberspace by logging in, almost certainly involving the individual entering their online name and their secret, personal password to be rewarded with their little home in cyberspace. The first moment in cyberspace is spent by nearly everyone in his or her own individualised place. Second, moving from this little home to other virtual spaces usually involves further moments of self-definition; for example, choosing an online name, choosing a self-description or outlining a biography. The experience of logging on occurs not only when entering cyberspace but is repeated across cyberspace as we enter name and password again and again. The two key areas where being an individual in cyberspace allows different actions to be taken than in offline life can be called identity fluidity and renovated hierarchies. These will be briefly explored in turn.

Identity fluidity is the process through which online identities are constructed. It remains true that in all sorts of online forums an individual's offline identity cannot be known with any certainty. With the reasonably well-documented instance of a conservative Jewish, teetotal, drug-fearing, low-key, sexually awkward, male, abled, psychiatrist convincingly posing as an atheistic, sexually predatory, dope smoking, hard drinking, flamboyant, female, disabled, neuro-psychologist are in the presence of a potential disconnection between online and offline identities. However, it would be a misconception to draw the conclusion that identity disappears online. Identities that constrain, define and categorise exist online, but these identities are made with different resources to offline identity. Broadly online identities are constructed out of two types of indicators: identifiers and style. Neither of these mandate that someone's offline identity must reappear within their online identity, though there are many ways in which a repressed offline identity may return in the midst of online fantasy.

Identifiers are the addresses, names, self-descriptions and more that designate contributions to cyberspace. Email addresses are the most common form of identifier and can illustrate the resources provided by identifiers for the construction of virtual identities.

The identity of the sender of an email can be constructed, in part, from their email address. All sorts of identifiers abound in cyberspace and there is no restriction on only having one, in fact there is almost a compulsion to creating several. Identifiers include the signatures people place at the bottom of their email, the often lengthy self-descriptions Muds and some discussion groups allow, the various names might choose or have imposed on for various lists, newsgroups and so on and even the visual avatars some are developing for three-dimensional shared virtual places. All these function as long or short, more or less freely chosen names; they are the virtual equivalent of seeing someone's face and being able to think male or female, black or white, old or young, and so on. The second type of resource for identity is style.

Many virtual places have resident celebrities whose styles are instantly recognisable to other participants and anybody who participates repeatedly will eventually come to have their style recognised. Groups also provide certain stylistic resources. Abbreviations are common in the typed world of online discussions, such as 'btw' for 'by the way' and groups sometimes generate their own specific abbreviations.

Online personalities are constructed through resources that are different to offline, preventing the use of many offline tactics for identifying identity. Online characters are constructed and judged through a number of markers that replace offline ones; addresses, handles, signatures, self-portraits and styles. Identity is both present in cyberspace and is different to non-virtual space, the only mistake here would be to assume that the powers the flow around offline identities-such as those around gender or race-are absent online, instead of identifying the particular forms of identity which exist in cyberspace and on which power takes hold.

Renovated hierarchies are the processes through which offline hierarchies are reinvented online, with many online resources undermining offline hierarchies while also defining new hierarchies. The second component of online life that appears obvious to the individual online is that it seems anti-hierarchical. Attempts to censor or restrict access to parts of cyberspace can often be by-passed.

Further, communication from many people to many people is close to the norm in cyberspace. This opens participation in decision-making, creating the potential for conclusions to be reached in more egalitarian ways than offline. Three ways in which hierarchies are affected will be noted; identity, many-to-many communication and anti-censorship.

Identities are one of the key building blocks in offline hierarchies, but if no-one knows are black or disabled online then cannot be placed in a hierarchy on that basis. This seems undoubtedly true, and to the extent that someone can keep their offline identity separate from their online then offline hierarchies based on identity can be dislocated. However, identity does not disappear online but is remade according to the rules of identifiers and styles.

This means that specifically online hierarchies can be expected, such as that noted by Branwyn who was told be an online sex enthusiast that 'In compu-sex, being able to type fast or write well is equivalent to having great legs or a tight butt in the real world.' All the various resources available for the construction of online identities will also function to create online hierarchies. Someone's witty and knowledgeable posts to a newsgroup, their style, may mean their claims are treated more seriously than a newcomer and can be reasonably certain that many may treat an email from billg as being of higher importance than many other emails we receive.

The second way hierarchies are dislocated is through many-to-many communication and its ability to include people in decision making. The inclusion of people in offline decision making is limited by the need to meet together, to only speak one at a time, to overcome the hierarchies of identity and so on. Offline hierarchies can be undermined through the broader access to information that cyberspace offers. In the UK in 1999-2000 there has been a discuss over the ability of patients to research their illness and treatment over the Internet and whether this is undermining the authority of physicians. Without entering into this particular debate, can note that it is one sign of the way the hoarding of information as a means of generating a more powerful position in society, particularly by professional bodies, can be undermined by cyberspatial communication.

Offline hierarchies are undermined in online life is by the censorship evading properties of the Internet. Not only is there a greater pool of expertise available but information that governments or courts might have restricted is almost impossible to hold back once it is free in cyberspace. The global nature of cyberspace is important here, as it only requires one country connected to the net to allow the publication of some information for that information to be let loose in cyberspace. Information restricted in an offline nation-state will then be available in cyberspace, subverting the national boundaries that have helped in the past to control access to information. A global informational space undermines regional or national attempts to restrict access to information.

While it is untrue to say that hierarchies are absent in cyberspace, it is also true to say that hierarchies there are made according to different rules than online hierarchies - rules that at their most hopeful make someone's ability to write creatively and knowledgeably the basis of higher positions in a hierarchy - and that many offline hierarchies are undermined by cyberspace's powers. Taken together identity fluidity and renovated hierarchies can also be seen to rely on the third component of cyberspace from the individual's viewpoint, because both rely on cyberspace's nature as an informational space. Sharing information allows the construction of identities; self-descriptions, signatures, styles are all constructed out of the words that pass between people. The renovation of hierarchies in offline life by cyberspatial communication results from different methods of sharing information and different access to expertise in cyberspace. When individuals experience cyberspace they come to the third recognition that life in cyberspace is fundamentally constituted by information.

If identity fluidity, renovated hierarchies and informational spaces constitute cyberpower from the viewpoint of the individual then power at this level must be understood as the possession of individuals, who can utilise the various abilities offered by these three to impose their will. If we pause and reflect on what it seems that cyberspace and the Internet offer as individuals, then the ability to remake our identity and to renovate the hierarchies are caught within make cyberspace appear as a place that offers various powers. These powers can used by individuals to take various actions they had not previously been able to; whether it is the desire of a woman to have gay sex with men or of a parent to understand the treatment their doctor is recommending for their child.

From this conclusion can understand the enormous hopes and commitment cyberspace sometimes draws from people, because viewed as a space based on individuals the main effects of cyberspace seem to be to offer various powers to act. It is from this perspective that the most hopeful visions of cyberspace derive. It is also a perspective based on the repeated and ongoing experience everyone has that entering cyberspace marks us as an individual, it is not a perspective that is simply naïve but it is one reinforced by the daily experience of millions who have virtual lives. Cyberspace is here understood as the land of empowerment of individuals, of reinventing identities out of thought.

Many people report a transformation, often slow, in their perception of online life. From an initial combination of bewilderment, glee and skepticism many come to accept the online world as normal - from MUD dragons to email. With stable online identities, in whatever forum they exist, people begin to have ongoing conversations, to meet the same people and learn their peculiarities. The particular rules of different corners of cyberspace become clear and normal, but then it is often realised that the individual is no longer the final cause of online life, for communities have emerged. The transformation is not magical but sociological. Even communities that begin by assuming the sovereign individual is primary soon come to realise that collective responsibilities and rules appear, created by many and over which no one person has control.

The idea of one person constituting a language or creating a society is strictly speaking absurd; anyone can invent a word but to have it understood means having a community. This transformation to seeing cyberspace as inhabited by collective bodies is not a simple opposition between individuals and collectives but an inversion of the relationship between these two. Individuals possessing cyberpowers can produce collective bodies, but individuals are here understood as being the fundamental constituent of community in cyberspace. What is often realised in contradiction to this individualism is that collectives may create the conditions under which certain forms of individuality can be realised.

The collective becomes the fundamental cause. At both levels of cyberpower both virtual individuals and virtual communities exist, but their relations are reversed. Cyberpower of the social derives from the belief that individuals have their possible actions defined by the collective bodies they are part of.

All of who use the Internet and enter cyberspace rely on a range of technologies. Any action can take in cyberspace, from changing a gender in a Mud to buying and selling stock, can occur only because we have entered an electronic space created and maintained by various technologies - IP, routers, personal computers, optic fibres, modems and so on. Our individual powers in cyberspace will be defined by the technology we are using and the capabilities this technology offers. The fundamental realisation that cyberspace is not just about powers individuals can use but also about the things that create those powers for all users, is essentially the same realisation as that there are collective bodies in cyberspace that both create and restrain the nature of individuality in cyberspace. This is because the communities that provide the basis for virtual individuals are essentially constituted by technologies. For example, the conditions for Usenet communities are primarily defined by the fact that Usenet technologies create discussion group made out of posts.

The nature of individuality in Usenet is constrained by the nature of its discussion group software and hardware. Different forms of individuality are possible in Muds, such as building virtual homes, and on the Web, such as use of graphics. All these powers that cyberspace offers the individual are based on communally created and experienced technologies.

If we assume cyberspace is the realm of societies and collectives, then a form of technopower becomes visible. Technopower is the constant shifting between objects that appear as neutral things - keyboards, monitors, email programmes - and the social or ethical values embedded in these objects by their designers and producers. Each questions the other. If email software allows many-to-many communication, we can ask why?, who made the software do this?, what results come from this? and in asking we may open up the inhumane appearance of the programme to find humans who embedded their ethics or ideals in a programme.

Technopower underpins the social structures of cyberspace through a constant shape-shifting between seemingly inert technology and seemingly alive values. This does not mean that every piece of technology was created with a form of technopower in mind. Not every technological thing we encounter or rely on has been purposefully designed to constitute the social life it actually constitutes. The unexpected result is always possible, like the emergence of teflon from the space race. But what will be found behind each thing will be humans in social spaces, making decisions within institutional and technological contexts. Dead technology always opens on the living, just as it is the living who create technology.

Technopower is constituted like an infinite series of Chinese boxes, each opening onto another little model of itself, and each layer composed of the same elements, inert seeming technology and alive seeming values. Technopower can also be seen in offline life; from car engines to ice cream, we live surrounded by technological artefacts that leak social values from every crevice. The difference between online and offline here is that online social forms are constituted fundamentally, if not totally, from technopowers. When we adopt the perspective of the social in cyberspace, we lose sight of individuals and their powers and bring into focus these impersonal technopowers that constitute the very possibility of cyberspace in the first place.

At the level of the social, cyberpower is a technopower. However there is more to say, as a particular direction to technopower can be defined. Technopower in cyberspace is governed by the ever increasing reliance by users on technological tools, that time after time appear as neutrally pointing the way to greater control over information but time after time result in different forms of information constituted by the values inherent in the new tools.

Information is endless in cyberspace and creates an abstract need for control of information that will never be satisfied. The direction of technopower in cyberspace is toward greater elaboration of technological tools to more people who have less ability to understand the nature of those tools. Control of the possibilities for life in cyberspace is delivered, through this spiral, to those with expertise in the increasingly complex software and hardware needed to constitute the tools that allow individual users to create lives and societies.

What can be called the technopower spiral is constituted out of three moments. First, there is the ongoing and repeated sensation of information overload in cyberspace. Cyberspace is the most extreme example of a general acceleration in the production and circulation of information. For example, cyberspace encourages people to produce more information rather than passively consume it. Information moves faster and in greater quantities in cyberspace than in other space.

Most powerfully, cyberspace increases information by releasing it from material manifestations that restrict its flow and increase its price. Ideas embodied in books have inherent costs and restrictions on the number that can be produced and the speed at which different people can obtain them. Information is largely freed of its material form in cyberspace. This constant increase in the sheer amount and speeding up of information leads to the experience of information overload. While the notion of having too much information might seem paradoxical, it is also the case that only a certain amount of information can be dealt with at one time. As early as 1985, Hiltz and Turroff estimated that computer-mediated communication resulted in what they call superconnectivity, whereby individuals' connections to each other increase ten-fold and this is a result reinforced by recent work.

Too much information or information too poorly organised leads to information overload. How many of know the feeling of signing up to an email list and then finding the constant flow of emails means messages have to be deleted before being read and the group resigned from? How many of search the Web for a particular topic only to end up with megabytes of files or piles of print-outs destined never to be read because there is simply too much? Cyberspace increases information's velocity and size to such an extent that information overload is a constant experience of virtual lives.

The second moment in the spiral in technopower is the attempt to master whichever moment of information overload has occurred. This can be done simply by switching off, but doing so removes all the powers the individual might feel they benefit from. Instead, information overload is constantly addressed with new technologies. Various solutions to the glut of information that cyberspace produces have been created, from news services that email news bulletins once a day to ticker tapes that produce a constant flow of stock prices or news flashes across a browser. Maes lists intelligent agents that schedule meetings, filter Usenet news and recommend books, music and other entertainment. All these share a number of traits. First, they interpose some moment of technology between user and information. This is always simultaneously a moment in which technopower is manifested and articulated because some technological tool, appearing as a thing yet operating according to values, is the method of controlling information overload. Second, the devices themselves produce information problems because they need to be installed and used properly. No matter how sophisticated such a device is the user will need to understand how to manage the device or risk being controlled by it.

Third, new tools nearly always make more information available and cyberspace easier to use, tending to create a new overload. This seems too paradoxical to be true, as the goal of many tools is to reduce the amount of information received by focusing or managing it in some automated way. However, the very success of any such tool tends toward the production of more information because it makes gaining information more efficient and there is always more relevant information waiting out there in the infinite reaches of cyberspace. Problems can be expected to re-emerge with the devices that have become essential to information management themselves producing too much information.

The technopower spiral is completed and re-initiated with the emegence of a new problem of information overload. This spiral of overload, tools, more overload and more tools is fundamental to technopower in cyberspace. It means that as individuals pursue their powers in cyberspace, they constantly demand more technological tools to master the seemingly infinite amount of information at their disposal. Technopower is constantly elaborated to meet the demand to control and manage information in cyberspace, thereby ensuring cyberspace constantly becomes more and more technologically complex. This, in turn, means that the ability to act in cyberspace is constantly elaborated by those who have technological expertise, either personally in figures such as hackers or by managing those who have expertise, as Bill Gates or Linus Torvalds do.

Accordingly, cyberpower of the social is a power of domination, through which an elite based on expertise in the technologies that create cyberspace increasingly gain freedom of action, while individual users increasingly rely on forms of technology they have less and less chance of controlling. If the cyberpower of the individual was a hopeful form of power, pointing as it does to the increasing range of actions cyberspace can help an individual to take, then cyberpower of the social is pessimistic because it reveals networks of interactions that increase the ability to act of an expertise-based elite.

Cyberpower encompasses both the perception that cyberspace offers power to the individual and that societies are defined by an expertise-based elite whose class power is ever-increasing. To complete this mapping of cyberpower, a third level needs to be outlined, for cyberspace exists not just in virtual lives and communities but also in dreams.

People are part of imaginary relationships that define societies and nations. A nation can be thought of as 'an imagined political community-and imagined as both inherently limited and sovereign'. It is imagined because it is impossible for all members of the community to meet, they must hypothesise their commonality. It is limited because there are always borders and beyond those borders there are other nations. Finally, it is a community because, regardless of actual inequalities between members of a nation, it is always conceived as a 'deep, horizontal comradeship' in which all are equal as members of the nation. A further recurrent characteristic of imaginaries is that they offer hopes and fears that appear as real projects just one or two steps away from completion.

Much of the urgency people draw from imaginaries stems from this sense of being nearly but not quite completed, meaning people feel a need to act quickly to either prevent the imagined disaster or bring on the imagined benefit. A similar imagined community exists in cyberspace and cyberspace's imaginary is driven by this compelling feeling that change is near. The content of cyberspace's imaginary is structured by a twinned utopia and dystopia that both stem from the claim that everything is controlled by information codes that can be manipulated, transmitted and recombined through cyberspace.

On the one hand, cyberspace gives rise to many hopes, including or especially the oldest human fantasy of immortality. Certain people believe that within our lifetime we will be able to separate our 'consciousness' from our body and upload it onto silicon. If the essence of our self can be made virtual, then what better home than cyberspace, where all the immortals would be able to meet.

In a related way, some believe cyberspace is becoming the one organic mind that will constitute a higher consciousness akin to god; a hope that has haunted the hippy mind at least since John Lennon declared everyone to be a god. On a less metaphysical plane, many see the cyberspace-based cyborg as the figure who will lead beyond the oppressions of this world - gender, class, race, sexuality and other - because the cyborg transgresses the oppositions between nature/culture, human/animal, and man/machine and in doing so helps to destroy the binary oppositions oppression is based on. Whether the heaven is a selfish one of personal immortality, a spiritual one of god-like hive mind or a materialist one of post-revolutionary utopia, cyberspace offers the possibility that this heaven is coming into existence.

On the other hand, cyberspace gives rise to many fears. Cyberspace is seen by many as the ultimate tool of surveillance. If repressive power operates according to the principle 'visibility is a trap', then cyberspace may make even our smallest interactions visible. A world is foreseen in which all interactions with the government, in education, in shops or any other institution will be carried out by electronic means and cyberspace will allow all these interactions to be linked, collated and examined. People will be considered guilty until proven otherwise because all interactions will be examined to see if they meet the expected pattern and if that pattern is not met then an investigation will be triggered.

More insidiously, information will be collected from everyone in the guise of serving their interests, such as with supermarket reward cards that offer special deals or money back in exchange for connecting the nature of our purchases to our socio-economic identity. We might also be implanted or tagged, cameras on public streets now constantly survey facial heat images looking for a wanted suspect and the USA and UK governments currently record and examine all fax, telephone and Internet communication in Europe and elsewhere.

All these nightmarish possibilities can be made real because cyberspace provides the perfect medium for collecting and transferring the phenomenal amounts of information that are necessary to this hellish vision of the totally supervised society. Both radical hopes and fears in cyberspace result from a belief that everything can now be manipulated through information codes. We may become immortal by turning our 'self' into an information code that can live in cyberspace or we may become prisoners in an open society because our 'self' can be defined by the information cyberspace draws together.

Certain particular visions are collectively imagined from the realisation that everything, even life itself in DNA, is an information code. This form of power operates not, as might seem obvious, to create or resist the imagined heavens and hells but by providing some of the unifying thoughts that allow individuals in cyberspace to recognise each other as members of the same community.

As different people come to grasp some parts of both sides of the imaginary, they come to recognise themselves as part of something larger than the individuals they meet or communities they participate in. Whereas cyberpower at the level of the individual offers possessions that enable people to act more widely and cyberpower at the social is a network that creates increasing power for a techno-elite, cyberpower at the imaginary constitutes the broad social order of cyberspace by providing dreams and nightmares through which individuals and communities come to recognise they are part of something greater than themselves.

Power is the condition and limit of politics, culture and authority. Cyberpower aims not at the immediately obvious forms of politics, culture and authority that course through cyberspace but at the structures that condition and limit these. A certain complex form of power that operates on the three levels of the individual, the social and the imaginary now careers through the virtual lands, directing conflict and consensus towards certain distinctive issues and social structures.

No one level of cyberpower determines or dominates the others. In particular, the powers of the individual and the social are in constant battle. The powers the individual gains in cyberspace, such as cryptography, may contradict the domination of a technical elite, just as the technopower spiral may lead individuals to increasing reliance on technological tools whose metaphorical bonnet they cannot hope to open. We can expect these two levels to swing back and forth, with individuals gaining powers against an elite only to find they have given birth to another part of the elite.

Informational libertarianism or anarchism gains its special place as the political discourse of cyberspace here because it emphasises both individual liberty, speaking to individuals and their powers, and that cyberspace produces the best possible outcomes through free markets, speaking to the elite as a justification for their growing control.

Libertarianism on the net has at its core a doubly articulated concept that connects individual liberty to free markets, allowing the one ideology to speak to both the elite and the grassroots. This does not mean libertarianism, or the sort of informational anarchism that permeates hacking, will be universally celebrated on the net but that it is a uniquely equipped ideology through which politics on the net will be played out. This analysis does not endorse libertarianism, it tries to identify why variants of libertarianism and anarchism have formed such a powerful political language in cyberpolitics. And many politically motivated hackers will be found endorsing sentiments of freedom of information flows in anarchistic language.

Cyberpower points not to the ultimate dominance of elites, though it clearly identifies the burgeoning power of an elite, nor does it predict the ideal of individual empowerment, though it makes conspicuous the ongoing creation of powers for individuals in cyberspace. Cyberpower points to these processes continuing, driven by dreams and nightmares. When examining cyberpower we must always be aware of the roar of battle and the complex conflicts that define virtual lives, elites and dreams.

Information Security in Cyberspace

If your are connected to the Internet, a firewall should be used to protect your data. However in today's marketplace, the presence of a firewall is currently not a certainty. In the last couple of years, the Internet has dominated technological news pages everywhere. But when companies start adding ".com" to their names and finally join the e-commerce marketplace, their problems are only just beginning. Many people don't realise that just linking two computers on a network, let alone setting up a website, causes a lot more difficulties than are immediately apparent. When one PC is connected to another to form a basic network, the security protecting the data on both machines is compromised. This means any sensitive information on one of the machines can be accessed by the user of the other. Needless to say, this should be the exception rather than the rule when it comes to data protection. Users and data should be filtered so that one doesn't have all-access rights to the other. An internal network can be divided using as many firewalls as deemed necessary, so imposing a graduated form of access to highly secretive information. It may help to think of a computer network like your company building.

Every employee has access to the building itself (the network), but only certain employees have a key to your office. Even fewer co-workers can open the file cabinet next to your desk, and only you know the combination to the strongbox within the cabinet that contains your emergency Mars bar supply. Here the Mars bars are the most protected data on the network (and quite rightly so). All of the files in the cabinet are slightly less protected, followed by the paperwork (and snacks) lying around the office. The least protected foodstuffs are the ones in the corridors and foyer of the building. However these still have access limitations, in that only employees of the firm are eligible to test their edibility.

Members of the public walking along the street outside the office building (non-users of your network) have no access to any of the data (or snackfoods) within it because the office doors keep them out. These doors are the firewall which protects your network from unknown and untrusted users outside the company. This perimeter firewall is needed if the network is connected to an external network, such as the Internet.

A firewall between the internal and external networks serves two purposes: it prevents any unauthorised communication from entering the internal network and stops any user of the internal network from accessing the external network without permission. This is, needless to say, extremely useful for scuppering company directors accessing unsuitable websites or spending their day surfing cyberspace. In the home environment, a firewall could act in loco parentis for children using their home PCs and block the viewing of certain pages on the Internet.

A firewall consists of two parts: the security policy and the physical implementation of that policy. The policy itself is the logical written statements allowing users their access rights to various facilities or parts of the network. It can conform to one of four general types. As the name implies, the paranoid is the most protective version forbidding every connection or communication attempt - not exactly an ideal scheme for a network. A prudent policy refuses any communication as a rule and only permits those communications through the firewall which have an explicit clearance status. The permissive type of network security is slightly more easy-going, having a default setting of accepting everything sent to it, unless the communication has been unequivocally forbidden and the final, promiscuous, kind allows every communication or connection request to enter. In the main the ideal security policy would be a combination of the prudent and permissive types, as the other two options would inhibit (completely) the performance of the network (paranoid) or endanger the security and integrity of the data stored on the network (promiscuous).

For the physical implementation of the firewall there are yet more choices depending on the security measures to be implemented. The oldest and most insecure form of firewall is a packet filter. This type of firewall checks the destination and source addresses of the communication packet (the data) requesting access to the protected network and decides, after consulting a set of rules, whether to permit the communication to enter the network. The primary disadvantage of this system, is that it can only distinguish the machine the request came from and not which user used that machine to send the packet, so connections can only be permitted or denied based on the locations sending and receiving the data.

Circuit level firewalls are a step up from packet filters in that they can distinguish between a connection request and a packet containing data. Only data packets relating to an existing, valid connection are allowed through the firewall. Any connection request must follow a handshake procedure to establish communication between two machines in order to pass through the firewall. Both machines must also be approved for communication with each other according a specified set of rules listed in the firewall's memory. A major disadvantage of this type of firewall is that the only communication protocol which follows the handshaking procedure is TCP/IP (Transport Control Protocol/Internet Protocol) the most common - but not the only - Internet communication protocol.

A yet more advanced form of security is the application layer firewall. Many examples of this type of firewall use proxy servers and clients to interact with the external network on the user's behalf. This means that the machine into which the user enters his commands never actually connects with the desired network directly; every request is filtered through another machine - the proxy - which processes and examines the packets sent. The proxy also checks whether the requests it sends and receives are permitted by the policy rules relating to the proxy.

The proxy server, protocol analysis and proxy client are the three invisible parts which together form the proxy service. A well set up proxy service will be transparent to the user and make him think he is interacting with the real machine partner. The only occasion when the user should be aware of the proxy is if the requests made are not permissable, and he is alerted to the fact. These three types of firewalls all have their advantages and problems. Although the proxy, application level firewall is generally considered the best protection, it requires twice as much processing time to complete the clearance checks on each data packet passed between machines. The circuit level firewall is quicker than the application level security checks, but only works with the TCP/IP protocol and testing the 'accept' and 'deny' rules is difficult. The fastest protection is provided by the packet filter type of firewall, but this only performs a cursory check on any communication packet and offers minimal security.

6

Communicative Interactions in Information Society

The information society is a new kind of society. Specific to this kind of society is the central position information technology has for production and economy. Information society is seen as successor to industrial society. Closely related concepts are post-industrial society , post-fordism, post-modern society, knowledge society, Telematic Society, Information Revolution, and informational society.

One of the first people to develop the concept of the information society was the economist Fritz Machlup. In 1933 Machlup began studying the effect of patents on research. His work culuminated in the breakthough study "The production and distribution of knowledge in the United States" in 1962. This book was widely regarded and was eventually translated into Russian and Japanese. The Japanese have also studied the information society joho shakai, which means the highest stage of societal evolution seen in analogy to biological evolution. This concept was discussed already in the 1950s and 1960s.

There is currently no universally accepted concept of what exactly can be termed information society and what shall rather not so be termed. Most theoreticans agree that we see a transformation which started somewhere between the 1970s and today and is changing the way our societies work fundamentally. Information technology is not only internet, and there are discussions how big the influence of specific media or specific modes of production really is.

Some people, such as Antonio Negri and Newt Gingrich, characterise the information society as one in which people do immaterial labour. By this, they appear to refer to the production of knowledge or cultural artifacts. One problem with this model is that it ignores the material and essentially industrial basis of the society. However it does point to a problem for workers, namely how many creative people does this society need to function? For example, it may be that you only need a few star performers, rather than a plethora of non-celebrities, as the work of those performers can be easily distributed, forcing all secondary players to the bottom of the market. It is now common for publishers to promote only their best selling authors and to try and avoid the rest- even if they still sell steadily. Films are becoming more and more judged, in terms of distribution, by their first weekends performance, in many cases cutting out opportunity for word of mouth development.

Another problem with the idea of the information society is that there is no easily agreed upon definition of the term, which can not only include art, texts, blueprints and scientific theories, but also lies, football results, trivia, random letters, mistakes and so on. Information is not necessarily productive or useful. It can even be harmful.

Considering that metaphors and technologies of information move forward in a reciprocal relationship, we can describe our society (and more specifically the Japanese society) as an information society because we think of it as such. One of the central paradoxes of the information society is that it makes information easily reproducible, yet corporations need to confine it, or demarcate it in some way, otherwise they cannot sell it and make a profit. This is also one of the central political struggles, will open source beat copy restriction, will all of the natural world be gradually copyrighted so that you cannot use biological functions without paying a licence fee. In many parts of the world it is hard for farmers to grow crops without paying agricultural companies for seeds. They cannot use saved seeds. One issue which makes information much more important than before is the integration of photography, film, etc. with the computer; which moves gradually from being a universal machine to being a universal media-machine. Another important issue is the close relation between information technology, modes of production and globalization.

Use of Communication Resources in Information Sociey

There is a growing interest in using the computer to enhance instruction and learning through shared activity, and to engage students in the same intellectual and cultural activities that sustain practicing scientists and engineers in knowledge building. A major part of this learning involves engaging the student in sense-making activities, such as conversations and talk about external representations that use concepts, symbols, models and relationships.

Brown, Collins, and Duguid argue that learning involves making sense of experience, thought, or phenomenon in context. They hypothesize that our representation or understanding of a concept is not abstract and self-sufficient but rather is constructed from the social and physical contexts in which the concept is found and used. Brown et al. have emphasized the importance of implicit knowledge in developing understanding rather than acquiring formal concepts. It is therefore essential to provide students with authentic experiences with the concept. Students can engage in learning conversations in distributed multimedia environments.

The technologies allow participants to use multiple modes and representations to construct new understanding that eventually leads to conceptual change. Learning is fundamentally built up through conversations between persons or among groups, involving the creation and interpretation of communication. Learning is established and negotiated through successive turns of action and talk.

Conversations are the means by which people collaboratively construct beliefs and meanings as well as state their differences. These conversations provide a common ground or mutual knowledge about beliefs and assumptions during conversation. Therefore, one of the major issues facing designers of communication systems concerns helping one person or group understand others and create and maintain common ground.

Suchman studied the ways writing and drawing activities interact with conversation. Such activities can be used to display understanding, facilitate turn taking, and in general serve as appendages to the verbal conversation. Some experimental video systems such as Videodraw have been used to create representations that express ideas.

Some studied how design emerges from social interactions among individuals and groups as they communicate to establish, maintain, and develop a shared understanding. He observed four practices that participants used to achieve design communication:

— negotiating understanding,

— tailoring communication,

— preserving ambiguity, and

— manipulating mundane representations.

Minneman noticed that: Talk, gesture, sketching, lists and tables, formal drawings, calculations, video, photographs, and embodiments all show up as contributing to the representational and communicative activity in group designing.

These studies suggest that a multi-channel communication system provides more information and better facilitates communication between users. However, several research studies show little or no evidence of a specific benefit of multi-channel communication to outcomes of a problem solving group. Chapanis found that restricting channel capacities had little impact on the outcomes of problem-solving tasks, but did influence the process through which the result was obtained. In educational environments, this distinction can be critical, as students are expected to learn how to work in a collaborative fashion.

Various forms of computer conferencing, coordination tools, and on-line knowledge databases are currently being explored to help augment learning activities. Computer-supported cooperative work (CSCW) systems are designed to provide an interface to a shared environment in which users are linked in multiple ways such that they will perceive themselves to be communicating as if they were in the same space. Using CSCW systems, collaborators make use of a host of tools such as networked chat and draw systems, file transfer, electronic mail, and audio- and video-conferencing to work together to solve problems. When applied to educational environments, students can communicate with collaborators from institutions worldwide; the students will experience and have to contend with, cultural, ethnic, knowledge, and other differences as if they were meeting face-to-face.

Advocates of CSCW systems claim that these technologies can be used to support conversations and enhance communication. Even for people involved in face-to-face communication, images, graphics and text can be used to support the process. The use of multiple representations and multiple communication channels provide opportunities for helping one person understand the other. The studies also suggest that there is a fit between the media and a particular task or social context. Designers of CSCW systems have to be aware of the complex nature of the communication process and the use of tools and channels to facilitate communication. As designers develop new communication tools, they need to be aware of how the CSCW system fits into existing workspace. Finally, designers have to be aware of the ways people experience or perceive these new media for communication.

In an effort to help improve the teaching of concurrent collaborative design and to help students learn to work in a collaborative context the Interactive Multimedia Group (IMG) and the College of Engineering at Cornell University, have been working on a multi-year project to implement and test a networked multimedia environment.

With the advent of any new technology, there usually follows a gestation period marked by evolving features and functions. Initially, the new technology replaces rather than improves the old technology, doing the same thing but perhaps faster or on a larger scale.

Computer mediated communications (CMC), for example, have been implemented largely as expensive teleconferencing systems. Eventually, however, CMC technology will come into its own as discover how to utilize the unique attributes of this medium for supporting change and improvement. In addition to the technical design challenges of collaborative and information systems, researchers should also address the social and psychological aspects of using on-line resources and collaboration.

The ideal collaboration system would support the advantages of social, psychological and technological information resources, including communication and data access tools, on-line mentoring and experts, multiple representations for clarity, and archived exchanges and records. However we can see that students do not make effective use of the database resources and communication tools. Users need training in communication and information seeking to effectively use these systems.

In the future, CMC technology will have a profound impact on how approach and engage in the processes of education and communication. Because group interactions are often unpredictable, need to design flexible systems that can readily adapt to change. By monitoring the individual, social, and cultural forces at work as users interact with these new systems, able to develop tools, programs, and technologies that are more responsive to the changing needs of individuals and to the changing circumstances in society.

Using the New Media Technologies

The new media are a lot like that. "What generally stand in the way of people's understanding of new media are the very terms media and medium. As commonly used, those terms are misnomers that block understanding." Simply don't confuse a medium with its Vehicles. Very few people understand the new media simply because what most people think are media are actually vehicles within a medium. Magazines aren't media nor is a magazine a medium. Television isn't a medium nor is radio nor are television stations media. A personal computer connected to the internet isn't a medium and the many computers that comprise the internet aren't media. Neither is the World Wide Web a medium nor is e-mail a medium nor is the internet itself a medium.

Newspapers, magazines, television, radio, telephones, billboards, personal computers, the internet, the World Wide Web, and e-mail all are vehicles for conveying information within a medium or media. They aren't the media or a medium in which they operate. To understand the difference between a communications vehicle and a communications medium, merely need to understand how the terms medium, media, and vehicles are correctly used when discussing transportation. Indeed, you will then also understand that only three communications media exist, what those three are, and how to use them. Only three transportation media exist.

Land was the aboriginal transportation medium; it was the first transportation medium. Humans have has walked on it since time immemorial. We still do. But we've also built vehicles to help convey us in this medium: carts, chariots, carriages, bicycles, trains, automobiles, trucks and lorries, etc.

Water is the second transportation medium. Its use as a transportation medium is almost as old as humanity's use of land, dating from whenever the first human attempted to ride a floating log or to swim across a stream, river, or lake. We've since created vehicles to convey use in this medium: rafts, canoes, barges, sailboats, ships, submarines, etc.

Before list the third transportation medium, note some characteristics of these two transportation media, because find that these characteristics have analogues in communication media:

— Note first that humans' use of those two ancient transportation media predated technology. The vehicles that human technology created have merely extended our speed and carrying capacities in those media.

— Also note that humanity's uses of these two media aren't necessarily dependent upon technology; most of us can walk and swim without any technology.

— And note that each of the vehicles for these media are limited by its medium. Trains don't operate on water nor do steamships operate on land.

Indeed, land and water have mutually exclusive transportation characteristics and reaches, mutually exclusive advantages and disadvantages. A person who needing transportation had to pick one or the other of these media based upon where that medium reached or upon that medium's carrying capacity. For examples, water vehicles have almost global reach but not to landlocked cities. Land vehicles can deliver door-to-door, a capability that water vehicle can't provide. But many water vehicles have much greater carrying capacities than do land vehicles.

Throughout most of human history, people were limited to those two transportation media and those media's mutual advantages and disadvantages. A third transportation medium was inconceivable. But in 1783 two French brothers named Montgolfier used their era's technology to vehicle that transported them into an entirely new medium. A hundred years later, Otto Lilenthal fabricated the technology of airfoils and began gliding over the German countryside, ponds, and lakes. And 20 years after that, two American brothers named Wright determined how to marry an engine to a glider. You probably know the rest.

Utilizing technology, these pioneers opened a third transportation medium that until then had been little more than a dream — the Sky. Other vehicles developed for this new transportation medium are balloons, parachutes, gliders, airplanes, helicopters, and lately, spacecraft. These are vehicles that can transport people anywhere on Earth. Though the transportation media of land and water have mutually exclusive reaches, this new transportation medium of the sky encompasses the reaches of both land and water, and generally without the complementary advantages and disadvantages of those two prior media. But note that this new transportation medium of the sky is entirely dependent upon technology, unlike the two prior media. The sky isn't a natural medium for humans; people can walk and swim but we cannot fly.

As with transportation media, two of those communication media are ancient and arose independent of technology. But the third medium is relatively new and its use is totally dependent upon technology. Oddly, the first and earliest of these three communications media is only one not to have a commonly accepted name. So, we'll call this first medium the interpersonal medium. This aboriginal medium arose in basic animal communications, predating both humans and technology. Human technology later extended its speed and reach. Interpersonal conversation is the basic form of this medium. The vehicles that human technology later built for it include the postal letter, telephone call, and electronic mail.

Just as the transportation media of land or water have some unique characteristics, so does the this interpersonal medium of communications. It notably has two hallmarks:

— Each participant has equal and reciprocal control of the content conveyed.
— And the content can be individualized to each participant's unique needs and interests.

However, those hallmark advantages come with equal disadvantages:
— The equal control and also the individualization of content degrade into cacophony as the number of participants increases beyond two, for example, try simultaneously holding different conversations with more than one person.

For those reasons, this interpersonal medium characteristically is used for communications between only two people. And why many academics who study communications media term it the 'one-to-one' medium. The mass medium is the second communications medium. Most people mistake the mass medium as a product of technology and don't realize how old it really is. Like the interpersonal medium, the mass medium predates technology. It originated with the utterances and speeches of tribal leaders, kings, and priests. Technology has merely extended its speed and its reach to global dimensions. Some vehicles in the mass medium are edicts, oratory, sermons, scriptures, plays, books, newspapers, billboards, magazines, cinema, radio, television, bulletin boards, and webcasting.

Communications in the mass medium generally go from a one person, for examples, a leader, a king, a priest, a publisher, or a broadcaster to many people (the audience, readership, listenership, viewership). This also is why many academics who study communications media term it the 'one-to-many' medium. The hallmark characteristics of the mass medium are:

— That the same content goes to all recipients.

— And that the one who sends it has absolute control over that content.

The corresponding disadvantages of the mass medium are:

— That its content cannot be individualized to each recipient's unique needs and interests and that the recipients have no real control over that content.

Like the interpersonal medium, the mass medium isn't necessarily dependent upon technology. For example, an actor or speaker can perform without any technology.

Before we list the third communications medium, let's note some contrasting characteristics of these two earlier communications media. Just as the transportation media of land and water have mutually exclusive characteristics, so do the interpersonal medium and the mass medium for communications:

— The interpersonal medium can deliver an individualized message but only to one person at a time.

— The mass medium can simultaneously deliver messages to an infinite number of people but its messages cannot be individualized for each recipient.
— The interpersonal medium allows each participant equal control over the content.
— The mass medium allows control over the content by only one person.

Those mutually exclusive characteristics of the interpersonal and mass media have been important because anyone who wants to individually communicate a unique message to each recipient has had to use the vehicles of interpersonal medium. And anyone who wants at once to communicate message to a mass of people has had to use the vehicles of the mass medium.

Just like using the sky as a transportation medium, for most of human history the possibility of any third communications medium existing had been inconceivable. Anyone needing to communicate had to choose between the mutually incompatible characteristics of the interpersonal and the mass media. But, Just like how several technologies converged nearly a century ago to make the sky a transportation medium, the evolution of several ostensibly unrelated technologies converged during the past century to create a third and entirely new communications medium. Among those convergent technologies were:

— The invention of digital communications during the late 1940s;
— The invention of the Transport Control/Internet Protocol ((TCP/IP) in the late 1960s;
— ARPANET's creation of the Internet during the early 1970s;
— The invention of the personal computer in the late 1970s

To lesser degrees of the importance:

— The invention of the HyperText Transport Protocol (HTTP) in the late 1980s;

— The opening of the Internet to the public in 1992;

— The invention of the Mosaic browser software in that same year.

These and other technological innovations converged to create a new communications medium that has characteristics inconceivable even a decade ago.

The hallmark characteristics of this new medium are:

— That individualized messages can simultaneously be delivered to an infinite number of people.

— And that each of the people involved shares reciprocal control over that content.

In other words, the new medium has the advantages of both the interpersonal and the mass media, but without their complementary disadvantages. No longer must anyone who wants to individually communicate a unique message to each recipient have to be restricted to communicating with only one person at a time. No longer must anyone who wants at once to communicate message to a mass of people be unable to individualized totally the content of that message for each recipient. Note that the new medium for communications, like the transportation medium of the sky, is entirely dependent upon technology, unlike the two preceding communications media. Like humans flying with technology, this form of communications can't be done with technology.

Because the new medium simultaneously encompasses both the characteristics and the reach of the two previous communication media and therefore can easily perform each of those media's individual tasks, many people mistake the new medium as merely an electronic extension of the interpersonal or mass media. Most people mistake it as a paperless or antenna-less form of the mass medium. Moreover, many marketing consultants often mistakenly refer to it as a 'one-to-one' medium.

But the academic and the consultants who truly understand this new medium and its possibilities to simultaneously deliver an infinite number of individualized messages while providing equal control over that content refer to the new medium as the 'many-to-many' medium — to distinguish it from the 'one-to-one' (interpersonal) or 'one-to-many' (mass) media. Mistakes, misnomers, and misperceptions of the new medium are easy to make because the vehicles of this new medium are only starting to appear, as are the true capabilities of this new medium.

Capabilities of new media

Just consider the converged technologies that make this new medium possible. For instance, the millions of computers interconnected through the internet can acquire, sort, package, and transmit information in as many ways as there are individual people. They can establish those communications simultaneously. And they allow each participant to share equal simultaneous control. This can result in unprecedented forms of communications.

Imagine that when a person visits a newspaper Web site, he sees not just the bulletins and major stories that he wouldn't have known to request information about but sees the rest of that edition customized to his own unique needs and interests. Rather than every reader seeing the same edition, each reader sees an edition that has simultaneously been individualized to his interest and generalized to his needs. Or imagine that each viewer who is simultaneously watching a broadcast can stop, rewind, or fast forward the program at will, or even change the denouement of the program's plot. Realize that these new medium forms of content inherently are forms of mass customization, something impossible with either the interpersonal medium or the mass medium. The existence of this new medium will catalyze, economize, and popularize entirely new vehicles for production and distribution, just as the invention of the medium of air did for transportation.

The new medium itself is merely a manifestation of a larger, revolutionary historical change underway that transcends just issues of communications. Analysts and pundits talk about this larger change as an Informational Revolution that is superceding the world of the Industrial Revolution in much in the same way that the Industrial Revolution itself superceded the Agrarian Revolution. But the terms Informational, Industrial, and Agrarian merely refer to characteristic products of these phases in the evolution of human society. Not to the natures of these revolutions themselves.

During the Agrarian world, which began about 5,000 to 10,000 years ago, a person who needed clothing had to make his clothing himself. Or another person made his clothing individually for him. Only one piece of clothing would be made at a time and each piece of clothing would be individualized to his own individual size and needs.

Then some 200 years ago, mechanical technology evolved to the point where factories could created, and the Industrial Revolution began. In the Industrial world, millions of pieces of clothing could be produced, but none could be individualized to the exact measurements of its ultimate consumer. Note how these complementary advantages and disadvantages of products from the Agrarian and Industrial ages are similar to the complementary advantages and disadvantages of the interpersonal medium and the mass medium.

This is because most of what we nowadays perceive to be the interpersonal medium dates from the Agrarian Revolution and most of what we nowadays perceive to be the mass medium dates from the Industrial Revolution. Now, new advancements have created technologies that unite the advantages of both Agrarian individualized production and Industrial mass production, with none of the complementary disadvantages. For example, companies using these new technologies,such as Levis Strauss & Co., have begun to mass-produce jeans that are individualized to each users exact specifications. This is similar to how the new medium can send instantly individualized messages to mass of recipients. Both the new medium and Levis Strauss & Co.'s abilities to mass produce of individualized jeans are manifestations of the Informational Revolution.

The Informational Revolution's effects upon society are being compared to those from the invention and promulgation of printing presses. However, the actual significance of the Informational Revolution is greater: The invention of the printing press was merely a technological amplification of the mass medium. By contrast, this new medium indeed is an entirely new medium; a quantum leap beyond mere innovations such as the printing press.

Returning to our analogy between transportation and communications media, the development of the air as transportation medium didn't entirely replace land or sea transportation. Neither will the development of this new communication medium entirely replace the interpersonal or the mass media. However, it will certainly and markedly reduce and limit those previous media, much as the invention of aviation did to land and sea transportation.

Synchronous Multi-user Textual Communication

The recent growth of Internet connectivity and popularity worldwide has been providing abundant opportunities to communicate and collaborate with peers and colleagues across national boundaries, which may bridge the national and cultural gaps among them. People with different cultural backgrounds can communicate over the Internet without noticing their surface-level differences such as differences in language, tone of voice, the amount of silence in conversation, eye-contact, meaning of gestures, proxemics (the use of space), etc., which are apparent and often become the cause of intercultural miscommunication in face-to-face situations.

On the other hand, people can discuss such deeper levels of difference as shared values and norms between cultures which are deeply embedded in their history, social structure, educational system, mass media and everyday rituals. Most people within a culture take these cultural assumptions for granted until they encounter a different culture. One of the utilities of international tele-collaboration is to make those assumptions explicit while communicating without realizing the surface level differences. Through dialogue with people from different cultures, people would recognize their taken-for-granted assumptions and develop more global perspectives.

The Internet has a great potential to facilitate international and intercultural understanding among people in different countries by sharing discourse and knowledge in a virtual space. In addition, with the Internet, people can collaborate regardless of time and space. Though such potential of the Internet as a ground for international tele-collaboration has been realized, few studies have been done on how people with different cultural backgrounds communicate and collaborate through the Internet.

CMC as a Synchronous Multi-user Textual Communication Tool

Computer-Mediated Communication (CMC) has been recognized as a means to establish an electronic environment that is accessible to participants who might otherwise be separated by time zones and physical distance. In addition, CMC is attractive to people who have trouble getting out of their homes to socialize-people who are disabled, feel socially insecure, live alone with young children, work at unusual hours, etc. Although available since the early 1970's, CMC was not in widespread use until the 1980s, when professionals and researchers began to acquire a large number of inexpensive stand-alone microcomputers and the convergence of computing and telecommunication technologies enabled independent microcomputers to talk with one another and to mainframe computers.

Since then computer-mediated communication has attracted a number of researchers' attention as a new mode of mediated communication. Some notes that CMC substitutes writing for spoken conversations and extends the domain of writing to cover areas of communication that previously were limited to face-to-face interactions, mail, and telephone. CMC, up to now, is mainly limited to textual communication where most of the "social context cues" are eliminated. Social context cues include aspects of physical environment that define the nature of the social situation and the actors' status relative to one another. Without such cues, CMC is said to lead to a kind of anomie, as seen in increased excited and uninhibited communication such as "flaming".

In order to somewhat complement the lack of contextual cues, people use sideways-oriented text pictures called "smileys", capital letters, asterisks, and exclamation points to indicate the intention of the message, to emphasize, and to communicate the tone of the text. At the same time, since 'phatic' aspects of face-to-face conversation are minimal in CMC, communication anxiety seems to be exacerbated when the sender gets no reply. This is the major reason why on-line communities place such an emphasis on active participation and are often critical of passive readers who are pejoratively called 'lurkers'.

The advantage of such text-based communication is that it reduces discriminatory communication patterns based on physical and social cues such as gender, race, job titles, social position, physical features, etc., and encourages equality of participation. In face-to-face conversations, it has been cited frequently in studies of groups engaging in problem-solving discussions that women are interrupted more frequently in their turns and speak less often than men in the same situation. In addition, studies suggest that dominant individuals, who have power, disagree more often than do less powerful individuals and offer fewer supportive statements than do those same individuals.

In CMC, however, people are less bounded by convention, less influenced by status, and unconcerned with making a good appearance. The tendency for an individual or a faction of a group to dominate group discussions dissipates in the CMC environment. Previous research has shown that when comparing with face-to-face groups, the proportion of talk and influence of higher status people was reduced when group members communicated by electronic mail.

In other words, CMC may undermine the established roles of individuals within a group or organization. As a result, CMC tends to destabilize existing hierarchies in relationships and rehierarchize communications according to criteria that were previously irrelevant.

In addition, due to the lack of social context cues to pressure individuals to agree with the existing or dominant paradigm of a discussion, the computer-mediated groups have more difficulty reaching consensus leading to disinhibition and occasional overly emotional or asocial interactions and make slightly riskier decisions than do the face-to-face groups.

Text-based communication also augments the interaction with ideas generated through the discussions. In face-to-face discussions, so much depends not on what is said but on who says it, how they make their intervention, what clothes they wear, their body language, facial and oral expressions, etc. In addition, pressures to conform to existing paradigms or to an emerging consensus are great. In CMC, however, all of this is absent; participants tend to focus more on issues and arguments than on the messenger.

Another important aspect of this standardized textual communication is an individual's great control of his/her self image. In many cases of synchronous computer-mediated communication, the only identity an individual user has is a "handle" name which may be, and most often is expected to be, fictional. So-called "digital persona" emerge as each individual uses multiple identities to reflect different aspects of their "real" personality. Anonymity may allow one to express one's true mind, or authentic self, unfettered by concerns of self-presentation, or even physical sanction.

Asynchronous CMC such as e-mail, bulletin board systems, and newsgroups is a convenient medium; we can send and read a message at convenience. This feature of asynchronous CMC-time independence-is especially helpful in international collaboration in which people have to communicate across different time zones. In addition, in asynchronous CMC, people can spend time reading, reflecting upon, and replying to a message. This feature is invaluable for those for whom the working language the group is using is not their native language. Because communication over the Internet is predominantly done in English, the asynchronous nature of CMC helps non-native English speakers participate in international dialogue.

Although asynchronous CMC is useful for international communication, as the past studies indicate, there are some disadvantages to the asynchronous nature of the medium, the biggest of which would be the lack of immediate response. It takes longer for a group to reach a consensus through asynchronous CMC because everybody has to wait for responses from the rest of the group.

If a group has to work with a limited time frame, asynchronous CMC may frustrate those engaged in the group work and tend to lead them to non-conforming behaviors. The degree of asynchronicity depends on the frequency of login by the members, and infrequent logins by one member may prolong the entire process of the group work.

In contrast to asynchronous CMC, synchronous CMC such as Internet Relay Chat (IRC) and Multiple User Dungeons (MUDs) have been used mainly for social and recreational purposes. The biggest obstacle of incorporating a synchronous CMC into tele-collaboration is its demand of coordination. Members of a group have to decide on a specific time to log on to communicate in real time. It is also somewhat tiring to stare at a computer screen for a long time while texts scroll up incessantly. In addition, at the current stage of technological development, a user-friendly client interface to the synchronous CMC is rarely available to users, and participants have to struggle with their typing skills. This serves as the biggest disadvantage in international tele-collaboration for those whose native language is not English.

Despite these disadvantages, if properly planned, synchronous CMC can be used for several aspects of tele-collaboration. First of all, the synchronous mode of communication serves better for brainstorming. It may take too long to brainstorm and participants may lose the spontaneity of brainstorming if they use the asynchronous mode only. Second, synchronous CMC is more suitable for decision-making than asynchronous CMC as decision-making requires a short turnaround time for responses. Generally, synchronous CMC is appropriate for activities which do not require lengthy arguments but require immediate responses to get going. In addition, synchronous CMC adds the excitement of interacting with others in real-time. Such excitement could be heightened if the participants were distributed across nations.

CMC as a Communication Medium in Tele-Collaboration

"Social presence" is the degree to which the medium facilitates awareness of the other person and interpersonal relationships during the interaction. It is said to depend on the number of channels or codes available within a medium; the fewer the channels, the less attention paid by the user to the presence of other social participants. Some argues that communication media can be characterized as "rich" or "lean" based on four criteria: speed of feedback, types of channels employed, personalness of source, and richness of language carried.

According to the media's capacity for processing equivocal information, media can be ranked in the media richness hierarchy. Equivocality of information means that multiple and conflicting interpretations exist within a situation. Low equivocality means the message has clear content that suggests a single interpretation. Richer media have the higher capacity to process equivocal information, while leaner media have the lower capacity.

Expressiveness of a medium is associated with the bandwidth of the channel, i.e., the extent to which the medium can carry nonverbal and paralinguistic cues. Interactivity of a medium is analogous to the synchronousness of the medium or the immediacy of responses in communicating. Expressiveness and interactivity have effects independent of each other. Communication media vary in their expressiveness and interactivity that eventually affect "social presence" of the media.

Although in the original model of social presence by Short, Williams and Christie CMC did not appear in their analysis of social presence of a communication medium, generally CMC had been considered to be at the lowest end of the media richness hierarchy among the various electronic media.

In terms of the two dimensions of the media richness, CMC has the lowest expressiveness compared with videoconferencing, videophone, audioconferencing, and telephone while it varies in its interactivity. In synchronous CMC, the interactivity is as high as other richer electronic media while in asynchronous CMC the interactivity can be as low as fliers and bulletins. In this sense, synchronous CMC will be more appropriate for communicating equivocal information than asynchronous CMC.

CMC and Cross-Cultural Communication

There is a vast amount of literature discussing difficulties in cross-cultural communication. However, most of them focus on the face-to-face interaction of people with different cultural backgrounds, and few studies have been done on cross-cultural communication in technology-mediated environments even though the opportunity of communicating with people with different cultural backgrounds through communication media, especially computer networks, is rapidly increasing. When asked if they were aware of any differences in the ways they interact online with those of another culture or nationality compared to how they interact with those within their own culture, 40% of the respondents had said yes.

The reason why the majority of the respondents in Ryan's practice have indicated little cultural impact on their interactions with others online may be explained by the lack of social and contextual cues of CMC. Without obvious social and contextual cues, it is hard to imagine the cultural background of a person one is communicating with. Besides this lack of social cues, online communication is usually ruled by its own set of social protocols and conventions which have been developed by a group of people. In a way, when people communicate over the Internet, they enter a new culture, a "virtual culture".

Virtual cultures on the Internet have been developed over the years. Norms are made explicit to some extent in the forms of netiquette and AUP. Implicit norms are made explicit when a person posts a message which is not within the implicit norms of the network community and that person gets a number of angry messages, or "flames." To what extent a virtual culture is independent of national cultures which communicators are affiliated with is unknown. However, anecdotal evidence shows that unique cultures are being developed over the Internet.

Microculture formed by members from different countries is called "international microculture", in which each member's use of a "sense of presence" plays an important role. A sense of presence is defined as a state of consciousness in which a person is psychologically present in the immediate task situation and is broadly aware of a range of ecological characteristics in it. In other words, a person who is sensitive to the 'ecology' of the immediate task and aware of his/her surroundings, has a sense of presence.

Though most of the discussion surrounding a sense of presence in the past has been within the context of international assignments in which people do face-to-face business with people from different cultural backgrounds, this concept can be extended to computer-mediated interaction among people across cultures. While a "sense of presence" plays an important role in creating an international microculture, in creating a virtual microculture what becomes important is a "sense of copresence," a sharing of the sense of presence among participants through communication media.

The difference between a sense of presence and a sense of copresence is that while the former involves a "broader focus more likely to include other potentially relevant characteristics of an ecology", the latter is more narrowly focused in its physical ecology but including an awareness of people's activities at a distance.

The concept of "copresence" itself is not new. In describing children's socialization process, some explains that, "copresence is established when two people are aware that they constitute part of the other's perceptual field." Here the definition of "a sense of co-presence" is expanded to include a person's intellectual ability to enter other's perceptual field as well as an awareness other person's existence in his/her own perceptual field.

In other words, a sense of co-presence in tele-collaboration requires conscious and intentional efforts as well as "intellective skills" to construct meaning from a symbolic medium and to interpret the text. While the medium (or media) of tele-collaboration is limited in conveying a variety of contextual and social cues, by employing a participant's intellective skills a sense of co-presence enables him/her to work together rather seamlessly at a distance.

Social presence affects task outcome rather indirectly through person-to-person interaction. It is assumed that a sense of co-presence also affects the virtual microculture through person-to-person interaction termed "telepresence," a concept originally from research on virtual reality and telerobotics. In the original context, telepresence is defined as "the psychological experience that results when simulator technology works well enough to convince users that they are immersed in virtual worlds".

Although this term has been narrowly used mainly in the operation of a remote robot, it can be extended to mean more broadly "the awareness of being somewhere else". If a participant communicates intensively with others at a distance through communication media, his/her awareness of being somewhere else will increase; his/her telepresence will be heightened.

Accordingly, it is hypothesized that telepresence closely relates to the communication intensity of the participants. The more intense the communication becomes (i.e., the higher frequency of communication), the higher the telepresence of a participant becomes. Telepresence is also affected by the interactivity of the medium, i.e., synchronous or asynchronous modes of communication. Usually, it is considered that telepresence is higher in synchronous than asynchronous modes of communication.

In sum, participants of tele-collaboration develop a virtual microculture through telecommunication media, which may be quite different from the microculture they develop in face-to-face encounters. It is theorized that in order to develop a virtual microculture, each participant has to develop a sense of co-presence; media of appropriate social presence need to be used; and the telepresence of each participant needs to be demonstrated.

The concepts of a sense of co-presence and social presence are the elements of tele-collaboration. A sense of co-presence may be operationalized broadly as individual skills and cultural orientation, and social presence as communication modality. Individual skills can be further operationalized as typing skills, English composition skills, and online skills. Cultural orientation can be operationalized as national culture or measures of some psychological and behavioral traits of individuals which are affected by the culture.

Social presence may be operationalized as communication modality in which expressiveness and interactivity of a medium are the dimensions of the communication modality. Telepresence occurs as a result of interaction between an individual's sense of co-presence and communication modality. It can be operationalized as interaction dynamics in which two dimensions of communication, its intensity and the amount of socioemotional communication, are measured. Virtual microculture can be operationalized as group performance. Group performance will be defined by the quality of its outcome and the effectiveness of its group process.

The finding of a significant positive correlation between the number of words exchanged among group members and the quality of final group papers may indicate that the more group interaction they had, the higher the quality of group performance would become. In that sense, the synchronous mode of communication may help the overall quality of group performance on the condition that the group does not have to waste time on coordinating the time for the synchronous communication.

However, it cannot be forgotten that synchronous CMC requires substantial typing skills to communicate effectively. And although synchronous communication may be useful for collaboration among those who speak the same language, it may be too difficult to incorporate it in international tele-collaboration. Only when all the participants obtain enough communicative competence in the same working language will synchronous CMC be utilized effectively.

The future system of instantaneous machine translation may hold some promise in resolving this language problem. However, to what extent such automatic translation of words could help facilitate intercultural tele-collaboration is unknown as human collaboration is a complex phenomenon. In a world which is becoming more interdependent, the facilitation of intercultural collaboration aided by available technologies should be explored further.

Electronic Mail as a Media Choice for Manager

In an organization, communication occurs between individuals who have a clearly established relationship, who are in some way connected. Wigand expands this comments:

> "Conceptually, the existence of a relationship between two individuals is constituted by the recognition of some constraint which restricts the behavior of one or both of

> the individuals. Such a constraint suggests one other characteristic of a relationship, namely, some interdependence between the individuals".

Such a relationship exists in organizations between managers and their subordinates and co-workers, and between other co-workers whose tasks and information are interdependent. In manager-to-subordinate communication, the purposes of such communication are believed to include: giving specific instructions about a job-related task; providing information about organization policies and procedures; providing evaluations of performance; and explaining how the subordinate's job-related tasks fit into the organization's operation. This communication is highly directive in nature and may often times include equivocal, ambiguous information. Between co-workers, communication concerning job-related tasks focuses on giving and receiving information necessary to complete assignments and fulfill individual job responsibilities. It may also involve traditional "grapevine," socio-emotional and otherwise non-job-related information.

Although there are many factors that influence the openness and ease of an organization's communication, including organization goals and members' personalities, research indicates communication channels or media that are readily accessible and universal throughout an organization may keep necessary information flowing to those who depend on it.

Organizational Communication through Electronic Mail Steinfield explains that organization design strategies have been developed that allow for increased vertical and horizontal communication flows so related individuals can best deal with complex and interdependent, task-related questions. A medium whose attributes give it potential to positively impact the way in which organization members communicate job-related, interdependent information is electronic (or computer mediated) mail.

Electronic mail, a type of interpersonal message service, is designed to transmit written messages from one point to another electronically, rather than by physical or personal delivery. For those organizations that have already moved into the age of office automation-with computer workstations available at every desk-electronic mail is a doable and affordable alternative to traditional mail delivery systems and other channels in its ability to improve organizational communication functions.

Supporters of electronic mail argue it can make the work environment more productive and help people more effectively handle information when it comes to them. It can also increase the number of communication relationships within an organization and create a new environment for sharing and disseminating job-related information.

Specifically, electronic mail allows for speedy interactions; dissemination of information to one or more individuals immediately and at any time of day or during any day of the week; cost effective distribution of information; permanent records of all communications, regardless of the origin. As a result, more and more organizations are introducing electronic mail to their employees as a means to improve office productivity and office communication.

The researchers note that pairs of individuals who have access to electronic mail interact more frequently with each other than those who only communicate in person, face-to-face. Similarly, some found that individuals in an organization use electronic mail in ways that increase their effectiveness in fulfilling organizational goals. Further, he states: "use of advanced information technologies leads to more available and more quickly retrieved information, including ... internal information ...". The presence of universally accessible electronic mail in an organization helps create a less centralized, less structured system of communication.

Today, there are a number of communication options for managers to consider, with electronic mail among them. But there are others, and there is now a growing body of research literature that discusses them and examines their impact on organizational communication. Henceforth this discussion will focus on electronic mail as a media choice for managers for their organizational communication needs, and it will also look at factors which enter into a decision to use or not use electronic mail.

Some scholars suggest the easier it becomes to communicate with individuals at diverse and distant locations, the more complex the process becomes. The reason for this deduction is in part because in organizations, choosing a medium for internal and external communication is not the simple, intuitive process it appears to be. Choosing the appropriate medium can make the difference between effective and ineffective communication. In some instances, a single medium is fine for communicating certain messages. However, rarely is a single medium appropriate for all communication. Media choice mistakes can impede successful communication.

Trevino et al. cite the Challenger space shuttle disaster as the result of a media choice mistake, referring specifically to the use of teleconferencing to make the decision to launch the Challenger in January 1986. They note the engineers had strong feelings against launching the Challenger. "It is possible that the teleconference medium was incapable of communicating the strength of the engineers' emotions and gut feelings to the managers who had to make the decision".

A question that arises, then, is what variables do and should influence a manager's decision about which medium to use in organizational communication? Researchers suggest the following three: (1) the equivocality of a message to be sent, (2) the context of the messaging situation, and (3) the potential symbolic cues that could be conveyed by the medium itself above and beyond the literal message the manager may have had in mind. Steinfield in particular asserts that the key contingency for determining which medium is appropriate is dependent upon the amount of equivocality in the message and the situation itself.

Equivocality-the existence of many and conflicting interpretations about an organizational situation-may be high when a message or situation is ambiguous to one or more parties involved. They further note that equivocality leads to the exchange of existing views among managers and related individuals to define the problems and resolve conflict through the development of shared meaning, meaning that can direct future organizational activities. Equivocality and ambiguity develop in organizational settings because people "come to a problem with different experience, cognitive elements, goals, values, and priorities... A common perspective does not exist".

With unequivocal or unambiguous messages, a consensus about meaning has been reached by the parties involved. Such information whose meaning is clear can be transmitted through most media without the threat of misunderstandings or confusion. Equivocality and its subsequent relation to media richness is emphasized here, particularly when addressing electronic mail as an organizational communication media choice for managers.

Communication media such as electronic mail have varying capabilities for resolving ambiguity and have been characterized as "rich" or "lean" based on their capacity to enhance shared meaning among the participants in the communication situation. Some note that communication that requires a long time to enable understanding or that cannot overcome different perspectives is high in ambiguity and requires a rich medium. They explain that rich media have the highest capacity to facilitate shared meaning, while lean media have the lowest capacity.

The media classifications are, in decreasing richness: (1) face-to-face, (2) telephone, (3) personal documents such as letters or memos, (4) impersonal written documents, (5) numeric documents. However, when they expanded this hierarchy in 1990, electronic mail was listed third, between the telephone and letters. They also listed four criteria that determine media richness: (1) the availability of instant feedback, which allows for quickly reaching a shared understanding, (2) the capacity of the medium to send multiple cues such as body language and tone of voice, (3) the use of real language rather than numbers, as is the case of quantitative office reports or spreadsheets, and (4) a focus on the people involved.

To this extent, researchers have suggested that electronic mail is varied in terms of its media richness. It has already been noted that electronic mail systems can provide rapid feedback, although such message exchanges may become a series of punctuated statements rather than an interactive discussion. However, there are some electronic mail systems that allow individuals to interact by sending to and receiving from each other messages at the same time, or in "real-time," but those messages cannot carry voice inflection or other non-verbal cues. However, emphasis cues and "flaming" in electronic mail may convey strong-felt emotions. Immediate feedback from body language, interruptions, or other cues we have developed as a society to aid the intercommunication process is lacking in this media.

The most important phenomenon to result from electronic mail use is the frequency with which a recipient reacts negatively or inappropriately when reading electronic mail messages-whether new messages or feedback-that might have been misinterpreted.

Considered another way, electronic mail contributes to a punctuation of responses. Generally, communication between two individuals is a continuous interaction, not a series of punctuated communication events. In electronic mail, however, this is not the case. Messages are sent and received individually. This is not a continuous interaction and, again, feedback through nonverbal cues is absent. The process may become one through which individuals cannot productively manage ambiguity.

While it may appear that electronic mail is not preferred for interpersonally involved communications, it is important to note that face-to-face interactions are not always viewed as the "cure-alls" to communication challenges. Face-to-face interactions may also not be the best to facilitate conflict resolution. In manager/subordinate communication, defensive behavior can result in a face-to-face situation if one or both individuals involved perceive the other's responses or behavior to be rehearsed. "Arousing defensiveness interferes with communication and thus makes it difficult...for anyone to convey ideas clearly and to move effectively toward the solution of...problems".

Yet, advanced information technologies such as electronic mail are making it possible for individuals within an organization, whether at the same location or at geographically diverse locations, to communicate amongst themselves without ever seeing and/or speaking with each other. But support for use of the medium for intra-organizational communication is not consistent. "People are used to reading body language, voice intonation, and numerous other cues when interpreting messages delivered in conversation ... Those cues are missing in electronic mail, and what was meant as a casual comment... is misinterpreted".

However, it is worth mentioning that electronic mail has been used for interpersonally involved messages. Steinfield found electronic mail was used for a variety of socio-emotional purposes in addition to more standard task-related applications. However, in this same study he found that electronic mail was not perceived to be an appropriate medium for discussing confidential or private communications. Private information was noted to include performance evaluations and information about job and promotion opportunities. People studied typically selected electronic mail as the medium by which to broadcast requests for information, get a message directly through to someone whose calls are normally screened, and to send a message in place of a phone call.

Thus far this discussion has examined message content as a factor for consideration by managers faced with a communication medium decision and how such a content-based decision, if inappropriate, may lead to the medium becoming a symbolic message. However, context is a remaining factor for consideration. Contextual attributes include "distance, expediency, time pressure, or simply the accessibility of a particular communication technology". The latter may include a travel budget or method of transportation that allows use of what may be perceived to be the most appropriate channel or medium, such as face-to-face interaction.

Steinfield and Fulk found that managers at geographically diverse locations used electronic mail more frequently than other media, despite message equivocality. Steinfield points out "the choice to use an inefficient medium for a task may be quite rational, in light of the social context".

In addition, especially with a new technology such as electronic mail, access to the technology and to an audience of skilled and willing users determined media choice. For example, it was previously mentioned that a reminder about a regular staff meeting could be transmitted via electronic mail. Since electronic mail is capable of transmitting such a reminder to all individuals concerned, with minimal effort by the manager, it may be the medium chosen for this communication simply because of its ability to reach many receivers at once.

Clearly there are several characteristics and attributes of messages, communication situations, and electronic mail as an organizational communication medium that managers must consider before deciding how to transmit their message. They must acknowledge that problems will arise when lean media are used for communicating information that requires interpersonal involvement, such as negotiations or conflict resolution.

As a guideline, however, Trevino et al. and Steinfield suggest electronic mail as a suitable medium for the following: (1) sending routine information, (2) broadcasting a question, and (3) conducting transactions that do not require high levels of interpersonal involvement. Electronic mail may be inappropriate for transmitting confidential or personal information, resolving disputes, or getting to know someone.

Although there is some grey area concerning what type of information managers will communicate to their subordinates via electronic mail, there is evidence to suggest that the introduction of electronic mail could result in an increase in the amount of information exchanged between managers and subordinates.

Communicative Interactions

The public/private distinction is a complex one, which in modern capitalism is so often confused by the extension of private control into the 'public sphere' as market place. The traditional pre-capitalist market place is not a place of private interests negotiating, but of the public good of exchange. Today the private exists in the public sphere as can the 'public' exist in the private. Privacy might be commonly thought of as being confined to the spaces of the home, but this is also increasingly the place where, paradoxically, individuals gain access to the public sphere. The fact of this is mutually generated: the less individuals engage in practices of interaction in 'public spaces', the more they are likely to be engaged in interactive practices in private spaces, and vice versa. Under these conditions, the household unit becomes a primary cell of modern social relations, the basic unit and building block from which social interaction occurs. When the public sphere has withdrawn to the home, where a 'dialogic' or two-way open interaction becomes impossible, interaction becomes more and more 'confined' to the family, the household, and where one works.

These conditions certainly did not obtain in pre-media society in which the frequency and intensity of embodied interaction are of an entirely different order. The origins of European modernity since the 18th century, are founded on the café as the bedrock of the emergence of a public sphere.

However, in media societies where the geographic and kinship ties of the parish, local neighbourhood, or the industrial slum have virtually disappeared, individuals have historically become very heavily dependent on media of many kinds to acquire a sense of belonging and attachment to others. The situation is one of separation and unity. Individuals are separated at a geographic level, locked away in their house allotment or unit fortresses, but united on scales of city or nation in their attachment to forms of media.

Ironically, the marketing calls for consumers to 'get connected' and 'travel on the Internet' instead of being 'stuck at home' are an exact reproduction of the social and urban consequences of broadcast technologies. On the one hand, individuals are told they can interact to overcome the tyranny and restraints of broadcast, but they do so only by reinforcing the domestic conditions of their atomised existence.

The question of whether interaction, once it is reduced to the electronically mediated and technologically-extended kinds of access to communication which is enabled from the home, constitutes participation in a public sphere is a pivotal one to ask in relation to CMC. Certainly the private/ public question becomes extremely vexed on the Internet. Some suggests that "If 'public' discourse exists as pixels on screens generated at remote locations by individuals one has never met and probably will never meet, as it is in the case of the Internet with its 'virtual communities', 'electronic cafes', bulletin boards, e-mail, computer conferencing and even video conferencing, then how is it to be distinguished from 'private' letters, printface and so forth."

Symbolically, as well as functionally, the cybercafé is extremely interesting. It strongly reaffirms the idea that the cellular network basis of gaining access to the public sphere predominates, where even one of the strongest institutions of embodied public life can be remade in terms of CMC. Nobody meets face-to-face at a cybercafé, as the face-to-screen precludes dialogic contact in any form other than electronic.

To understand whether electronically-mediated communication, of either the broadcast variety or network form, is capable of constituting a public sphere, the difference between these forms needs to be discussed. The contention that the Internet, and CMC in general, have radically altered the nature of public communication is largely built on the assumption that they are progressively coming to usurp the power of broadcast media.

Theorists of the second media age argue that both broadcast and interactive communication apparatuses have together constituted the primary forms of cultural mediation in information societies since the second world war. The important point here is that it is not possible, in this view, to understand the second media age without first understanding the first media age. The dependence on media of both first and second media are interrelated. However theorists of cybersociety such as George Gilder in Life After Television, Sherry Turkle in Life on the Screen,

Mark Poster in The Second Media Age, contend that the second media age has arisen on the back of the conditions produced by the first. These conditions, the production of an indeterminate mass by broadcast, the separation of individuals from the means of producing their own contributions to public communication, and the disintegration of traditional community, are all hailed to be overcome by the Internet.

The Internet is, above all, a decentralised communication system. Like the telephone network, anyone hooked up to the Internet may initiate a call, send a message that he or she has composed, and may do so in the manner of the broadcast system, that is to say, may send a message to many receivers, and do this either in 'real time' or as stored data or both. The Internet is also decentralised at a basic level of organisation since, as a network of networks, new networks may be added so long as they conform to certain communications protocols.

According to the second media age perspective, the tyranny that is attributed to broadcast lies in its hegemonic role in the determination of culture as well as individual consciousnesses, which derives from its predominantly vertical structure. This structure is one in which the individual is forced to look to the image and the monopolisation of information and entertainment to acquire a sense of assembly and common culture.

The second media age, on the other hand, bypasses this 'institutional' kind of communication and facilitates instantaneous, less-mediated and two-way forms of communication. For the romantic variety of cyber-utopians, on the other hand, it 'restores' such communication.

At the level of interaction, the second media age utopians point out the empirical increase in the take-up of the Internet and other network technologies, and the fact that empirically it is true that the Internet is mainly interaction and very little broadcast whilst television is mainly broadcast with very little interaction, as evidence for the 'ontological' nature of the second media age as a distinctive trend, movement and modality of social integration.

The importance of the fact that the many can interact with the many in cyberspace is almost exclusively related to the way it is said to break the 'lock-out' predicament which individuals face in broadcast interaction. The walls that are erected by the power of broadcast rapidly disintegrate as a form of electronic communication is made available which is adequate in speed, form and complexity to the abstractness of the social forms which have denied mediated interactivity by way of broadcast.

In broadcast communication, the individual receiver of messages is subject to one-way communication from the 'elite' producers of messages. The horizontal connection with other consumers of the same messages, is generally only possible via the fetish of the image or the celebrity, in whom 'concrete consciousnesses are concentrated'. Conversely, with the Internet, the message producers are by-passed, as the walls that are erected at the horizontal level effectively disappear.

These 'media' walls are the result of the architecture of broadcast itself. The more the individual looks to the media for acquiring a cultural identity the less they look 'sideways' for interaction. Conversely, the less the individual looks sideways for social solidarity and reciprocity, the more this mode of association becomes weak and de-normalised, and so the alternative dependence on a centralised apparatus of cultural production becomes imperative.

In the second media age, however, the walls separating individuals at a horizontal level are said to be overcome, as the individual looks directly to others for a sense of millieu and association.

The Internet lifts individuals out of the isolation created by media walls - particularly as these walls are reinforced in urban contexts. In information societies, individuals increasingly interact with computer screens, developing face-to-screen relations rather than face-to-face relations, but this opposition is no longer significant, some argues, when the larger cultural contexts of post-industrial societies are eroding the boundaries between the real and the virtual.

The extent to which the Internet is hailed as an overcoming of fragmentation and individualism is quite remarkable in recent literature. In some cases it is attributed with an integrative function which is able to correct a tendency that is over two hundred years old. The message of redemption which is promoted in the second media age thesis, be this for public or private, is a resounding one - a message whose dreams of unity has theological undertones.

The success of any argument claiming a special role for the Internet in the constitution of a new public sphere rests on its ability to establish an imaginary unity in which all participants have equal opportunity for 'observation' and communication. This postulated imaginary unity, most well known in the phrase 'virtual community', seldom reconciles itself with the fact that 'the Internet' is not at all technically homogenous and is segmented into quite a range of properties and capabilities, each of which carry different sociological and communicative potentials and effects.

It is true that, unlike television, the Internet is a network as well as 'dialogical' capable of a two-way dialogue, and for this reason is applauded as a universalising structure of communication. But its network properties are rarely realised in communication directly, rarely do they become meaningful qua network because, individuals only ever 'use' the Internet within well-defined sub-mediums. Trevor Barr usefully breaks down the different kinds of interaction on the Internet into six categories:

— one-to-one messaging (such as email);
— one-to-many messaging (such as 'listserv');
— distributed message databases (such as USENET news groups);
— real-time communication (such as 'Internet Relay Chat');
— real-time remote computer utilisation (such as 'telnet'); and
— remote information retrieval (such as 'ftp', 'gopher' and the World Wide Web').

It can be seen from this list that the Internet provides a generic environment for a number of different modes of interaction which can vary according to real-time/stored time, symmetrical versus asymmetrical dialogue, broadcast sending and receiving and information posting and retrieval.

But each of these modes of interaction relate very differently to the possible constitution of an 'electronic public sphere'. Moreover, the information and communication possibilities of the Internet are more often than not parasitic of broadcast-mediated communication. The growth of companion websites which accompany media organisations, newspapers, consumer products, sporting events etc, provide an astonishing array of reasons why information retrieval, listserv, and interactive databases available on the Internet are turned to.

When CMC is broken down into specific sub-media's rather than reduced to the indeterminacy of 'the Internet' as a communication environment, a more sophisticated appreciation of the change technological transformations of the public sphere is enabled, and the advancement of new accounts of context-specific partial publics is one outcome. However, at the same time, the global reach and mobility of all forms of Internet communication, regardless of the specificities of their sub-media also needs to be accounted for.

Why this is significant is that, whereas broadcast generates an instant 'international context' of social connection, there are few ways in which individuals can achieve meaningful interaction to make tangible these global connections. There are telephones and other 'narrow-band' ways of communicating, but none of these is quite able to provide a multi-media context for any given interaction. The Internet, it is argued by its promoters, changes all of that.

In accounting for the growth of CMC via the Internet, both national and global statistics become significant. Given that the experience of community on the Internet is not limited to national boundaries, the shape and structure of this virtual community becomes significant. In 1996, five years after the Internet became fully commercially available, only 7% of Australian homes had connected to the Internet, whilst 25% already had access in their workplace.

In 1998, the domestic connection figure had almost tripled to 19%. The number of Internet users worldwide at the end of 1998 was 147,800,000 of which 52% were American. World wide, therefore, the number of Internet users had increased from approximately 25 million in July 1995 - almost a sixfold increase.

Besides being hailed as a technology which can deliver the 'global village'. The Internet is also promoted as a singular medium which allows for democratised processes which were not previously possible in the era of broadcast. But what kinds of democracy are being postulated here? Traditionally, and more than ever now, democracy is heavily aligned with the nation state. Because of this, nonsense is made of the claim that the Internet enables universal participation in democratic process.

The point here is that practices of communication afforded by CMC may be able to substitute some of the functions of the mass media - for example in the formation of pre-instutional public opinion' - but do not necessarily exert pressure on the institutional apparatuses of politics. Of course the mass media itself, as a means of electronically mediated communication, can never replace the institutional apparatuses of politics and, as numerous studies have shown, has been just as much used by politicians as it has influenced them.

The Internet can properly be classified as a 'global' technology, which enables connections with individuals and institutions overseas just as easily as is does nationally, regionally or locally. If there is an imagined community on the Internet, it is definitely not the nation state. State-bounded kinds of citizenship cannot be considered coterminous with the kinds of citizenship which are achieved on the Internet. However, this is not to argue that a global sense of citizenship, even if it too is an 'imagined one', cannot exist. Recent protests against international financial insitutions such as the World Bank were organised almost entirely through Internet media—a case of not so visible electronic assemblies producing very visible embodied assemblies.

John. B Thompson's book "The Media and Modernity", he argues that it is not possible to arrive a satisfactory understanding of the nature of public life in the modern world with a conception of 'publicness' which is spatial and dialogical. By seeing the public sphere in only these terms are invariably obliged to 'interpret the ever growing role of mediated communication as an historical fall from grace'. Thompson argues that this is so because the widespread conception of publicness used by political and communication theorists alike is one based on mutual face-to-face relations. To problematise this, Thompson takes issue with Habermas' model of the public sphere which is criticised for being metaphysically flawed.

Thompson's critique of 'political science' accounts of the public sphere, even those which try to accommodate the significance of media, is that they are invariably modelled on a theoretically inflexible yardstick of mutual presence.

The deficiencies of such a framework begin to reveal themselves when start to differentiate between different socio-technical bases of interaction. The following is an outline of Thompson's model.

John B. Thompson's Three Types of Interaction

1. Face-to-Face (mutually embodied presence)
   — dialogical
   — mutual presence
   — a high degree of contextual infomation (body language, gestures, symbolic cues, deitic expressions 'here' 'this'
   — reciprocal
   — interpersonal specificity
2. Mediated Interaction (technical mediums like writing, telephoning)
   — dialogical
   — extended/ not mutual
   — restricted degree of contextual infomation
   — reciprocal
   — interpersonal specificity
3. Quasi-Mediated Interaction
   — monological
   — extended
   — produced for an indefinite range of recipients
   — senders and receivers of messages nevertheless form bonds
   — narrowing of the range of symbolic cues.

The value of Thompson's classification is that it is able to distinguish between the social dynamics of the different sub-media of the Internet. On the Internet some forms of communication are clearly produced for an indefinite range of recipients, whilst others are produced for one or a few others. Some forms of information retrieval and transmission are one-way and not dialogical. What is most instructive however, is the fact that mediated interaction, be it the Internet or television, depart from the face-to-face, or 'mutual presence' insofar as it involves a definite narrowing of the range of symbolic cues. Thompson's commentary on this is to suggest that communicative acts do not require their own in-built contexts in order to be meaningful or provide information.

However, when cues are 'filtered-out' because the context is removed, so too is the fragmentation which derives from the fact that all cues-based communication is always localised and incapable of universalisation. Thus, paradoxically the more there is a narrowing of cues by way of the constraints of a technical medium, the greater the prospect for semantic standardisation, by which communicative competence and consensus can be achieved.

The merit of models like John. B Thompson's, of specifying levels of interaction according to a range of communicative qualities, is that it reveals the folly of putting forward a theory of a unitary public sphere based purely on technological possibility. The almost theological status of the Internet as a redemptive agent of 'civil society' in the late 1990s is exemplary of this tendency as is the earlier view of some thinkers like Jean Baudrillard that the mass media had replaced the public sphere in post-industrial societies.

To privilege either 'broadcast' or interactive mediums like CMC as one-dimensional domains which can deliver a universal public sphere is fraught with methodological problems. Perspectives on media epochs—'the video age', the 'age of the Internet' or the 'second media age', are too simplistic and read as much too technologically determinist insofar as they neglect the sub-media's and sub-cultures which are internal to apparatuses of electronic media, both broadcast and interactive. Such models tend to be one-dimensional in that they view forms of public association, be they by images and broadcast or by information and interactivity, as mutually exclusive.

It is true that certain mediums, particularly ones like CMC which enable global reach, provide the individual with mobilities of communication which enable associations beyond what persists in modern life as the most powerful sense of a pre-given public frame—the nation state. And moving beyond the nation-state in a global rather than 'inter-national' sense, also expands the numbers of those with whom would want to participate in a public sphere with. However, it is also true that individuals are mobile across communicative mediums and continuously participate not in a pre-given public sphere, but in the process of constructing publicness across a range of mediums.

Bibliography

Abbott, E. A. "The electronic farmers' marketplace: new technologies and agricultural information". Journal of Communication. For upscale and younger farmers, videotex and teletext are emerging as a "best source" for relatively perishable or highly volatile information like market prices but otherwise seem to complement rather than replace existing sources of more stable information.

Adkins, M., & Brashers, D. E., "The Power of Language in Computer-Mediated Groups". *Management Communication Quarterly*, 8(3), 289-322 1995.

Adrianson, L., & Hjelmquist, E.. *Group Processes in Face-to-Face and Computer-Mediated Communication*. Behaviour & Information Technology, 10(4), 281-296

Ahuja, M. K., & Carley, K. M. "Network Structure in Virtual Organizations". *Journal of Computer-Mediated Communication*, 3(4) - Find evidence of a heirarchy and other structures in a virtual organization 1998.

Allen, T. J., & Hauptman, O. "The Influence of Communication Technologies on Organizational Structure" *Communication Research*, 14(5), 575-587

Baym, N. K. *The Emergence of Community in Computer-Mediated Communication*. In S. G. Jones (Ed.), Cybersociety Computer-Mediated Communication and Community (pp. 138-163). Thousand Oaks: Sage, 1995a.

____________, "The Performance of Humor in Computer-Mediated Communication". *Journal of Computer-Mediated Communication*, 1(2), 1995b.

Bikson, T. K., Eveland, J. D., & Gutek, B. A. "Flexible Interactive Technologies for Multi-Person Tasks: Current Problems and Future Prospects". In M. H. Olson (Ed.), Technological Support for Work Group Collaboration Hillsdale: Erlbaum, 1989.

Bimber, B. The Internet and Political Transformation, 1996

Black, J., & Bryant, J. Introduction to Media Communications. Chicago: Brown & Benchmark, 1998.

Carey, J. W. *Communication as culture: essays on media and society.* Winchester: Unwin Hyman, Inc., 1989.

Chilcoat, Y., & DeWine, S., Teleconferencing and Interpersonal Communication Perception. Journal of Applied Communication Research, 13(1), 14-32 - testing the degree of social presence for various media -

Knapp, M. L. *Essentials of Nonverbal Communication.* New York: Holt, Rinehart and Winston, 1980

Rice, R. E. "Contexts of Research in Organizational Computer-Mediated Communication". In M. Lea (Ed.), *Contexts of Computer-Mediated Communication* (pp. 113-144). New York: Harvester Wheatsheaf, 1992.

Siegel, J., Dubrovsky, V., Kiesler, S., & McGuire, T. W. Group "Processes in Computer-Mediated Communication". *Organizational Behavior and Human Decision Processes,* 1986.

Walther, J. B., "Interpersonal Effects in Computer-Mediated Interaction, A Relational Perspective". *Communication Research.* 19(1), 1992.

Index